Father of Liberty

AMERICAN POLITICAL THOUGHT
Wilson Carey McWilliams and Lance Banning
Founding Editors

Father of Liberty

JONATHAN MAYHEW AND

THE PRINCIPLES OF

THE AMERICAN REVOLUTION

J. Patrick Mullins

 University Press of Kansas

© 2017 by the University Press of Kansas
All rights reserved

Published by the University Press of Kansas (Lawrence, Kansas 66045), which was organized by the Kansas Board of Regents and is operated and funded by Emporia State University, Fort Hays State University, Kansas State University, Pittsburg State University, the University of Kansas, and Wichita State University

Library of Congress Cataloging-in-Publication Data

Names: Mullins, J. Patrick, author.
Title: Father of liberty : Jonathan Mayhew and the principles of the American Revolution / J. Patrick Mullins.
Description: Lawrence : University Press of Kansas, 2017. | Series: American political thought | Includes bibliographical references and index.
Identifiers: LCCN 2016056650
ISBN 9780700624485 (cloth : alk. paper)
ISBN 9780700624492 (ebook)
Subjects: LCSH: Church and state—United States—History—18th century. | United States—History—Revolution, 1775–1783. | Mayhew, Jonathan, 1720–1766. | Clergy—Massachusetts—Boston—Political activity.
Classification: LCC BR516 .M75 2017 | DDC 320.092—dc23
LC record available at https://lccn.loc.gov/2016056650.

British Library Cataloguing-in-Publication Data is available.

Printed in the United States of America
10 9 8 7 6 5 4 3 2 2 1

The paper used in this publication is recycled and contains 30 percent postconsumer waste. It is acid free and meets the minimum requirements of the American National Standard for Permanence of Paper for Printed Library Materials Z39.48-1992.

For my wife, Corinne—
ani ohev otach ba'olam

CONTENTS

Preface, *ix*

Introduction, *1*

1 The Right of Private Judgment, *19*

2 The Right of Resistance, *44*

3 Virtue and Liberty, *66*

4 Power and Corruption, *96*

5 Sceptre and Surplice, *123*

6 The Whig Dilemma, *151*

Conclusion, *177*

Notes, *183*

Bibliography, *213*

Index, *229*

PREFACE

Father of Liberty is the first book on the politics of Dr. Jonathan Mayhew, pastor of the Congregationalist West Church in Boston from 1747 to 1766. This work contends that Mayhew was the most politically influential clergyman in eighteenth-century America and the intellectual progenitor of the American Revolution in New England. Among the handful of leaders who set the cultural context for colonial America's political resistance to British authority in the 1760s, Mayhew ought to be counted along with Patrick Henry, Samuel Adams, and James Otis. And yet he is little remembered today. The corridor of time between the 250th anniversary of his death in 1766 and the 300th anniversary of his birth in 1720 is a fitting moment to reexamine and reassess his historical significance. This book aspires to stimulate a renewal of scholarly and public appreciation for Mayhew's contributions to American thought and culture—and for a life of the mind lived always in fierce dissent.

This book does not purport to be an intellectual biography of Jonathan Mayhew, let alone a comprehensive account of his life. As the clergyman's protégé John Adams remarked in 1818, "To draw the character of Mayhew would be to transcribe a dozen volumes." It is, rather, a study of his political thought and political activism, understood in the context of his personal experiences and intellectual influences, as well as the cultural developments and political events of his time, in New England and the wider Atlantic world. Its object is to analyze and assess Mayhew's contribution to eighteenth-century New England political culture in general and to the intellectual origins of the American Revolution in particular.[1]

Father of Liberty is the product of many years of research in primary sources, from microfilmed newspapers to archival documents. I made extensive use of the Jonathan Mayhew Papers, kept in the Bortmann Collection at Boston University's Mugar Memorial Library. I found it fruitful to draw upon archives at the Massachusetts Historical Society, Harvard University's Houghton Library, and the Huntington Library. My access to and acquisition of the primary and secondary sources for this project relied upon the yeomen's work of librarians, library staff, and archivists from these institutions as well as Liberty Fund, Marymount University's Reinsch Library, Marquette Library's Raynor Memorial Library, and the University of Kentucky's Young Library.

The shortcomings of this work are entirely my own, but its merits I must share with the many heads and many hands contributing to its completion. For the manuscript's thorough and insightful review, I am deeply grateful to Rosemarie Zagarri, Chris Beneke, and Colin Nicolson. In various forms and stages of development, this book project benefited from lively conference chats, e-mail exchanges, editorial assistance, critical feedback on chapters, and moral support from several colleagues, among them, Michael Zuckert, Jack P. Greene, the late Pauline Maier, J. C. D. Clark, Joyce Lee Malcolm, Craig Yirush, William W. Freehling, Conrad C. Wright, James Ceaser, Robert A. Ferguson, Michael Winship, Jonathan H. Scott, Hans Eicholz, Robert G. Ingram, C. Bradley Thompson, Edward Stringham, Thomas G. West, Holly Brewer, Brad Jarvis, Paul Teed, Suzanne Carson, and Amanda Bourne. The late, incomparable, and much-missed Lance Banning directed much of the research on which this monograph is based, and to him I will always remain in debt.

During his tenure as director of the University Press of Kansas, Charles Myers also served as acting editor for the American Political Thought series, carrying on the brilliant legacy of Lance Banning and Wilson Carey McWilliams. Chuck embraced my Mayhew project from the start and pushed for it every step of the way. He did a magnificent job, and I thank him—as well as Joyce Harrison, Mike Kehoe, Larisa Martin, Karl Janssen, Martha Whitt, and the rest of the editorial, marketing, and production teams at the University Press of Kansas—for turning this project from an idea in my mind to the book in your hands. I appreciate financial support for my research, writing, and revision of the book from Marymount University, the University of Kentucky, and Liberty Fund. For their encouragement, I am grateful to my friends, Jack F. Wakeland, Margaret Tseng, and Charles R. Smith, as well as my parents, Donald W. Marshall, the late Nancy D. Marshall, and John P. Mullins, Jr., my first history teacher, who showed me the power of ideas to move the world. I am grateful to my stepdaughter, Shir Bloch, for enduring patiently my pontifications about Jonathan Mayhew over most of her lifetime. And thanks goes to my son, Jonathan Henry Bloch-Mullins, for always giving my spirits a lift when I needed it most—and for being the only member of the family willing to join me, with his ingenuous gusto, in a hearty toast and three stout huzzahs to the 250th anniversary of the repeal of the Stamp Act. And, at last, I thank my wife and favorite Marquette colleague, Corinne Bloch-Mullins, for seeing this book through from beginning to end, for always believing in me, and for making life so dear and peace so sweet. She is first in my heart, and my first book belongs to her.

Introduction

On the night of August 26, 1766, a "number of rude Fellows"—in the words of the *Boston Gazette*—rallied around a bonfire on King Street in downtown Boston and formed a torchlit mass of indignation. The crowd divided into two teams, ransacking the private homes of two officers of the British Crown. The mob then re-formed and marched to a three-story Palladian mansion, the home of Thomas Hutchinson, chief justice and lieutenant governor of Massachusetts. An eyewitness, lawyer Josiah Quincy, Jr., documented the riot in a diary entry the following day. As the crowd surged into Hutchinson's house, the lieutenant governor fled with his daughter. Quincy believed that Hutchinson's life would have been forfeit had he not made this narrow escape. The "Rage-intoxicated Rabble," Quincy recalled, swept into the house and destroyed or stole everything of value. Over hours of steady work, the rioters pulled down interior walls and tore its stately cupola from the roof. They left a gutted shell behind and dispersed with the approach of daylight. Historian Bernard Bailyn described the Hutchinson Riot as "more violent than any yet seen in America, more violent indeed than any that would be seen in the entire course of the Revolution." In the weeks that followed, mobs followed Boston's example in cities up and down the Atlantic seaboard, from an assault upon the royal governor's home in New York City to raucous street rallies in Charleston. The Hutchinson Riot was the spark that set Britain's Thirteen Colonies on fire, turning American opposition to the Stamp Act of 1765 from a genteel affair of legislative petitioning into a violent popular uprising with the potential for armed revolution. Publicly, Lieutenant Governor Hutchinson blamed the attack on mistaken gossip that he was a supporter of the hated new stamp tax. Privately, he blamed Jonathan Mayhew.[1]

As crowds gathered around the ruins of the Hutchinson mansion on August 27, the rumor spread in some social circles that this attack upon the private residence of the second-ranking Crown officer in Massachusetts, unprecedented in its destructiveness, had been incited by Dr. Jonathan Mayhew's sermon on August 25. In that sermon, the forty-four-year-old pastor of the Congregationalist meetinghouse in Boston's West End obliquely addressed the subject preying on the minds of all Bostonians: Parliament's universally hated stamp tax, scheduled for implementation on November 1. Mayhew offered his flock an explanation of the principle of civil liberty, which requires that the laws "are made by common consent & choice; that all have some hand in framing them, at least by their representatives, chosen to act for them, if not in their own persons." If people are "governed contrary to, or independently of, their own will & consent," then they are "in a state of slavery." Moreover, Britain's American colonists should be considered slaves rather than freemen, he contended, "if they are to possess no property, nor to enjoy the fruits of their own labor, but by the mere precarious pleasure of the mother [country], or of a distant legislature, in which they neither are, nor can be represented." While denouncing taxation without representation and government without consent, he also cautioned his congregation against the lawlessness of mob rule, which negates civil liberty as surely as parliamentary oppression.[2]

Mayhew's caveat regarding the dangers of anarchy was omitted from accounts of the sermon offered by Thomas Hutchinson and Governor Francis Bernard. Rev. Henry Caner, the King's Chaplain in Boston, wrote to the archbishop of Canterbury that, the day before the Hutchinson Riot, Mayhew "distinguished himself in the pulpit upon this Occasion (it is said) in One of the most seditious Sermons ever delivered, advising the people to stand up for their rights to the last drop of their Blood." It is unlikely that any of the rioters were moved to action by the sermon on civil liberty, and Mayhew denied vociferously the slander that he had instigated this violence. Such colonial champions of royal prerogative as Hutchinson, Bernard, and Caner were, however, inclined to blame Mayhew for the August 26 riot. His sermon on the Stamp Act had been only the latest political act in a long and controversial career of challenging authority and asserting liberty from the pulpit.[3]

❖ ❖ ❖

Mayhew died on July 9, 1766, less than a year after the Hutchinson Riot, and almost exactly ten years before two of his disciples, John Adams and Robert Treat Paine, signed the Declaration of Independence on behalf of Massachusetts. Adams and Paine justified armed resistance to the British Crown in the name of political ideas: the Real Whig principles of natural human rights, popular sovereignty, a consensual government of limited and delegated powers, liberty of conscience, and the people's right to resist tyrannical government. They first encountered these principles as young men in Mayhew's sermons. Long after his retirement from the US presidency, Adams wrote his friend Thomas Jefferson that Mayhew's first political pamphlet, *A Discourse Concerning Unlimited Submission to the Higher Powers*, served as his political "Chatechism," which he read at the age of fifteen and reread "till the Substance of it was incorporated into my Nature and indelibly grafted on my Memory." In 1818, Adams claimed, "If the orators on the 4th of July really wish to investigate the principles and feelings which produced the Revolution, they ought to study ... Dr. Mayhew's sermon on passive obedience and non-resistance." Adams considered Mayhew, along with Samuel Adams and John Hancock, one of the five men who started the American Revolution in New England. Paine, who regularly attended Mayhew's services, called the clergyman nothing less than "the father of civil and religious liberty in Massachusetts and America."[4]

Mayhew's sermons and discourses shaped the political thinking not only of John Adams and Robert Treat Paine but many other "friends of liberty" in Massachusetts in the 1760s. Mayhew influenced politically such secular Yankee leaders as Paul Revere, James Otis, Jr., Samuel Allyne Otis, Mercy Otis Warren, Josiah Quincy, Jr., and his brothers Edmund and Samuel, James Bowdoin, Benjamin Church, Richard Cranch, Harrison Gray, *Boston Gazette* co-publishers Benjamin Edes and John Gill, and such clergymen as Samuel Cooper, Andrew Eliot, and Charles Chauncy, as well as New Yorker William Livingston and Pennsylvania's chief justice, William Allen. Mayhew's political writings also drew fire from "friends of government" on both sides of the Atlantic, among them Francis Bernard, Thomas Hutchinson, the Episcopal clergymen Henry Caner and Samuel Johnson, as well as Thomas Secker, the archbishop of Canterbury. Selling well in England, his tracts won the admiration of Catherine Macaulay, Joseph Priestley, Thomas Hollis, Richard

Price, and other English champions of the Enlightenment and the American cause. Within his lifetime, printers in both Boston and London produced multiple editions of some of his most popular books and pamphlets. Most of his published works were moral or theological in nature, but his political sermons attracted the greatest public attention (both positive and negative). According to historian Carl Bridenbaugh, by the 1760s, Mayhew "had won for himself a transatlantic reputation as the champion of British Nonconformity, and it is doubtful if even Benjamin Franklin had as many readers."[5]

This study examines Mayhew's political thought and activism in the context of the ideas and events of his time and place, demonstrating his critical contribution to the intellectual origins of American Revolution in Massachusetts. In the process, it illuminates the meaning of the Revolution as a political and constitutional conflict informed by the religious and political ideas of the British Enlightenment. It also corrects a historic injustice in recovering the largely forgotten achievement of "this transcendental genius," as John Adams called Mayhew, who "threw all the weight of his great fame into the scale of the country in 1761, and maintained it there with zeal and ardor till his death, in 1766." It is the conclusion of this book that no clergyman in eighteenth-century America dared more, struggled more, and succeeded more in advancing the cause of liberty than Dr. Jonathan Mayhew. If the principles of the Declaration were indeed "self-evident" for most New Englanders by 1776, this was due in no small part to the exertions of the West Church pastor, who preached those principles with fiery eloquence and forceful logic in the transatlantic press from 1747 to 1766. He should rightly be numbered with Patrick Henry, James Otis, and other early intellectual leaders of the American Whig opposition who set the cultural conditions and intellectual parameters for colonial resistance to Britain's new imperial policies following the French and Indian War. More than any other clergyman, Mayhew helped prepare the New England conscience for disobedience to British authority in the 1760s.[6]

Raised in Massachusetts by a Puritan missionary and educated at Harvard at the height of the Enlightenment, Mayhew believed that the essence of Protestantism is the individual believer's application of reason to the interpretation of Scripture and practice of the classical virtues from Christian motives. Persuaded that Scripture must be interpreted in the light of reason, the young Congregational minister rejected the main tenets of Calvinism. In the 1750s, he was the first American to repudiate publicly the doctrine of the Trinity as unscriptural and irrational. Embracing the "natural religion" of the British Enlightenment, Mayhew maintained that God is rational and benevolent, and that God created humans with the natural capacity for reason, virtue, and happiness. In accordance with the low-church Protestant doctrine of "the right and duty of private judgment," he argued that humans should be free to think, worship, live, and seek happiness according to their own judgment. While most of his fellow Boston divines were Calvinist and Trinitarian and found Mayhew scandalous, the theologically heterodox pastor remained committed to New England Congregationalism, as he thought congregations should govern themselves independent of the control of unelected bishops (whether Anglican or Catholic, appointed by a king or a pope). In printed sermons of the 1750s and 1760s, the West Church pastor criticized orthodox Calvinist Congregationalists, evangelical New Lights, and high-church Episcopalians as bad Protestants for usurping the individual's right of private judgment in religious and moral matters. Alienated from most of his colleagues in New England, Mayhew found intellectual kinship with anti-Trinitarian Presbyterian clergy in London, who feted him as one of their own and arranged an honorary doctorate from a Scots university.

From 1750 to 1766, Mayhew used press and pulpit to affirm the principles of natural rights, popular sovereignty, delegated powers, consensual government, and the right of resistance, which he thought to be under attack from the high-church Episcopal clergy in America and England. Considering these Whig "revolution principles" the theoretical basis for Britain's Revolution of 1688 and the succession of the Hanoverian dynasty, he sensed no contradiction between preaching the right of the people to overthrow a tyrannical monarch and professing patriotic loyalty to the British Crown. During the French and Indian War, Mayhew celebrated Britain as the bulwark of constitutional monarchy and enlightened Protestantism against Catholic, absolutist France. But he remained ambivalent about the British Empire, fearful that Britain was becoming increasingly corrupt, and that the American people's virtue would be corrupted by their imperial connection with Britain. Mayhew's outspoken criticism of what he called "*high-church, tory-principles* and maxims" earned him the enmity of Francis Bernard, royally appointed governor of Massachusetts. An affair of honor between the two men convinced the pastor that tyranny and corruption had already reached New England's shores. He began working in tandem with James Otis's Whig legislators to combat encroachments on liberty by the Bernard administration.[7]

In defending the transatlantic Protestant interest against the Catholic Church and Protestant nonconformity against the Church of England, the controversial minister won appreciation from theologically orthodox Congregational and Presbyterian clergy in New England, as well as Presbyterian admirers in New York and Pennsylvania. The archbishop of Canterbury's proposal to establish an Anglican bishop in the American colonies sent ripples of anxiety through the colonial clergy of Protestant denominations dissenting from the king's Church. Taking the lead against this plan, Mayhew's pamphlets argued that it assumed the principle that the Church of England had jurisdiction over America's churches and that Parliament had legislative supremacy over America's legislatures. He rallied low-church Protestant clergy against the episcopate as a danger to civil and religious liberty, compelling the archbishop and his colonial allies to back down. Mayhew's campaign not only helped to unify low-church Protestant clergy politically despite their theological differences, but also to alienate them from Britain and keep them wary of a broader British conspiracy against American rights.

Although he had long preached popular sovereignty, the right of revolution, and the British menace to American virtue and liberty, Mayhew was taken aback by the intensity of public protest against the Stamp Act of 1765. He was the only New England clergyman to denounce the tax act from the pulpit. When Boston rioters destroyed Lieutenant Governor Thomas Hutchinson's home the following day, Hutchinson and Bernard blamed Mayhew's sermon for inciting the violence. While his sermon likely did not play a role, he was genuinely heartsick over the riot and the rising threat of civil war between Britain and her colonies. He was immensely relieved by repeal of the Stamp Act, but he did not retreat from his lifelong commitment to Whig revolution principles and his warning to Americans to remain vigilant against future British encroachments on their liberty. Mayhew never seemed to acknowledge that his career as a Real Whig political propagandist, and particularly his agitation of the episcopate issue, helped create in New England the cultural conditions for a violent public response to the Stamp Act. Mayhew sowed the wind, but the American people reaped the whirlwind.

In an often quoted 1825 letter to Henry Lee, Thomas Jefferson remarked that the object of the Declaration of Independence was "not to find out new principles, or new arguments, never before thought of," but "to place before mankind the common sense of the subject." With respect to American rights and British violations of them, he claimed, "there was but one opinion," such that "All American Whigs thought alike on these subjects." Congress meant the Declaration to be "an expression of the American mind," whose authority rested upon "the harmonizing sentiments of the day, whether expressed in conversation, in letters, printed essays, or in the elementary books of public right, as Aristotle, Cicero, Locke, Sidney, &c." Scholars and other commentators have long debated the intellectual sources of the American Revolution. Perhaps a greater mystery is the cultural process by which such radical moral abstractions as natural human rights, popular sovereignty, consensual government, and the right of resistance ever became so broadly accepted by the majority of eighteenth-century Americans as not simply true but "self-evident."[8]

In his 1781 work, *The Origin and Progress of the American Revolution*, Peter Oliver, former chief justice of Massachusetts and Loyalist refugee to England, blamed the Congregational clergy for turning the people of New England against Britain and its colonial Crown officers unjustly. Oliver called the clergy the "black regiment" of the Whig opposition movement, and he styled Mayhew and his friends Charles Chauncy and Samuel Cooper the "sacerdotal Triumvirate" that led this regiment into political war against lawful government. He blamed the three pastors for "encouraging Seditions & Riots, until those lesser Offences were absorbed in Rebellion." Perpetuating the claim by Caner and Hutchinson that Mayhew had incited the notorious Boston riot of August 26, 1765, Oliver wrote, "on the day preceeding the Destruction of Mr. *Hutchinson*'s House, he preached so seditious a Sermon, that some of his Auditors, who were of the Mob, declared, whilst the Doctor was delivering it they could scarce contain themselves from going out of the Assembly & beginning their Work." Oliver accused Mayhew and his fellow clergy, along with James Otis and other secular Whig leaders, of setting the Revolution in motion not so much by teaching bad principles to the people as by appealing to such passions as fear, greed, and resentment of their social betters.[9]

In the nineteenth century, New England intellectuals (mainly Unitarians) taught a Whiggish version of Oliver's Tory interpretation. They praised Congregationalist clergymen for contributing to the Revolution's intellectual origins by educating public opinion in the principles of civil and religious liberty (as grounded in rationalist theology). Following the death of his foremost advocate, John Adams, in 1826, Mayhew's role in the Revolution was perpetuated in public memory by pastor Alden Bradford's 1838 biography. On the eve of the Civil War, Congregationalist clergy seemed anxious to hold up Mayhew as evidence that Yankees had well preceded Southerners in intellectual leadership of the Revolution. In 1856 Cyrus Bartol (associate minister of the West Church) praised Mayhew as a champion of liberty, noting that his "hand was felt at the helm of our bewildered vessel of state, before the voice of Patrick Henry, in Virginia, was heard rising above the storm." Unitarian minister and abolitionist Theodore Parker memorialized Mayhew as "a profound and bold thinker, one who feared not the truth." Massachusetts lawyer and antiquarian John Thornton Wingate demonstrated the Revolutionary-era clergy's commitment to liberty and union in an 1860 collection of political sermons, *The Pulpit of the American Revolution*, which opened with Mayhew's 1750 *Discourse Concerning Unlimited Submission*. New Hampshire journalist Frank Moore edited a similar collection in 1862, *The Patriot Preachers of the American Revolution*, opening with Mayhew's 1766 political sermon, *The Snare Broken*. This Whiggish interpretive tradition, advanced by gentleman historians, culminated in 1910 with *The Heralds of a Liberal Faith*, by Boston Unitarian minister Samuel A. Eliot. Emphasizing Mayhew's precedence in preaching revolution principles, Eliot honored Mayhew as "the torchbearer who lighted the fires of his country's liberties," who was "not the associate, but the inspirer of the leaders of the patriot cause in the days before the Revolution."[10]

In her 1928 monograph, *The New England Clergy and the American Revolution*, Duke University historian Alice M. Baldwin gave the old Whig interpretation its first full presentation in academic scholarship—and its last, for decades to come. Herself the daughter of a Maine Congregationalist minister, Baldwin aimed for her study "to show how the New England clergy preserved, extended and popularized the essential doctrines of political philosophy, thus making familiar to every church-going New Englander long before 1763 not only the doctrines of natural right, the social contract, and the right of resistance, but also the fundamental principle of American constitutional law, that government, like its citizens, is bounded by law, and when it transcends its authority it acts illegally." Baldwin's book contended that the political preaching of New England's Congregational and Presbyterian clergy "may explain, in some measure, why these theories were so widely held, so dearly cherished, and so deeply inwrought into American constitutional doctrine." Highlighting the clergy's great and persistent influence over their congregations in the eighteenth century, she credited them with popularizing the political ideas of thinkers as diverse as Aristotle, Cicero, Algernon Sydney, John Locke, and Benjamin Hoadly. The clergy provided one of the "lines of transmission" by which the political ideas of the seventeenth century were communicated in New England's political culture over the generations to the Revolutionary era. Mayhew figured prominently in Baldwin's study as a minister who "had long been writing in support of liberty, both civil and religious, and was known all over America and in England for his bold attacks in behalf of the right of resistance." She denied that natural rights political philosophy was "foisted upon the people by a few book-learned political leaders when the Revolutionary ferment began." In New England, the nonconformist clergy had rendered these radical doctrines mere common sense for the average Yankee, such that there was "not a right asserted in the Declaration of Independence which had not been discussed by the New England clergy before 1763." Moreover, they gave these political ideas "the sanction of divine law," making them seem sacred and undeniable to a religious population.[11]

In Baldwin's hands, the old Whig account of the nonconformist clergy's political leadership provided a compelling explanation for how Whig revolution principles became so widely accepted by the Yankee populace over the decades preceding the Declaration of Independence—and why New England so frequently stood in the vanguard of American resistance to British authority, dragging the southern and mid-Atlantic colonies along. But Baldwin knew in 1928 that she was writing against the historiographic tide. At least since the 1913 publication of Charles A. Beard's *Economic Interpretation of the Constitution of the United States*, the Progressive interpretation had gained dominance in academic historical scholarship. Bringing a materialist worldview and positivist methodology to their analysis of the past, Progressive historians had little patience with the role of ideas and intellectuals—let alone religious ideas and clergy—in their analysis of the Revolution's origins. In their studies of the Revolution's origins, scholars such as John C. Miller and Philip Davidson found Whig political writing to be mere propaganda for social classes scrambling for power and economic groups competing for advantage in largely quantifiable terms. Over the first half of the twentieth century, Jonathan Mayhew and the New England clergy gradually faded from scholarly consideration and public memory.[12]

In the second half of the twentieth century, though, some historians embraced John Adams's interpretation of the Revolution as an intellectual movement, a "radical change" in "the minds and hearts of the people." Repulsed by the totalitarian ideologies of Nazism, fascism, and communism in the wake of the Second World War and early Cold War, "neo-Whig" scholars rediscovered the importance of ideology as motivation for colonial resistance to British tyranny, taking seriously the colonists' own explanation of their motives in political literature. In his 1953 *Seedtime of the Republic*, Clinton Rossiter profiled the intellectual leadership of six colonial thinkers—including Mayhew—who explained and popularized those "liberal" political ideas from which the generation of American Revolutionaries would later draw guidance. Concurring with John Adams's assessment of the pastor's historical role, Rossiter found Mayhew "easily the most striking representative of the dissenting preachers who from the 1740s onward proclaimed Locke and Sidney from their pulpits and prepared the mind of New England for the Revolution." Rossiter's analysis of Mayhew's political writing began the gradual rehabilitation of his reputation as a historically significant figure.[13]

Building on Rossiter's rediscovery of Mayhew eleven years later, Charles W. Akers published *Called unto Liberty*, the only scholarly biography of the West Church pastor to date. Akers joined in Rossiter's neo-Whig approach to Mayhew as a radical in both religion and politics, a boldly independent thinker whose attachment to Real Whig political principles followed logically from his rejection of Calvinism and Trinitarianism in favor of a rationalist form of Christianity. He found Mayhew "the boldest and most articulate of those colonial preachers who taught that resistance to tyrannical rulers was a Christian duty as well as a human right." Akers concurred with Adams's Whig view of Mayhew as foremost among the New England Congregational clergy who promoted Whig ideology and laid the groundwork for popular resistance to Crown authority in the 1760s.[14]

In exploring the intellectual origins of the American Revolution, other neo-Whig historians evaluated the cogency of colonial Whig claims of a British conspiracy against their liberties in the 1760s, reconsidering the New England Congregational clergy as a conduit for Whig political thought. In his 1962 study, *Mitre and Sceptre*, Carl Bridenbaugh argued that religion was "a fundamental cause of the American Revolution," finding that conflict over church-state relations provided the century-long context for conflict over relations between Britain and the American colonies. Bridenbaugh assessed Mayhew as foremost among the Congregational political activists of the 1760s who convinced New Englanders and their British co-religionists that Episcopal militancy was a threat to civil liberty. While Bridenbaugh highlighted religious zeal and sectarian fears as compelling motives for colonial resistance, Trevor Colbourn's *Lamp of Experience* treated the Revolution as "the achievement of literate politicians who enlightened and informed American public opinion" through the appeal to reason and historical facts. Colbourn devoted a chapter to the Congregational clergy's role in this cultural process, finding Mayhew "the most outstanding of New England's politically minded clerics" who "led New England clerical criticism of England."[15]

A fundamental pivot in the historiography of the Revolution came with Bernard Bailyn's ideological interpretation, later dubbed "republican revisionism," which attributed colonial political resistance primarily to the influence of American Whig political thought. In 1965, Bailyn published his edited collection of *Pamphlets of the American Revolution, 1750–1776*. He took Mayhew's *Discourse Concerning Unlimited Submission* as the first pamphlet in his collection and the beginning of the great debate on the nature of government that culminated in the Revolutionary War. In Bailyn's estimation, the *Discourse* was the "most famous sermon preached in pre-Revolutionary America," and "the American Revolution itself" was "the fulfillment and application" of the arguments in Mayhew's *Discourse*. Through the *Pamphlets* and his 1967 monograph *The Ideological Origins of the American Revolution*, Bailyn's work elevated the intellectual interpretation of the Revolution's origins to historiographic dominance and won new scholarly attention for Mayhew and the clergy as part of that story. Focusing on colonial political pamphlet literature rather than political sermons, however, the republican revisionists tended to neglect religion, interpreting Whig political thought in largely secular terms.[16]

❖ ❖ ❖

Fueled by academic fascination with the mass protests of the late 1960s and early 1970s, a new body of scholarship explored the centrality of religion to early American history. Leading the way in his 1966 work *Religion and the American Mind*, literature professor Alan Heimert located the antiauthoritarian impulses of the colonial Whig opposition in the New Light revivalism of the First Great Awakening. He characterized the rationalist critics of the Awakening—Mayhew prominent among them—as a self-serving establishment hostile to egalitarianism that aimed to keep the common people under control and maintain the sociopolitical status quo. Heimert revived the nineteenth-century Whig thesis that the Revolution had been led by rationalist clergy only to stand it on its head. "The image of Jonathan Mayhew as a 'fiery liberal' also has every virtue except consonance with the facts," Heimert wrote.[17]

Other work in early American religious history incorporated the republican revisionist literature on colonial Whig political literature. In his 1977 study *The Sacred Cause of Liberty*, Nathan O. Hatch outlined the political thought of the New England's Congregational clergy. Mayhew figured in his work as one among many pastors who used sermons to promote Real Whig ideas in New England's political culture. Hatch denied that theological liberals like Mayhew, Chauncy, and Cooper were the vanguard of the Revolution, and he also denied that the Revolution was a product of the Great Awakening. He found the political beliefs of the Congregational clergy to be uniformly Whiggish, regardless of theological persuasion. In her 1986 monograph *Under the Cope of Heaven*, Patricia Bonomi agreed that the Congregational and Presbyterian clergy helped lead colonial resistance to British measures, finding the root of their commitment to antiauthoritarian, liberal politics in Protestant dissent's resistance to Episcopal domination. But for Bonomi, theology made a significant difference in the politics of the clergy. She rejected Heimert's view that the Revolution was a product of the Awakening. "Attacks on episcopacy and on blind obedience to government," Bonomi noted, "came most often from rational-minded liberals of the educated elite," of whom Mayhew was one of the most influential. She maintained that both evangelical and rationalist clergymen provided the laity with political leadership in the 1760s and 1770s, but theological liberals like Mayhew took the lead within the clergy itself. Harry Stout's *New England Soul* concurred with Bonomi, Hatch, and Baldwin that "New England's Congregational ministers played a leading role in fomenting the sentiments of resistance and, after 1774, open rebellion." Hatch trumpeted Mayhew's "unparalleled success in setting forth a theology and ideology of resistance that all New England could endorse," his political sermons standing "as the apotheosis of Revolutionary preaching in New England."[18]

While early American historians in the 1980s rehabilitated the importance of Protestant dissent for the intellectual origins of the American Revolution, scholars of British history elaborated upon the connection between Protestant dissent and political radicalism in eighteenth-century Britain. In a prodigious body of scholarship, J. C. D. Clark reinterpreted British history from the Restoration to the early nineteenth century as an ancien régime characterized by dominance of monarchy, aristocracy, and episcopacy. Over the long eighteenth century, Britain remained an Anglican confessional state, undergirded by a traditional culture of deference to authority. The principal constituency for reform of this status quo, Clark found, was the Protestant dissenters, a view that largely jibed with James E. Bradley's study of the British dissenters' political activism. Clark, however, found the root of political radicalism in the anti-Trinitarian theology of the heterodox dissenters. Their assertion of a right of private judgment gave rise to an individualistic worldview incompatible with the Anglican insistence upon hierarchy and authority. In response, Bradley noted the theologically orthodox dissenters within the reform movement. Downplaying theology, he attributed the political radicalism of British Protestant dissenters to the egalitarian and contractarian character of their ecclesiology and their resentment of disenfranchisement and marginalization under Anglican hegemony.[19]

In the 1990s, historians of early modern British religion outlined a religious persuasion they called "Rational Dissent" or "Enlightened Dissent," a synthesis of rationalist theology with congregational or presbyterian ecclesiology. Challenging the long-standing view of the Enlightenment as hostile to Christianity, Knud Haakonssen and other Rational Dissent historians contended that rationalism, individualism, and religious liberty originated, in part, from liberal forms of Protestantism. Providing a critical context for understanding Jonathan Mayhew and his fellow heterodox clergymen, John Corrigan has drawn upon the insights of this and earlier literature to demonstrate the presence of the Rational Dissent persuasion among the Congregational clergy in New England by the early eighteenth century.[20]

While Alice Baldwin found natural rights political philosophy pervasive in New England political sermons, the republican-revisionist interpretation of the Revolution's intellectual origins marginalized natural rights in particular and individualism in general. Eager to carve out a place for "Lockean liberalism" within early American political discourse, some scholars of political thought rehabilitated the Baldwin thesis in the late twentieth and early twenty-first centuries. Steven Dworetz, Michael P. Zuckert, and Thomas G. West pointed toward the political sermons of New England Congregationalist clergy as proof of the prominence of natural rights in the Revolution's intellectual origins. The clergy were attracted to John Locke's natural rights philosophy, Dworetz observed, because they had already adopted the theological assumptions of the Enlightenment, particularly natural religion. Zuckert acknowledged that there were other intellectual sources for the Revolution, such as Real Whig political thought and classical republicanism. But, he maintained, these various strands of political thought were synthesized into an "amalgam" of American political thought to which Lockean natural rights provided the "cornerstone." Zuckert argued that Mayhew and the heterodox Congregational clergy broke with Protestant tradition by embracing Locke's rationalism. West concurred with the main thrust of the Dworetz-Zuckert thesis but offered a corrective, observing that New England rationalism should be understood as part of the broader American Protestant tradition.[21]

In the 1990s and 2000s, with the collapse of Communism and the rapid globalization of evangelical Protestantism and Islamic militancy, Western intellectuals could no longer take the secularization of society as an inevitable aspect of modernity. Historians came to recognize religiosity as central to any plausible account of the intellectual origins of the American Revolution. Over the last twenty years, republican revisionism has largely conceded the historiographic high ground to an eclectic postrevisionism that aims to synthesize republican revisionism with other twentieth-century interpretations of the Revolution, including the well-documented role of religion. Postrevisionist historians such as Mark Noll and Eran Shalev have found the Revolution's intellectual roots in a synthesis of British Whig or classical republican political thought with Protestantism. James P. Byrd agreed with Shalev that colonial Whigs used biblical language to communicate Whig revolution principles to the people. The clergy were the most effective purveyors of Christianized resistance theory, and Byrd cited Mayhew as a consummate example of this "apostolic patriotism."[22]

Other postrevisionist studies have explored the interrelation of Enlightenment rationalism with Protestantism and Whiggism. In his 1997 analysis of the American Enlightenment, Robert Ferguson defined the European Enlightenment in terms of secular rationalism. But he found that colonial Whig writers such as Thomas Jefferson, John Adams, and Jonathan Mayhew selected their ideas from several traditions by an active intellectual process and synthesized them in their own New World contexts. Ferguson concluded that Mayhew's political sermons, like the American Revolution as a whole, synthesized Enlightenment rationalism with Protestant religion. In his 2012 study, *The Religious Beliefs of America's Founders*, Gregg Frazer claimed that the American Revolutionaries, including Mayhew, espoused "theological rationalism," a "new religion" of the Enlightenment that "denied every fundamental doctrine of Christianity" but jibed well with their preexisting commitment to Whig political principles. In convincing the colonists that the Bible conveyed a right of resistance, "Mayhew's service to the Revolutionary cause was immeasurable." Frazer saw the Enlightenment clergy as playing a critical role in the intellectual origins of the Revolution by converting a Christian populace to theological rationalism and Lockean political philosophy. By contrast, most scholars have, like Ferguson and Corrigan, found Mayhew, the Enlightenment clergy, and the American Revolutionaries to be both Protestant and rationalist.[23]

In this postrevisionist landscape, a few historians have come to consider religion as one of the principal causes of the American Revolution. Seeing the conflict between Britain and the colonies as driven by the conflict between high-church and low-church Protestants, J. C. D. Clark mused that the American Revolution was "a war of religion." Taking Clark's cue in 2008, James B. Bell argued in *A War of Religion: Dissenters, Anglicans, and the American Revolution* that the denominational conflicts over a colonial episcopate and Episcopal missionary efforts raised constitutional questions about the relation of the colonies to king and Parliament. Jonathan Mayhew's controversies with Anglican authorities figured prominently in Bell's account, but he credited Samuel and John Adams with framing this sectarian conflict in political and constitutional concerns that helped alienate the people against Britain. Bell found that the Church of England, "by the very nature of its Englishness, was one of the causes of the American Revolution."[24]

In his 2010 account of the outbreak of the Revolution in New England, T. H. Breen warned against historians' focus on "the Founders" like Adams and Jefferson and instead considered the arguments for resistance that were heard, received, and applied by "ordinary Americans." Like Baldwin eighty-two years earlier, Breen saw the political sermons of the Congregational clergy as the most successful cultural mechanism for the popularization of Whiggism. Ministers like Andrew Eliot recast Locke's philosophy of natural rights—and argument for the right of resistance—in biblical terms that made war with Britain seem like a Christian duty, turning Yankee farmers into "popular Lockeans." Bell and Breen were concerned mainly with New England, where the religious interpretation of the Revolution's origins seems most persuasive. But Joseph Tiedemann applied the Clarkian interpretive model to the Middle Colonies. He found that mid-Atlantic Presbyterians tended to become Whigs, while Anglicans tended to become Tories, with preexisting denominational conflicts helping to draw party lines in the years before war. Denominational differences and corresponding ethnic differences were compelling factors in a mid-Atlantic colonist's politics, Tiedemann argued, but human motivation is complex, and religion was "not the only or always the determinant force." Fresh scholarship on the role of religion for the Revolution in the southern colonies would be the next step toward determining whether the notion of the Revolutionary War as a religious war can be sustained.[25]

With the emergence of a religious interpretation within postrevisionist historiography, scholarly opinion on the origins of the American Revolution over the last two centuries has ironically cycled back around to where the journey began. In exploring the origins of the American Revolution, historians now give serious consideration to the claims of John Adams and Peter Oliver for the importance of religion in general and the Congregational clergy in particular. Growing scholarship on this subject has gradually rehabilitated Jonathan Mayhew's historical reputation, approaching a critical mass at which an extended examination and reassessment of Mayhew's politics is not only possible but timely. The arrival of the 250th anniversary of Mayhew's death and approach of the 300th anniversary of his birth render the moment for such a reassessment not only timely but urgent.

Father of Liberty is the first book devoted to examining Jonathan Mayhew's political thought and activism and to outlining Mayhew's role in the intellectual origins of the American Revolution. Its claims derive from years of rigorous research in archival sources, but those claims are informed and conditioned by the discoveries and interpretations of commentators ranging from Bell, Clark, Zuckert, Bonomi, Bailyn, and Pauline Maier on back to Oliver and Adams. *Father of Liberty* offers a postrevisionist interpretation of Mayhew's politics that draws upon and integrates many interpretations.

At the beginning of the twenty-first century, there is a rough consensus among scholars of the origins of the Revolution that, in interpreting British imperial policy and deciding about their own course of action, colonial Whigs sought guidance from multiple political traditions, such as Locke's modern natural rights philosophy, classical republicanism, and Real Whig political thought. Their political deliberations were, in turn, shaped by multiple philosophic traditions, such as Enlightenment rationalism and British Protestantism. Their religious and political thinking were, moreover, shaped by and shaping the political events and cultural developments of a transatlantic English-speaking world, from the French and Indian War to local provincial politics and street protests. There is no historiographic consensus, though, as to how such often conflicting and competing intellectual traditions fit together in the minds of Americans, let alone how they congealed into anything resembling what Jefferson called "the harmonizing sentiments of the day."

In *The Snare Broken*, his last published sermon, written two months before his death at the age of forty-five years, Mayhew looked back poignantly on his youthful enthusiasms. "Having been initiated, in youth, in the doctrines of civil liberty," he wrote, "as they were taught by such men as Plato, Demosthenes, Cicero and other renowned persons among the ancients; and such as Sidney and Milton, Locke and Hoadley, among the moderns; I liked them; they seemed rational." He went on to cite the example of the heroes of the Old Testament who combated tyranny. Mayhew concluded, "I would not, I cannot now, tho' past middle age, relinquish the fair object of my youthful affections, LIBERTY; whose charms, instead of decaying with time in my eyes, have daily captivated me more and more."[26]

Mayhew took a synoptic approach to sources as disparate as Cicero, Locke, and the Bible. The quality attracting him to these ancient and modern authors was what he perceived as a shared rationality, and what he took away from them (among other things) were arguments on behalf of "civil liberty." As a young man at Harvard College in the 1740s, he was "initiated" in these readings, but he actively extracted from them what he found persuasive and useful, and then synthesized these distinct elements into an ironbound fasces of fundamental principles. This passage from *The Snare Broken* suggests that passionate commitment to rationality and its free and responsible exercise is the key to Jonathan Mayhew's personal character and his religious and political principles. It seems this commitment to reason preceded his politicization, and he deduced early on that there could be no free and responsible exercise of reason—both in contemplation and in moral action—without religious and civil liberty.[27]

The American mind of Jonathan Mayhew might provide scholars with a model for how eighteenth-century American colonists adopted, reconciled, and applied intellectual influences from the ancient and modern, sacred and secular strains of the Western cultural heritage. In any event, rationality was the first cause of Mayhew's political activism, and liberty was the final cause, pulling him forward into battle. Mayhew held fast to his rationalism and libertarianism with fervor and lifelong consistency, although he continually adapted the practical application of his principles to new contexts and shifting events. *Father of Liberty* demonstrates how Mayhew struggled to reconcile the Reformation with the Enlightenment, classical moral thought with modern political thought, a respect for monarchy with a thirst for freedom, an attachment to Britain with a love for New England. We will see how his religious and political principles motivated, guided, and sustained a remarkable life of "practical religion" and political activism. We will consider the ways in which Mayhew inspired a generation of young Yankee gentlemen to embrace his principles as their own and act on them with integrity. Unlike his friend Samuel Cooper, Mayhew did not live to become one of the Sons of Liberty. But, in an intellectual sense, he was their father.

08/05/2024 11:52 AM
Santa Rosa County Library System
Gulf Breeze Library
(1)(850)981-7323

Patron Barcode: 223651101828xxx

Title: Father of liberty : Jonathan Mayhew and the principles of the American Revolution /
Barcode: 33801013119120
Due Date: 09/13/2024
Library Name Administration Center

Number of Check Out: 1

You saved $50.00 by using the library today. During the past year, you have saved $50.00 by borrowing from the library.

Serving our community - Committed to excellence

1

The Right of Private Judgment

At his Harvard College commencement in July 1792, a young Bostonian named Thomas Paine—no relation to the famous pamphleteer—recited his poem, *The Nature and Progress of Liberty*. When he addressed the origins of the American Enlightenment, Paine solemnly intoned:

> Then mental freedom first her power displayed,
> And called a Mayhew to religion's aid.
> For this dear truth, he boldly led the van,
> That private judgment was the right of man.
> Mayhew disdained that soul-contracting view
> Of sacred truth, which zealous Frenzy drew;
> He sought religion's fountain head to drink,
> And preached what others only dared to think. . . .[1]

Jonathan Mayhew had died almost thirty years earlier. The boy poet learned of the pastor from his father, Robert Treat Paine, a Massachusetts attorney and signer of the Declaration of Independence, who had attended services frequently at Mayhew's Boston church. This insightful verse laid open the essence of Mayhew's personal character. From youth to premature death, he rejected any tradition or authority that contradicted his own judgment and preached openly heterodox doctrines that some New England ministers, like his friends Charles Chauncy and Ebenezer Gay, "only dared to think."[2]

Mayhew's upbringing and education fueled his confidence in the efficacy of his own mind—and of human reason as such. His father, the widely admired missionary Experience Mayhew, was a teacher of Arminian theology who believed that "God dealeth with men as with reasonable creatures." At Harvard College in the 1740s, missionary's son studied the "natural religion" of the British Enlightenment, including the Arminian theology of John Tillotson and the anti-Trinitarian theology of Samuel Clarke. In his first book, *Seven Sermons*, Mayhew declared his independence from the orthodox Calvinism of his fellow Boston clergymen (rejecting Trinitarian Christianity soon after). *Seven Sermons* propounded the basic premises of eighteenth-century natural religion.

According to Mayhew, God is rational and benevolent, desiring the happiness of his mortal creatures. God created man with natural faculties—among them, a rational faculty and an innate "moral sense"—suited to the identification, pursuit, and attainment of happiness. Because God created all humans with the capacity for rational deliberation and moral agency, every individual has both the duty and the right to think rationally and live virtuously. By practicing the classical moral virtues out of a sincere love for God and man, humans are justified before God and can attain happiness on earth and in heaven. Anyone who imposes his own moral and religious judgments on another person violates the natural right of private judgment and therefore God's will for mankind. Understood in this heterodox Protestant framework, the right of private judgment ultimately had radical political implications, leading Mayhew to such "Real Whig" principles as individual natural rights, popular sovereignty, consensual government, and the people's right of resistance to tyranny. Sacralizing reason, worldly happiness, and moral virtue, the natural religion of *Seven Sermons* provided the vision of human nature and moral right on which Mayhew erected an individualistic conception of liberty and an equalitarian conception of civil government.

On October 8, 1720, Jonathan Mayhew was born to solidly Puritan parents with the solidly Puritan names of Experience and Remember Mayhew. Rev. Experience Mayhew was a poorly educated minister who lived in genteel poverty on Martha's Vineyard, an isolated island off the coast of the Province of Massachusetts Bay, sparsely populated by Wampanoag Indians and a few

Englishmen. For sixty-five years, Experience labored with quiet devotion as missionary to the natives, as his father, grandfather, and great-grandfather had done before him. Despite his lack of formal learning, Rev. Mayhew published in 1709 a translation of the Psalms and the Gospel of John in the Indians' native tongue. His mission work won him the admiration and support of such Puritan luminaries as Judge Samuel Sewall and Rev. Cotton Mather, who said of Mayhew, "in the Evangelical Service among the Indians, there is no man that exceeds this Mr. Mayhew, if there by any that equals him." The Praying Indians of Martha's Vineyard provided a rare example of success in the mission of the Massachusetts Bay Puritans to convert the indigenous population to English Protestant Christianity.[3]

The theology of John Calvin provided New England Puritanism with its hard core, and potential Indian converts were often baffled by the Calvinist tenets that human nature is totally depraved by original sin, God's will predestines most humans to damnation, and one can do nothing to earn salvation or even know for certain if one is counted among those souls divinely elected for salvation. Catholic missionaries in Canada and the Great Lakes had greater success with Indian conversion, teaching that Christians can access God's saving grace through faith combined with good works, such as participation in the sacraments of baptism and communion. In the late sixteenth and early seventeenth centuries, William Ames and other English Protestant theologians softened Calvinism by wrapping it in covenant theology, the doctrine that God's will is sovereign and he saves whomever he pleases, but he pleases to limit his own will by entering into a contract with mankind, offering humans the terms of salvation: faith as well as obedience to his revealed laws. Flourishing among the Massachusetts Bay Puritans, covenant theology struck a balance between divine power and human responsibility. By the early eighteenth century, this delicate balance tipped increasingly toward an emphasis on human responsibility, thanks to introduction of the "natural religion" of the British Enlightenment, which held that God's perfect rationality and benevolence limited his will and power and left room for humans to please God through their own rationality and benevolence. In his struggle to win Wampanoag souls for Protestantism, Experience Mayhew drifted unawares into the forbidden waters of rationalist heterodoxy.[4]

On November 23, 1718, Rev. Mayhew gave a sermon in Boston entitled *A Discourse Shewing That God Dealeth with Men as with Reasonable Creatures.*

In the familiar idiom of Puritan covenant theology, he took as given that God's covenants provide mankind with moral laws. The theme of his sermon was that, "while GOD does thus deal with Men in a Covenant-way, He Dealeth with them as with Rational Beings." Because God has "made Man a Creature capable of thinking" and imbued him with "such noble and excellent Powers" as "Reason and Understanding," Mayhew observed, men and women are "capable of the highest Views, and the most Excellent Employments and Enjoyments." In stressing God's rationality and his intent that man also live by the guidance of reason, the missionary tread dangerously close to the thin line separating Puritan covenant theology from Enlightenment natural religion.[5]

In emphasizing the rationality, justice, and benevolence of God, Experience Mayhew inadvertently crossed that line. "As GOD made us Rational Creatures," he instructed his Boston audience, "so He condescends to Reason and Argue with us, about things that are of the greatest importance and concernment to us; He is willing that Reason should decide every case wherein He has to do with us; And if there be any matters of Controversy betwixt Him and us, He invites us to argue with Him upon them." God takes pains to reveal the reasons behind his judgments, so that not even the damned can fairly claim his decrees to be "merely Arbitrary, without respect to Reason and Justice." John Calvin and the English covenant theologians claimed that there is no justice above God's sovereign will. Mayhew taught on the contrary that, while "GOD's Justice and Sovereignty are distinguishable one from the other, so it is not to be supposed that GOD ever so exerciseth His Sovereign Power as to act any ways contrary to Justice or Equity." It was not simply that God chose not to act in an arbitrary or mysterious fashion, but that God "neither does nor can act any thing contrary to His Infinite Wisdom, and Unalterable Truth." Rev. Mayhew insisted that "there are some things that are in their own Nature unjust, and therefore such as GOD neither can nor will do."[6]

This contention—that there is a natural truth and natural justice to which even God is subject—was a radical departure from orthodox Calvinism. By assuming that promise-keeping is a moral virtue that God *would not* violate, covenant theology brought Mayhew to the rationalist conclusion that there is a natural moral order, existing independent of God's will, that God *could not* violate without acting against his own perfection. Despite its heterodoxy, the missionary's sermon was published without controversy in Boston in 1720, and Harvard College rewarded the humble Indian preacher with an honorary degree. That same year, his son Jonathan was born.

Remember Mayhew died two years later from complications in childbirth; Experience never remarried. Like the Puritan Jehovah, his presence pervaded his son's life on Martha's Vineyard inescapably. Like the benevolent deity of the British Enlightenment, however, Experience treated his children as reasonable creatures, preferring persuasion to the rod. Jonathan loved and deeply respected his father. In 1764, five years after Experience's death, the younger Mayhew wrote of "the irreproachable memory of my father," whom he honored as "a good man, who spent a long life in the laborious and his patrimony in the humble and laborious, tho' apostolical employment of preaching 'the unsearchable riches of Christ' to *poor Indians*." Experience hoped his eldest son, Nathan, would carry on the family tradition of ministering to the Vineyard Indians. Having long called for an educated ministry in the Indian missions, he sent Nathan to Harvard College on scholarship, but the young man died only two years after his graduation. Experience's second son, Zachariah, eventually took up his father's mission work, but he was not well suited for higher education. Jonathan, the youngest son, displayed a dazzling intelligence and a special talent for classical languages. Greek and Latin were the principal subjects of the college entrance examinations. Despite his apparent lack of formal preparation, Jonathan passed his exams in July 1740 and secured a scholarship, beginning his education at Harvard that August at the age of nineteen, much later than most boys.[7]

Young Jonathan's belief in the power of natural reason, following from his upbringing by Rev. Mayhew on Martha's Vineyard, was affirmed by his program of study at Harvard. In the first decades of the eighteenth century, New England's foremost college came under the leadership of moderate Calvinist Congregationalists who softened the hard edge of Puritan orthodoxy with gentility of manners and a "catholic" spirit of tolerance. Among these moderate Calvinists were college presidents John Leverett and Edward Holyoke, pastors William Brattle and Nathaniel Appleton, and the long-serving Hollis Professor of Divinity, Edward Wigglesworth. In recommending Holyoke for the college presidency in 1737, Rev. John Barnard told the Massachusetts governor, "I think Mr. Holyoke as orthodox a Calvinist as any man; though

I look upon him too much of a gentleman, and of too catholic a temper, to cram his principles down another man's throat." One could not better convey the liberal spirit of New England's moderate Calvinists.[8]

Their moderation lay not in dilution of Calvinist doctrine but in willingness to let students exercise free inquiry in the pursuit of religious truth, confident that reason would lead them back to the faith of their Puritan fathers. Assigned reading immersed students in natural theology—the systematic inference of God's existence and attributes from the "design" of the natural world—and natural religion, the systematic deduction of moral law from man's divinely created nature. By the 1720s, one could find on the Harvard College library's shelves the works of Archbishop John Tillotson and Dr. Samuel Clarke, two Episcopalian champions of natural religion considered dangerously heterodox by orthodox Calvinists. While John Locke's *Essay Concerning Human Understanding* did not find its way into the Harvard curriculum until 1743, college tutor John Whiting taught its philosophic principles and methods of thinking as early as the 1710s. Dr. John Winthrop, first Hollis Professor of Mathematics and Natural Philosophy, introduced New England's elite youth to the inductive reasoning and naturalistic worldview of Robert Boyle, Isaac Newton, and Edmund Halley. As sound Protestants themselves, though, the students were less interested in science for what it said about nature than for what it implied about God's nature. Thanks to these liberalizing reforms, the germ of an American Enlightenment—simultaneously religious and rational—grew quietly but steadily in Harvard Yard over the course of the eighteenth century.[9]

The British Enlightenment's infiltration of the New England mind spurred orthodox Calvinists like Rev. Jonathan Edwards to put the old doctrines into new bottles and warm them with an evangelical appeal to emotion. Within a month of departing the sleepy isolation of Martha's Vineyard, Jonathan Mayhew found himself caught up in the First Great Awakening. Religious revival struck Boston in 1740 with the sudden violence of a northeaster. On September 16, a cross-eyed evangelist from England named George Whitefield brought the good news of God's mercy to Boston's anxious sinners. He preached nineteen times in eleven days, appealing to their fear of damnation and hope of deliverance. As many as 15,000 hungry souls gathered to hear Whitefield speak on Boston Common. During his sermon at the Old South Church, the frenzied crowd trampled five Bostonians to death. On

September 24, Whitefield addressed some 7,000 on Harvard's College Yard. A month later, he left the city to carry his message throughout Britain's colonies. American evangelist Gilbert Tennent came to Boston on December 13 to stoke the revival's smoldering coals. In the midst of a blizzard, he preached hellfire to enraptured thousands.[10]

That same month, Harvard tutor Henry Flynt observed approvingly a group of thirty-odd students—among them Jonathan Mayhew and his friends James Otis and Samuel Cooper—who "prayed together, sung Psalms, and read good books." In the autumn of 1741, after the spiritual fever had passed, a literal fever swept Harvard. Following a student friend's death, Mayhew contracted the illness. He recovered from his brush with annihilation convinced that God spared his life so he might preach the Gospel. News of religious revival sent Jonathan into ecstasies. "How thankful we should be to our Glorious Redeemer," he wrote his older brother Zachariah in December 1741, "that he is thus riding forth in the Chariot of his Word, conquering and to conquer. But happy, yea thrice happy, shall we be, if made partakers of these Blessings ourselves." Having felt that God had indeed made him a partaker in the outpouring of his grace, Jonathan urged his brother to testify to his own love of Jesus Christ before men. The young man's warm zeal received a cool reception from Zachariah. Disappointed by his brother's silence, Jonathan wrote again, reminding his brother just how "awful would it be for us to dye in Raptures, expecting to be convey'd by Angels into Abraham's Bosom, when Death has dissolved the Vital Ban, & to find ourselves in the merciless Embraces of ghastly Fiends, to be convey'd to the Regions of Horror and Despair." Jonathan's first attempt to convert a soul through the evangelical methods of Edwards and Tennent proved to be his last.[11]

By late 1743 at the latest, Jonathan had passed out of this phase. Familial influence may have played a role but not a decisive one. Despite drifting unintentionally into heterodoxy, his father was at heart a Puritan of the seventeenth century. Experience Mayhew's 1744 work *Grace Defended* drew criticism from Boston's Calvinist establishment for its Arminian implications, but the old missionary considered himself a conservative proponent of New England covenant theology. He sent Jonathan to Harvard to learn and carry on that family tradition. In response to his son's decision to become a clergyman, Experience exhorted Jonathan "to be diligent in reading and Studying the Oracles of God, which are able to make you wise unto Salvation thro'

Faith which is in Christ Jesus." He encouraged Jonathan to seek "knowledge of the Holy," which comes only through direct experience of God's grace, and warned him against relying for his knowledge of God upon "the light of Nature or Reason," as "unholy" people do. Although an "Old Light" critic of the Awakening's excesses, Experience Mayhew was not opposed in principle to the revivals and their reinvigorated Calvinism. The influence of Experience and Zachariah Mayhew may have contributed to the young man's rejection of evangelical religiosity, but his program of study at Harvard provided the intellectual antibodies with which Jonathan decisively fought off the revivalist fever. To his father's dismay, Jonathan soon developed an immunity to orthodoxy of all kinds.[12]

One can get a general sense of young Mayhew's undergraduate reading from an alphabetical list of assigned books that he recorded in 1741. The surviving third volume of his copybooks, stocked with quotations he extracted from his reading, offers a window into his intellectual development. Of the twenty-nine books on Mayhew's 1741 reading list, only about a half-dozen titles are primarily concerned with revealed religion or religious devotion, and fewer still with orthodox Calvinist theology. Of the remaining books, twelve best qualify as works of natural theology, natural religion, or natural philosophy, while nine are concerned with the improvement of one's natural faculties of reason and will. If some of his father's sermons were implicitly heterodox, Harvard offered him an alternative worldview in the explicitly anti-Calvinistic principles of the British Enlightenment.[13]

The first quotation that Mayhew printed in his college copybook states that "the determinations of Reason are Gods law to man." In this passage from *The Reasonableness of Scripture Belief*, the mid-seventeenth-century Presbyterian layman Charles Wolsey explained that we should obey the voice of reason as "the voice of God within us"; to "neglect or oppose" one's own rational judgment is "a sin."[14] In one of Mayhew's copybook quotations from Richard Steele's *Ladies' Library*, early eighteenth-century England's arbiter of good taste expounded:

For God having implanted in us a *rational* Faculty, . . . he expects we shou'd follow it, as the Guide and Director of our Lives and Actions; and whatsoever this Faculty does naturally, and in its due Exercise dictate to us, is as much the Voice of God as any Revelation. For whatever it naturally dictates, it must dictate by his Direction, who is the Author of its Nature, and who having fram'd it to speak such a Sense, and pronounce such a Judgment of Things, has thereby put his Word into its Mouth, and does himself speak thro' it, as thro' a standing *Oracle*, which he has erected in our *Breasts*, to convey and deliver his own Mind and Will to us."[15]

Since God endows his creatures with a rational faculty, the dictates of reason are another form by which God reveals his will to men, using natural rather than supernatural means. This sacralization of reason provided one of the basic premises of natural religion.

By exercising reason in the control and direction of our choices and actions, Mayhew's reading taught him, men and women can acquire moral knowledge and act accordingly. "It is the Cultivation of our *Reason*," the Presbyterian minister Dr. Isaac Watts explained in the assigned textbook *Logick*, "by which we are better enabled to distinguish *Good* from *Evil*, as well as *Truth* from *Falsehood*: And both these are Matters of the highest Importance, whether we regard this Life, or the Life to come." In his *Improvement of Reason*, another one of Mayhew's required books, Joshua Oldfield agreed that the goal of logic was "the prudent ordering of our selves, our Enquiries, Undertakings, and Pursuits," including our "inferior Employments." Mayhew dutifully recorded Richard Steele's contention that, since reason is the voice of God within us, we should submit to it as "the supreme Regent of all our other Powers, . . . as the *Rule* of our *Will*, and the Guide of all our animal Motions." So far from being totally depraved by original sin, man has the power—through his natural reason, without the assistance of divine grace—to master his "appetites" and direct them toward good ends.[16]

Mayhew's reading on natural religion at Harvard largely equated Christian morality with such classical moral virtues as wisdom, justice, fortitude, and temperance, which Steele explained were various applications of reason to action. Through the guidance of such virtues, humans can attain happiness on earth. Following Steele's extract on temperance, Mayhew transcribed into his copybook a passage from the *Works* of John Tillotson. The archbishop of Canterbury noted "ye wonderful Advantages of truth and Integrity, to ye Prosperity of even our worldly affairs." While reason leads to virtue, Mayhew learned, virtue leads to happiness. So far from confining salvation to a divinely elected few, the Enlightenment's benevolent God created all humans with the natural capacities for rational deliberation and moral agency—thus bringing happiness within everyone's reach. Isaac Watts called reason "the common Gift of God to all Men," while Steele added in *The Ladies' Library* that reason is God's gift to women as well.[17]

Mayhew's studies also provided the proper method of practical reasoning. He transcribed into his copybook a condensation of "Some general Rules for the Improvement of Knowledge," the first chapter of *The Improvement of the Mind*, Isaac Watts's supplement to his textbook *Logick*. "Once a Day," Watts recommended, "especially in the early years of Life and Study, call yourself to an Account what new Ideas, what new Propositions or Truth you have gained, . . . and let no Day pass, if possible, without some intellectual gain." The English pastor advised his young readers to maintain "a constant Watch at all Times against a dogmatical Spirit," because it "stops the Ear against all further reasoning upon that subject, and shuts up the mind from all further improvements of knowledge." He urged upon them "Humility and Courage enough to retract any Mistake and confess an Errour," as well as the courage to challenge the errors of their own times. Mayhew carefully recorded Watts's advice to be intellectually ambitious: "Let the Hope of new Discoveries, as well as the Satisfaction and Reason of known Truths, animate your daily Industry. Don't think that Learning in general is arrived at Perfection, or that the Knowledge of any particular Subject in any Science cannot be improved, meerly because it has lain 500 or 1000 Years without Improvement.—May there not be a Sir Isaac Newton in every Science?"[18] Watts himself had displayed Newtonian boldness in repudiating a 1,400-year-old dogma. Like Samuel Clarke and many Protestant ministers in early eighteenth-century England, he was an Arian, one who rejects the mystery of the Trinity as contrary to reason and Scripture and describes Jesus Christ as a supernatural being but not God himself.

Steele, Watts, and other Enlightenment writers on moral and intellectual self-improvement fueled Mayhew's confidence in his own mind and in human reason in general. He internalized Watts's "general rules" for practical reasoning, using it as his model in *Seven Sermons* for the proper exercise of "private judgment." By applying this method in his study of Scripture and theology, Mayhew soon came to radical conclusions about some of Christianity's most venerable articles of faith. Through its emphasis on logic, self-improvement, and natural religion, midcentury Harvard inadvertently trained Mayhew and others of his generation—like Samuel Cooper and

James Otis—to assert their epistemological independence against standing authority, inherited tradition, and arbitrary dogma of all kinds. During the 1740s and 1750s, most of Harvard's professors, tutors, and students were Calvinists, albeit of the moderate, "catholic" variety. The tolerant faculty and liberal curriculum, however, made it easy for independent-minded young Yankees like Mayhew to reject Calvinism, discover natural religion, and adopt it as an alternative worldview. In the example of Mayhew's intellectual development at college, one can see how Harvard contributed to the Enlightenment's gradual transformation of the New England mind, helping to turn the Calvinistic Puritans of the seventeenth century into the Unitarian Yankees of the nineteenth century.

On July 5, 1744, Mayhew graduated with a bachelor's degree, and he began three years of graduate study, still on scholarship. Enjoying full access to the college library, he immersed himself in the mental world of the British Enlightenment. During his research as a divinity student, Mayhew greedily devoured the theological tracts of the Episcopal theologians Samuel Clarke and Joseph Butler, philosopher John Locke's collected works, Bishop Benjamin Hoadly's tracts, and the recent sermons of George Benson, Nathaniel Lardner, James Foster, and other English Arian Presbyterians. This graduate study completed the mental revolution that his undergraduate education had begun. On the afternoon of July 1, 1747, he took his oral examination, the final requirement for his master's degree in divinity. For his thesis, Mayhew argued that reason accorded with faith in Christianity. His classmate, Abraham Williams, responded that a religion that upheld the doctrine of original sin could not be rational. According to one witness, Mayhew replied in Latin, "Master, that is true."[19]

During those three years of graduate study, Mayhew worked rigorously to prepare himself for service in the Congregationalist clergy. On March 11, 1746, he wrote his father that he had hoped to visit home in the spring, "but if I should begin to preach in about 3 or 4 Months (which at present I have Thoughts of doing) I shall need to improve my Time with the greatest Diligence to prepare for such difficult work." He got some practice giving guest sermons at Boston's First Church and Brattle Street Church, invited by two theological liberals, his college chum Rev. Samuel Cooper and Dr. Charles Chauncy.

In March 1746, the Congregational church at Worcester needed a new minister and invited Mayhew to preach. By October, the congregation narrowed its choices to Mayhew and Thaddeus Maccarty, a New Light revivalist. On January 19, 1747, a majority of the Worcester congregation decided by two votes in favor of Maccarty. On a strong recommendation from Rev. Ebenezer Gay, the liberal pastor of Hingham's First Church, the congregation at Cohasset unanimously invited Mayhew to apply as the pastor of their new church. There was another, more prestigious pulpit open, however, at the Congregational meetinghouse in Boston's prosperous West End neighborhood.[20]

On January 25, 1747, Mayhew gave a guest sermon at the West Church, and his plain style and liberal theology won over its affluent congregation. On Friday, March 6, the congregation elected him pastor by a vote of forty-four to two. By a unanimous vote, they offered him a salary of fifteen pounds per week, plus rent and firewood—as much as any pastor in Boston. Mayhew accepted the generous offer, and the Cohasset pulpit passed to his friend and fellow liberal, John Brown. The West Church set May 20 as the date for Mayhew's ordination and issued invitations to the clergy. Of the clergy outside of Boston, the West Church invited Mayhew's father, Ebenezer Gay, and Nathaniel Appleton of Cambridge. Of the nine other Congregational churches in Boston, though, the deacons sent invitations exclusively to the First Church and Brattle Street Church, the only churches in the city that had seen fit to invite Mayhew to preach. As the members of the West Church saw it, Boston's ministers had snubbed Mayhew, and they were happy to return the snub.

This was not the first time that the West Church had clashed with Boston's other churches. In 1737, seventeen upwardly mobile Bostonians, led by the merchant Harrison Gray, founded the meetinghouse as an asylum for liberal theology within the fortress of Calvinist orthodoxy. Unable to find liberal preachers in Boston, they gave the new pulpit to a Scottish immigrant named William Hooper, educated at the University of Edinburgh, cradle of the Scottish Enlightenment. Religiously liberal Bostonians who did not live in West End went out of their way to join Hooper's congregation. Irritated by the laity's desertion and suspicious of the new pastor's theology, no Boston clergyman would preach at Hooper's ordination. Against New England convention, Hooper preached at his own ordination. From the moment of the West Church's birth, a pattern was set of hostility between its congregation and the other Boston churches. In 1740, the Boston Association of Ministers accused Hooper of criticizing the Calvinist view of God. Fed up with the Congregationalist clergy's commitment to Calvinism, Hooper resigned his pulpit in 1746 and received ordination in London as a minister of the Episcopal Church of England. He returned to Boston as pastor of Trinity Church, the second oldest Episcopal congregation in Boston. The West Church congregation blamed Boston's orthodox ministers for hounding their much-loved minister into Episcopal conformity. The congregation got their revenge by embracing the heterodox Rev. Mayhew as Hooper's replacement and refusing to invite more than two Boston ministers to his ordination.[21]

The result, predictably, was a scandal. Mayhew had been invited to preach at the First and Brattle Street Churches by the junior pastors there, but the senior pastors declined invitations to his ordination, and Cooper and Chauncy deferred to the authority of their superiors. The ordination ceremony had to be rescheduled when Experience Mayhew was delayed on the long journey from Martha's Vineyard. Rather than conciliate the offended Boston clergy, the West Church invited fifteen country parishes but not a single Boston church to the rescheduled ordination. Eleven of the fifteen clergymen accepted, among them Mayhew's father, Gay, Appleton, and such noted liberals as Lemuel Briant of Braintree, William Rand of Kingston, and John Hancock of Lexington. Agreeing upon "the Soundness of *Mr. Mayhew's* Principles," the assembled pastors unanimously approved the congregation's choice on June 17 and ordained him a pastor of the Congregational church. That October, he wrote his father that the ordination scandal left him ostracized by his Boston colleagues. With characteristically stubborn independence, he added that, "thro' God's Goodness to me, I live very happily and contented without them." The young reverend took heart that the "People of my Parish seem to be well united—none having left us since my Ordination." The feisty West Church congregation loved their twenty-six-year-old minister all the more for refusing to yield his private judgment to pressure from the orthodox establishment.[22]

The mouthpiece of that establishment, the Boston Association of Ministers, voted to decline him membership, an act without precedent. One of the institutions of Boston's religious life was the Thursday Lecture, and only association members could participate. Mayhew defied the association by offering his own series of competing Thursday lectures, from June through August 1748. Whether attracted primarily by his message, notoriety, or reputation for eloquence and wit, audiences for Mayhew's lectures in the West Church were much larger than those typical for the regular Boston Thursday Lecture. The town's orthodox Calvinist clergy failed in their gambit to quarantine his heterodoxy. The local printers, Rogers and Fowle, published a Boston edition of *Seven Sermons* in 1749.[23]

The first of the book's sermons presented and defended the basic premises of natural religion. Mayhew identified three "universal truths which concern all times and persons and places alike," namely that the difference between truth and falsehood and right and wrong derive from nature, that humans possess the natural faculties to understand these differences, and that humans have an "obligation" to use their faculties and "to judge for themselves in things of a religious concern." Properly understood, Mayhew explained, truth is "a knowledge of things as they really exist," so truth "exists independently of our notions concerning it." If right derives from truth, and truth is objective, then it should be possible to deduce from our knowledge of objective reality a code of moral values, virtues, and rights that are themselves true, immutable, universally binding, and accessible to all human beings, regardless of religious confession.[24]

Seven Sermons offered three principal arguments for the grounding of moral right in the natural order of things. Drawing on premises from John Locke, Samuel Clarke, and Joseph Butler, Mayhew proposed "happiness" and "misery" as the characteristics that distinguish moral good and evil, characteristics of natural human experience he noted that do not even require the existence of God, let alone belief in a particular religious creed. The existence of God provides a second source of moral obligation. As the British Enlightenment's natural theology taught, one may infer from the Newtonian "beauty, order, harmony and design" of the physical universe that "the Author of the world must be a wise and good being." This wise and good Creator operates the natural world "in such a manner as to communicate the greatest possible happiness to his creatures considered collectively." Again echoing Clarke, Mayhew reasoned that all other beings capable of reason and benevolence must strive to imitate God's perfection in these attributes. From this imperative derives the "obligation to practice what is usually called *moral virtue*; for by this we imitate God: and fall in with his benevolent design in creating and governing the world."[25]

The third source of obligation, which he considered the most compelling and immediate of the three, is mankind's "moral sense," an innate faculty of moral intuition. Mayhew derived this hypothesis from Clarke, but his understanding of it also owes something to Butler's doctrine of conscience. As with happiness and misery, the moral sense gives humans an understanding of the difference between moral good and evil, "antecedent to all consideration of all human laws and compacts, yea, to the consideration of the will of God himself." It is a source of moral obligation grounded in human nature, independent of any consciousness, even God's.[26]

In the second lecture of *Seven Sermons*, Mayhew defended his proposition that all human beings have the natural ability to know good and evil, without divine grace, scriptural revelation, or ecclesiastical authority. The finite nature of human consciousness leaves some truths beyond the reach of man's reason, hence the need for revelations from God. Moreover, not all humans possess the capacity to make moral judgments to the same extent, as there is a "great variety in their intellectual faculties." People of "the lower class," for instance, have little time to think about religious and philosophical issues, but "even these may have the power of judging in *some degree*." And whatever effect the sin of Adam and Eve may have had upon the natural faculties of their descendants, it was not true that original sin crippled the human mind.[27] Echoing both Isaac Watts's *Logick* and Richard Steele's *Ladies' Library*, Mayhew offered a rhapsody to man's capacity for reason. He wrote:

> Let us retain a suitable sense of the dignity of our nature in this respect. It is by our reason that we are exalted above the beasts of the field. It is by this that we are allied to angels, and all the glorious intelligences of the heavenly world: yea, by this we resemble God himself. It is principally on account of our reason, that we are said to have been *created in the image of God*. So that how weak soever our intellectual faculties are, yet to speak reproachfully of reason in general, is nothing less than blasphemy against God. Let us, therefore, instead of contemning this inestimable gift, in which consists the glory of our nature, employ it to the ends for which it was designed, in the service of the great Father of our spirits.[28]

Mayhew's Enlightenment view of man as the rational creature of a benevolent Creator was a radical break from the Calvinist view of man as totally depraved by original sin and dependent upon the grace of an inscrutable God.

In the third of his *Seven Sermons*, "The Right and Duty of Private Judgment Asserted," Mayhew explained what it means specifically and practically to exercise natural reason in search of truth and right. To form objective judgments about reality, a person must begin by suspending his "judgment intirely concerning the truth or falsehood of all doctrines; and the fitness or unfitness of all actions; 'till such time as he sees some reason to determine his judgment one way rather than the other." Only once his mind is in such a state of impartiality can it "be determined solely by reason and argument. He does not bring his old prejudices and prepossessions to determine the point; but comes prepared, by an unbiassed mind, to receive the impressions of reason, and of reason only." The next step, Mayhew explained, is "the exerting of our own reason in weighing arguments and evidences that offer themselves to us, or that are offered by others." We must be "active and vigorous in the pursuit" of knowledge, "inquire into facts" and consider a proposition from different perspectives, "not taking up the arguments that are brought to support any doctrine or practice." The pursuit of truth is useless, he insisted, "unless we follow it wherever it leads" and accept its conclusions without regard for "whatever notions it may contradict; whatever censures it may expose us to." The pastor warned his flock to "have no superstitious veneration for *great names*" and guard against the temptation "to believe as our forefathers did, or as any particular body of men does at present." Finally, one should make one's belief in a given proposition proportional to the evidence available for it. By this method, which Mayhew learned from Isaac Watts's *Logick*, one can become an independent thinker, an intellectually and morally autonomous individual.[29]

According to Mayhew, each individual not only can guide his life by reason—he must. What man *is* determines what he *ought* to do. All of man's natural organs and faculties have "an apparent *final cause*." Just as eyes are for seeing and ears are for hearing, so our minds exist to search for truth. "Our obligation, therefore, to inquire after truth, and to judge what is right," the minister contended, "may be found within us, in our own frame and constitution. This obligation is as universal as reason itself; for every one that is endowed with this faculty, is, by the very nature of it, obliged to exercise it in the pursuit of knowledge; especially of moral and religious knowledge." Lifting Locke's statement in his *Essay Concerning Human Understanding* that "we may as rationally hope to see with other Mens eyes, as to know by other Men Understandings," Mayhew declaimed that each person must rely upon the judgment of his own mind because one can no more "see only with another's eyes" than one can "think, and judge, and believe, with another's understanding." Within his own sovereign mind, each man stands alone or not at all.[30]

The exercise of "private judgment" is a "duty" dictated by human nature, but not a selfless duty; its principled practice serves one's self-interest. For Mayhew, there is no necessary conflict between duty and interest. The fundamental moral issue that all humans must explore, he preached, is the nature of personal happiness. The pastor asked rhetorically: "What is my chief good? Where is the road that will convey me to my happiness? Where shall I find this inestimable jewel?" Independent thinking is man's basic means of identifying, pursuing, and attaining happiness, and happiness by its nature is individual, personal, and private. Mayhew explained:

> Each individual has an interest of *his own* depending. We find, by experience, that we are all capable of being happy or miserable to a great degree. Pain and pleasure, at least, are private and personal things. And even they that arrogate to themselves the right of *judging for us*, do not pretend to *feel for us* also. Now if it be of any importance to us to be happy for ourselves, it is of importance to judge for ourselves also; for this is absolutely necessary, in order to our finding the path that leads to happiness.[31]

Having begun with the premise that man is naturally capable of independent thinking, he quickly arrived at the conclusion that each individual is morally obligated to think independently, for his own benefit.

Just as there is no necessary conflict between duty and interest, Mayhew insisted in the first of his sermons, so there is no necessary conflict between personal happiness and the happiness of others. Considering happiness an intrinsic good and misery an intrinsic evil, Mayhew concluded that "it is in itself right to do good to others, as well as ourselves, happiness being as valuable to them as it is us." From this principle, he reasoned, one may infer all of the classical moral virtues, such as "fidelity, justice, charity." The pastor observed that, "by the steady, uniform practice of these virtues, both the good of individuals, and of the publick, is promoted." Because virtue promotes the worldly happiness of "mankind," humans are obliged to practice it, even "without the consideration of there being a God" or afterlife. The individual's pursuit of worldly happiness is not a threat to the public good. "For publick happiness is nothing but the happiness of a *number* of *individuals* united in society," the minister contended. "So that if the individuals of which the society consists, be happy, the community must necessarily be happy also. And, on the other hand, the *community* is rendered miserable in the same degree that *individuals* are so." Self-interest—if pursued in accordance with reason and virtue—contributes to the good of the whole.[32]

The moral duty to judge for one's self and act accordingly implies a moral right to exercise that judgment without the interference of others. "If a man has a right to judge for himself, certainly no other has a right to judge for him," Mayhew maintained, "And to attempt it, is to strike at the most valuable interest of a man considered as a reasonable creature." Since God commands the exercise of private judgment and the spread of Christianity requires "free examination," those who try to impose their own opinions on others violate divine will as well as human nature. Mayhew accordingly condemned those "spiritual invaders" who "throw their chains and fetters upon the mind" as "incroachers upon the natural rights of mankind" and "enemies to truth."[33]

He specified these "enemies" by naming their methods. "Those that are guilty of this crime in the highest degree," he said, "are such as inflict capital punishments upon those that embrace opinions contrary to their own." For this first degree of evil, he indicted the Roman Catholic Church—"the *mother of harlots*"—which murdered Christians for their faith through the cruel offices of the Holy Inquisition. Those who commit this crime in the second degree are those "who punish *dissenters* and *nonsubscribers*, by fines and imprisonments" and by depriving them of civil privileges. Mayhew did not have to tell his audience that he was speaking of the Episcopal Church of England, which in the eighteenth century still excluded Presbyterians, Congregationalists, Baptists, Quakers, and other Protestant dissenters from public office through the Test and Corporation Acts. Mayhew said that a "practice akin to those mentioned above" is the making of creeds to serve as "human tests of *orthodoxy*, instead of the infallible word of God." Like Roman Catholics and Episcopalians, New England Calvinist clergymen assault the individual's right to think for himself when they threaten him with hellfire for refusing to accept "the grossest absurdities" that are "not to be examined *with reason*, but to be believed and adored *without it.*" Mayhew did not fail to include his Boston tormentors among the enemies of intellectual freedom.[34]

The West Church divine claimed that one effect of religious tyranny is "to prevent all improvements in religious knowledge, and to entail ignorance, error, and superstition upon future generations." Had such restrictions been placed centuries ago on the arts and sciences, he suggested, they would have suppressed "the greatest and most enterprising *Genius's*" and deprived mankind of the blessings of material progress. Religious coercion serves to establish and propagate only "*ignorance* and *hypocrisy.*" Considering the tendency of most people "to follow the multitude," Mayhew found little need to keep "people in the old beaten track by the terror of penal laws, gibbets, inquisitions, *spiritual* courts, and *carnal* curses."[35] Indeed, he declared, such methods are incapable of making people religious, because the conviction of the mind cannot be forced. Mayhew satirized the vicious futility of intellectual coercion. Alluding to Louis XIV's deployment of dragoons against the Huguenots, he sardonically quipped:

> To attempt to *dragoon* men into sound orthodox *Christians*, is as unnatural and fruitless as to attempt to *dragoon* them into good *poets, physicians* or *mathematicians.* A blow with a club may fracture a man's skull; but I suppose he will not think and reason the more clearly for that; though he may possibly believe the more *orthodoxly,* according to the opinions of some. And upon this account it must be confessed that those who make use of these methods to propagate their sentiments, act very prudently; for their doctrines are generally such as are much more readily embraced by a man after his brains are knocked out, than while he continues in his senses, and of a sound mind.[36]

Force can destroy a man's mind, but it cannot change it. Samuel Clarke had also argued that "nothing affects the *Understanding* and the *Will*, but *Reason* and *Persuasion,*" such that "the *inward* Acts of the mind, *cannot* be forced." Blind faith begets tyranny while reason takes its stand with liberty.[37]

Anticipating objections to these arguments in his fourth sermon, Mayhew posited that truth prevails when the mind is free. "Free examination, weighing arguments *for,* and *against,* with impartiality, is the way to find the truth," he observed, and this is as true with religion as with natural science. "The cause of error and superstition may suffer by a critical examination; its security is to lurk in the dark," he declaimed, "But the true religion flourishes the more, the more people exercise their right of private judgment." That some people may fall into error is insufficient grounds for depriving them of their freedom to think and choose for themselves. "We may as well pick our neighbour's pocket, for fear he should spend his money in debauchery," Mayhew reasoned, "as take from him his right of judging for himself, and chusing his religion, for fear he should judge amiss and abuse his liberty." The pastor's confidence that Christianity would thrive in a state of intellectual liberty depended upon his view of man as capable of reason and of his religion as based on nature.[38]

Since Martin Luther's defense of "Christian liberty" in 1520, Protestants have affirmed the individual's freedom to read and interpret Scripture without human interference. Luther taught that humans are justified before God by faith alone, such that salvation does not require the freedom of action to perform good works. In *Seven Sermons*, however, Mayhew did not confine the right of private judgment to the pursuit of moral and religious knowledge. "That which renders it a matter of the highest importance to examine with freedom into moral and religious subjects," he posited, "is not so much the advantage simply of *knowing* what is *true* and *right*, as the necessity of this in order to true and right *action*." Building on John Tillotson's formulation of the right and duty of private judgment, the West Church pastor expanded religious liberty to protect both the beliefs of the mind and the actions of the body dictated by those beliefs. "We have not only a right to think for ourselves in matters of religion, but to act for ourselves also," he maintained in *Seven Sermons*. "Nor has any man whatever, whether of a *civil* or *sacred* character, any authority to controul us, unless it be by the gentle methods of argument and persuasion." This broad construction of religious liberty followed from the natural religion that both Mayhew and Tillotson espoused.[39]

In the last three lectures of *Seven Sermons*, Mayhew assailed the Calvinist doctrine of justification by faith alone on behalf of justification by faith and good works, a doctrine that orthodox Calvinist critics associated with the Protestant Arminian heresy as well as Roman Catholicism. The West Church pastor preached a "practical religion" consisting of "such conduct as may render us acceptable to our creator, and lay the foundation for rational happiness here and hereafter." Mayhew repudiated the Calvinist doctrine of justification by faith alone without falling into Catholic doctrine. He equated "good works" not with participation in the sacraments of an institutional Church, but with justice, charity, moderation, and the other classical moral virtues—so long as these virtues follow from "Christian motives": sincere, heartfelt love for God and one's neighbor.[40]

Because Mayhew believed that religious belief required the practice of moral virtue, he concluded that the right to judge implies the right to act according to one's judgments. Due to his heterodox association of faith with works, Mayhew's commitment to religious liberty led him to civil liberty as it had not led Martin Luther. *Seven Sermons* was a book of moral philosophy, not political philosophy, but it asserted "the cause of *religious liberty*" as "of no less importance even to the present happiness of human society, than that of civil liberty, in opposition to arbitrary power." Mayhew would always maintain that, as faith must not be separated from works, moral judgment must not be separated from moral action, and man's spirit cannot be separated from his living body, so religious and civil liberty must rise or fall together.[41]

By sacralizing natural reason, worldly personal happiness, and classical moral virtue, Mayhew's natural religion telescoped "the right and duty of private judgment" to include the whole sphere of man's moral life, giving this principle radically individualistic and equalitarian implications for politics. Less than a year after the Boston publication of *Seven Sermons*, he published his first and most controversial political pamphlet, *A Discourse Concerning Unlimited Submission and Non-Resistance to the Higher Powers*. In terms borrowed from John Locke, Mayhew characterized political authority as "originally a *trust*, committed by the people" to their governors, "neither God nor nature, having given any man a right of dominion over any society, independently of that society's approbation and consent to be governed by him." The divine insisted that "the people know for what end they set up, and maintain, their governors, and they are the proper judges [of] when they execute their *trust* as they ought to do it." For one to say the people are "not proper judges when their governors oppress them, and play the tyrant," he growled, "is as great *treason* as ever man uttered; it is treason,—not against one single man, but the state—against the whole body politic;—'tis treason against mankind;—'tis treason against common sense;—'tis treason against GOD." His belief in the people's natural capacity for rational deliberation and moral agency, and in their God-given right of private judgment, guided him to the "Real Whig" principles of individual natural rights, popular sovereignty, consensual government, and the right of resistance to tyranny. Mayhew's heterodox religious views, as propounded in *Seven Sermons*, laid the foundation for his radical political views.[42]

The Boston clergy received *Seven Sermons* with contemptuous silence, but it delighted heterodox Protestant dissenters in Britain. Just before his death in 1749, Jeremiah Bollan, "a friend to the dissenting cause," gave copies of *Seven Sermons* to two English champions of the right of private judgment: Benjamin Hoadly and Benjamin Avery. Mayhew lauded Bishop Hoadly in *Seven Sermons* as "the noted scourge of civil and ecclesiastical tyranny." Hoadly was still considered the Church of England's principal defender of the rights of Protestant dissenters, and Dr. Avery was chairman of the Dissenting Deputies, a private association that lobbied Parliament for repeal of the laws depriving Protestant dissenters of their full civil rights. While Hoadly asked Avery to convey his compliments to Mayhew, Avery lent his own copy of *Seven Sermons* to Dr. George Benson, an Arian Presbyterian minister and a leader of London's nonconformist community. "They breathe the noble spirit of liberty & extensive charity, & give us a pleasing prospect of such a spirit's being diffused in N. England," Benson exulted in a letter to Mayhew, "I love you, tho' unknown; & sincerely wish you successes in your studies & labors." To encourage his lonely campaign against New England's Calvinist orthodoxy, Avery, Benson, and two other London ministers, Nathaniel Lardner and James Foster, secured Mayhew an honorary doctorate from the University of Aberdeen in January 1750. By that summer, the London press had printed the first British edition of *Seven Sermons*. The young pastor from Martha's Vineyard, snubbed by his colleagues in Boston, found himself the toast of dissenting Britain.[43]

Published in 1755, Mayhew's second collection of sermons touched off a theological controversy by assaulting systematically the doctrine of justification by faith alone as well as repudiating the mystery of the Trinity, which he blamed for the failure of Christians to win over "*Jews* and *Mahometans*." Although merely building upon the Arian theology he learned at Harvard from the works of Samuel Clarke and George Benson, Mayhew was the first colonial American clergyman to challenge Trinitarian Christianity explicitly and publicly. Anticipating the outcry, he told his readers, "I will not be, even *religiously* scolded, not pitied, nor wept and lamented, out of any principles which I believe upon the authority of Scripture, in the exercise of that small share of reason which GOD has given me." The *Sermons* of 1755 horrified New England's Calvinist colossus Jonathan Edwards and drew criticism from such staunch Calvinists as Ebenezer Pemberton, pastor of Boston's Old Brick Church, and Edwards's son-in-law, Aaron Burr, president of the College of New Jersey. They could not, however, contain the rationalist heresy that Mayhew's *Sermons* had unleashed. In a 1755 letter, one minister wryly lamented the recent appearance of "Mayhewmetans" among New England's once orthodox clergy.[44]

While Mayhew could count only Chauncy and Cooper as friends among the Boston clergy, he had immense appeal to certain independent-minded young Yankees, many of them Harvard graduates entering secular professions. According to legend, Paul Revere's strict Calvinist father forbade his son to go hear Mayhew's sermons (perhaps the popular series of public Thursday lectures he gave in the summer of 1748), and the boy received a paternal beating for attending anyway. Whether this family anecdote is true or not, Paul Revere became a full member of the West Church and made its pastor the subject of his first copper engraving. Robert Treat Paine, Mayhew's friend at Harvard, frequently attended services at the West Church. Mayhew often visited his two sisters in Braintree, a village just outside of Boston, where he won the affection of John Adams's young Quincy cousins, Josiah II, Edmund, and Samuel. The latter two were full members of the West Church, and Edmund became a dear friend of the pastor. Mayhew won the heart of Richard Cranch, John Adams's future brother-in-law, who reluctantly left the West Church to move to Braintree. Mayhew regularly exchanged pulpits with his friend Lemuel Briant, pastor of Braintree's Congregational church, giving young John Adams "an Opportunity often to hear him in the Pulpit." The West Church pastor was an electrifying influence on these future leaders of the New England's Whig opposition movement, particularly Adams.[45]

While Mayhew enjoyed the firm support of his congregation at the West Church, Briant's Arminian preaching provoked a revolt within his Braintree congregation in the early 1750s. John Adams followed the Briant controversy closely, and the council of ministers that ultimately condemned Briant convened in the home of Adams's father, a deacon of the Braintree church. With

Briant's premature death in 1753, Mayhew became the primary influence on Adams's religious and philosophical views. The young Harvard graduate recorded in his diary on March 17, 1756, that one minister "told me very civilly that he supposed I took my faith on trust from Dr. Mayhew." That October, Adams wrote fellow Mayhew disciple Richard Cranch that he had considered a career in divinity, but the "frightful engines of ecclesiastical councils, of diabolical malice and Calvinistical good-nature never failed to terrify me exceedingly whenever I thought of preaching." So he decided in favor of a legal career, in which "I shall have liberty to think for myself without molesting others or being molested myself."[46] In his capacity as a young lawyer, Adams followed Mayhew in applying the right and duty of private judgment to political and constitutional issues. While preparing for a court case in 1761, he wrote:

In Protestant Countries and especially in England and its Colonies, Freedom of Enquiry is allowed to be not only the Priviledge but the Duty of every Individual. We know it to be our Duty, to read, examine and judge for ourselves, even ourselves what is right. No Priest nor Pope has any Right to say what I shall believe, and I will not believe one Word they say, if I think it is not founded in Reason and in Revelation.... Every Man has in Politicks as well as Religion, a Right to think and speak for himself. No man either King or Subject, Clergyman or Layman, has any Right to dictate to me the Person I shall choose for my Legislator and Ruler. I must judge for myself.[47]

For Adams as for Mayhew, the right and duty of private judgment implied a radically individualistic understanding of civil and religious liberty as personal autonomy.

To understand how Dr. Jonathan Mayhew emerged as colonial America's most politically influential clergyman and why he specifically advanced such an individualistic and equalitarian understanding of liberty, one must first examine his fundamental philosophic premises about God, human nature, epistemology, and morality, as well as such theological issues as original sin and justification. His conclusions on these religious and philosophic matters shaped his vision of man as capable of rational deliberation and moral agency, endowed by his benevolent Creator with certain individual and natural rights. This vision prompted Mayhew to adopt and preach revolutionary political principles like the right of resistance and the sovereignty of the people. In the West Church pastor and such young "Mayhewmetans" as Robert

Treat Paine, Paul Revere, Edmund Quincy, Richard Cranch, and John Adams, one can see how the moral and religious principles of the British Enlightenment guided eighteenth-century Yankees toward the political principles of the British Real Whigs. More generally, one can see an example of the role of philosophic ideas in inspiring and motivating political radicalization.[48]

2

The Right of Resistance

In a letter of February 13, 1818, retired US president John Adams offered Hezekiah Niles, a Baltimore newspaper editor, some reflections on the nature and origins of the American Revolution. He insisted that the term "American Revolution" should apply not to the war with Britain but to an intellectual change that preceded and caused that war. "The Revolution was effected before the war commenced. The Revolution was in the minds and hearts of the people; a change in their religious sentiments of their duties and obligations," Adams contended. "*This radical change in the principles, opinions, sentiments, and affections of the people, was the real American Revolution.*" Stung by a biographer's recent claim that the Virginian orator Patrick Henry initiated this intellectual change in 1763, the proud old Yankee argued that a handful of Massachusetts Whigs were the true fathers of "*the real American Revolution.*"[1]

This process of "radical change" began, Adams explained in his letter to Niles, with "an awakening and a revival of American principles and feelings" provoked by intrusive new British policies. He counted "Dr. Mayhew" as fifth among the seven men—including Samuel Adams, John Hancock, and James Otis—who were "the most conspicuous, the most ardent and influential in this revival, from 1760 to 1766." The clergyman's contribution to the revival of "American principles," however, began earlier still, with "a sermon in 1750, on the 30th of January, on the subject of passive obedience and non-resistance, in which the saintship and martyrdom of King Charles the First are considered, seasoned with wit and satire superior to any in Swift or

Franklin. It was read by everybody; celebrated by friends, and abused by enemies." The Massachusetts Bay Puritans had suffered under the reigns of Britain's Stuart princes, "and Mayhew seemed to be raised up to revive all their animosities against tyranny, in church and state, and at the same time to destroy their bigotry, fanaticism, and inconsistency." Mayhew "had great influence in the commencement of the Revolution," and it was in his *Discourse Concerning Unlimited Submission* that the "real" Revolution had its earliest stirrings.[2]

Adams considered the Revolution itself—and Mayhew's particular contribution to it—as conservative. The Revolution was "radical" in the sense of a return to colonial America's roots, a revival of its first principles. The retired president explained in one 1818 letter to his former law clerk, William Tudor, that "independence" from the English state and the Church of England was "the fundamental principle of the first colonization. . . . When we say, that Otis, Adams, Mayhew, Henry, Lee, Jefferson, &c. were authors of independence, we ought to say they were only awakeners and revivers of the original fundamental principle of colonization." Beginning with his *Discourse* in 1750, Mayhew's contribution to the intellectual origins of America's war with Britain consisted not of introducing new ideas of government but of reviving the political principles of seventeenth-century Puritan Commonwealthmen and early eighteenth-century Real Whigs, volatile ideas that increasingly lost respectability in Britain as the eighteenth century wore on.[3]

The most controversial component of Mayhew's first political publication was its denunciation of King Charles I and vindication of Parliament's revolution against him—including the king's execution on January 30, 1649. No New England clergyman had dared defend the regicide explicitly since Rev. John Cotton in 1651. The sanguinary rhetoric of Mayhew's *Discourse* was shocking to many, at a time when British subjects on both sides of the Atlantic lived comfortably and complacently under the relatively benign rule of King George II. Why then did Mayhew think it necessary to assert the natural right of a people to overthrow and kill their ruler?[4]

Ironically, Mayhew conceived his revolutionary pamphlet as a conservative defense of Britain's Hanoverian dynasty, and of Protestant dissent as a bulwark of its legitimacy. Upholding the right of resistance and the sovereignty of the people, he reaffirmed these "revolution principles" as the proper grounding for the Revolution Settlement of the 1690s and therefore the House of Hanover's claim to the Crowns of England and Scotland. In this paradoxical and roundabout way, the Congregational pastor sought to clear those English Protestants who dissented from the Church of England of the accusation of disloyalty to the Crown leveled by high-church Episcopal clergy. Mayhew found the revival of Tory obedience principles by high-church clergy in the late 1740s disturbing, and he was determined to pull up these slavish doctrines by the roots before they spread in New England. Although conservative and anglophilic in its intentions, Mayhew's bold assertion of the sovereign people's right to depose and execute their own king struck some Episcopalians as profoundly radical not in the conservative but the subversive, seditious, and insurrectionary sense of the word.

New England's Congregational clergymen and Episcopalian missionaries both had long memories, understanding their denominational competition for Yankee souls in the historical context of Britain's religiously charged politics. For Mayhew and his Congregational colleagues, the Episcopal threat to their churches in New England began with the persecution of their Puritan ancestors by Charles I's archbishop William Laud in the 1630s and resumed with the restoration of the Stuart dynasty and the Episcopal Church of England in 1660. Since the Restoration, Episcopal clergy held sermons on the anniversary of King Charles I's execution on January 30, 1649. These anniversary sermons praised the king's memory, condemned parliamentary resistance and the English Republic, and solemnly reaffirmed the political principles of the absolute divine right of kings, the indefeasible hereditary succession of kings, the apostolic succession of bishops, and the people's duty of passive obedience and nonresistance to tyrants. Anniversary sermons also gave Episcopal divines the opportunity to excoriate Presbyterians and Independents (called Congregationalists in America) as the vanguard of the Parliamentarian and republican causes.[5]

In 1662, the reestablished Episcopal Church of England expelled from its ranks all those clergymen who refused to subscribe to its creed, the Thirty-Nine Articles. The expelled Puritans were thereafter known—together with professed Presbyterians, Congregationalists, Baptists, Quakers, and other Protestant sectarians—as dissenters or nonconformists. Subjecting them to the same Penal Laws as Roman Catholics, Parliament implemented a battery of new laws—including the Uniformity Act, Conventicle Act, Test Act, and Corporation Act—that prohibited Protestant dissenters from worshipping independent of Episcopal discipline, voting for or holding civil office, and receiving degrees or teaching at royally chartered universities. The Episcopalian ruling class thereby hoped to protect the English Church and Crown from destruction by the same sectarians whom it blamed for the national catastrophe of civil war, regicide, and parliamentary rule in the 1640s and 1650s.[6]

Within the Episcopal Church of England, though, low-church clergymen such as John Tillotson and Samuel Clarke thought that the only hope of reunifying English Protestants under one national Church for the common struggle against international Catholicism lay in reconciliation between the established national Church and the Protestant dissenters. These "latitudinarians" in the Episcopal clergy emphasized reason and morality over theology in their sermons so as to minimize the factional differences among English Protestants and make the Church more hospitable for dissenters with tender consciences. They also asserted a natural "right and duty of private judgment" by which all men as rational creatures can and should form their own interpretations of Scripture independent of any creed and worship according to their own lights independent of Episcopal discipline. While high-church Episcopal clergy were politically allied with the pro-Stuart Tory Party in Parliament, latitudinarians tended to be sympathetic to the Whigs, members of Parliament who asserted the political principles of popular sovereignty, consensual government, the right of resistance to tyrants, and religious toleration for Protestant dissenters.[7]

The rising specter of Catholicism did indeed have the effect of reunifying British Protestants of all persuasions, if only briefly. The Stuart king James II's ambition to put Catholicism on an equal footing with Protestantism in Britain drove high-church Episcopalians, low-church Episcopalians, and Protestant dissenters into an alliance against this common threat. They welcomed military intervention by the Dutch Protestant prince William of Orange, which prompted King James to flee the country. The Glorious Revolution of 1688–1689 and Parliament's subsequent Revolution Settlement of the 1690s left British Protestants quite unsettled, however.[8]

Committed to hereditary succession and popular nonresistance, high-church Episcopal clergymen could not recognize William of Orange as Britain's de jure king. Most grudgingly accepted him as the de facto king, but a few "non-jurors" preferred to leave the Episcopal Church than break their oath to King James and swear fealty to the new ruler. Both "high-flyers" like Henry Sacheverell and Jacobite nonjurors like Charles Leslie bitterly resented King William, his low-church supporters in the Church, and his Whig supporters in Parliament for suspending enforcement of the Penal Acts against Trinitarian Protestant dissenters with the Toleration Act of 1689. They despised dissenters and Whigs together as secretly republican in their political principles and subversive of the divine right of kings and bishops to rule the state and Church.[9]

In the 1690s and early 1700s, religious commitments and resentments continued to fuel political conflict between Whigs and Tories over the Revolution Settlement, a set of laws that included the Toleration Act, the Bill of Rights, and parliamentary recognition of the Hanoverians' claim to the Crown to the exclusion of all Catholic heirs. In defense of the Revolution Settlement, the low-church divine Benjamin Hoadly preached the "revolution principles" by which many Whigs justified the Glorious Revolution against James II: popular sovereignty, contractual and consensual government, and the natural right of resistance. In the latitudinarian tradition of John Tillotson and Samuel Clarke, Hoadly also used his power as a bishop to champion the rights of Protestant dissenters to full religious liberty and equal civil rights, going so far as to advocate the Episcopal Church of England's disestablishment. In the name of "the right of private judgment," English Protestant dissenters like George Benson and Benjamin Avery lobbied Parliament for repeal of the Test and Corporation Acts, finding sympathetic allies in Bishop Hoadly and the Whig minister Lord Barrington.[10]

Proclaiming "the Church in danger" from dissenters and their friends, Henry Sacheverell used the pulpit to reaffirm Tory obedience principles, associate Whigs and dissenters with republicans and regicides, and question the right of Parliament to exclude Catholics from the royal succession. In 1710 Robert Walpole and other Whig politicians prosecuted Sacheverell for sedition against the British Crown. When the trial turned into a propaganda victory for the Tories, Walpole concluded that the right of resistance was too controversial for public debate. When Tory statesmen like Lord Bolingbroke and high-churchmen like Bishop Francis Atterbury were implicated in the abortive Jacobite Rebellion of 1715 and subsequent plots, the incoming Hanoverian king, George I, looked to the Whigs and Protestant dissenters as natural allies.[11]

Over the decades that followed, Walpole and ministerial Whigs consolidated control of government, but they spoke less and less about the right of resistance. They came to understand the Glorious Revolution as a triumph of parliamentary, not popular, sovereignty. Locked out of power, self-styled "Real Whigs" like John Trenchard and Thomas Gordon denounced the Whig party leadership for corruption and abandonment of principle. In their political tracts *The Independent Whig* and *Cato's Letters*, Country Whig writers Trenchard and Gordon pleaded for dissenters' rights and the old revolution principles, but theirs was a voice in the wilderness. Meanwhile, Congregationalists and Presbyterians in New England identified with the English Protestant "dissenting interest," believing that repeal of the Test and Corporation Acts would put their own civil and religious liberties on a better legal footing within the British Empire. Their clergymen were unanimously devoted to the Glorious Revolution, the Protestant Succession, the Toleration Act, and the Whig party, believing that dissenters' rights would rise or fall with the fortunes of the Hanoverian dynasty.[12]

During the reign of King George I, high-church Episcopal clergy were less vocal in preaching Tory obedience principles from the pulpit. Easily smeared for disloyalty to the Hanoverian dynasty as Atterbury had been, most of them reluctantly accepted the Protestant Succession and the Toleration Act. But they answered the pleas of Protestant dissenters for repeal of the Test and Corporation Acts with contempt, accusing nonconformists of being as dangerous to the British constitution as their regicidal forebears. When James II's Catholic grandson, the Young Pretender, landed a French-financed army in Scotland in 1745 and marched within two hundred miles of London in 1746, all of the old fears of the 1680s and 1710s broke out in the open again. The Jacobite Rebellion gave high-churchmen a providential opportunity for full rehabilitation. By denouncing the Forty-Five in terms of divine right and passive obedience, they sought to free Tory ideology from its old association with Jacobite disloyalty.

One can detect this revival of high-flying Toryism in the anniversary sermons that ministers made immediately in the wake of the Jacobite Rebellion. On January 30, 1746, Dr. Andrew Trebeck reaffirmed the divine right of kings in his anniversary sermon to the House of Commons. Calling kings the "Viceregerents [sic] of God" and "the Anoited [sic] of the Lord," he saved his most lavish praise for "the blessed Martyr of this Day." "Most of those Virtues and Graces, which were admired singly in others, were united all, and shone eminently in him," said Trebeck of Charles I. Identifying the Parliamentarian resistance of 1641 with the Jacobite Rebellion of 1745, Trebeck warned Britons against "entertaining such Principles, as tend to encourage such rebellious Practices." On January 30, 1747, the bishop of Carlisle stood before the House of Lords, extolling the "excellent virtues [that] shone in the Royal MARTYR" and blaming his "barbarous Murder" on Puritan fanaticism and "the Madness of the People." On January 30, 1749, Dr. Thomas Pickering echoed these sentiments in his sermon to London's mayor and aldermen in St. Paul's Cathedral. He eulogized Charles as superior to his enemies "in Birth—in Virtue—in the Goodness of his Cause—I wish I could add, the Success of it too—But at last Enthusiastic Frenzy prevailed over true Courage." Of the fallen king, Pickering intoned: "He was swifter than an Eagle—stronger than a Lion.—But . . . Lions have been destroyed by Vermin."[13]

Pickering observed that the hundredth anniversary of the regicide held profound lessons for midcentury Britain. Describing the Puritan Parliamentarians as "a disorderly Rabble of Enthusiasts scrambling for Power in every Part of the Kingdom," the London vicar proposed that the dissenters of his own day—asking for the right to vote and hold office—were no different. "The only sure Method, that I know of (with the Blessing of God) to prevent all such Disorders and Confusions for the future," he maintained, "is for the Members of the Established Church to look upon the Test Act as an essential—most sacred—most inviolable Law." The Episcopal Church of England did not wish to revoke the Toleration Act and resume persecution of Protestant dissenters. "But then, on the other Hand, it would be great Imprudence, and downright Folly, . . . to trust them with Power." He urged London's mayor and aldermen "to be most industriously watchful—and to oppose vigorously all Schismatical Designs—all Antimonarchical Principles. Be extreamly cautious lest such Principles as these should ever revive, and insinuate themselves under the same, or newer and more specious Disguises, to attempt and accomplish the same Mischiefs for the future."[14]

Far from providing the ideological foundation of the Protestant Succession, these divines claimed, Whig revolution principles were subversive of the British constitution. Far from serving as the bulwark of Hanoverian legitimacy against Jacobitical treason, Protestant dissenters were no more to be trusted than Catholic dissenters. By this reasoning, high-churchmen stood Whig ideology on its head. Once disgraced by its association with Jacobitism, Toryism found a new respectability in British political culture. The revival of obedience principles after 1746 was not confined entirely to England. Some missionaries of the Society for the Propagation of the Gospel in Foreign Parts, like Rev. Charles Brockwell, carried those political ideas with them to the American colonies, challenging the Whig consensus in Congregationalist New England.

Commissioned King's Lecturer by the bishop of London, Brockwell had the task of preaching the afternoon sermon at King's Chapel in Boston. While Henry Caner, the rector of King's Chapel, gladly accepted invitations to perform the Episcopalian liturgy in Boston's Congregational churches, Brockwell considered it "a sin" to do so, refusing even to enter a meetinghouse. His bigoted resentment of Congregationalists likely had some connection to his personal attachment to the memory of King Charles I. When Brockwell was on his deathbed in 1755, he gave the attending physician an ancient Bible as his parting gift. "I value it very much," he explained. "It was given to my father by King Charles the First, who presented it to him with his own hand, after having taken it down from a shelf in his library, when my father was there with the royal martyr." On January 30, 1749, Brockwell gave a sermon in King's Chapel commemorating the "royal martyr." Its text does not survive, but one may surmise from his description of the sermon in a letter to the bishop of London, and from Jonathan Mayhew's response, that it resembled Pickering's anniversary sermon in praising Charles for his saintly character, denouncing the regicide, and casting suspicion upon the loyalty of Protestant dissenters.[15]

Aggravated by the high-church rehabilitation of Tory principles in general and by Brockwell's Boston performance in particular, Mayhew resolved to vindicate Protestant dissent and Whig revolution principles with a retaliatory strike. The West Church pastor grumbled that he would not have addressed the controversial subject of Charles I's death "were it not that *some men* continue to speak of it, even to this day, with a great deal of warmth and zeal; and in such a manner as to undermine all the principles of LIBERTY, whether civil or religious, and to introduce the most abject slavery both in church and state; so that it is become a matter of universal concern." In preparation for his response to Brockwell, Mayhew researched a first edition of Bulstrode Whitelocke's *Memorials of the English Affairs*, a Cromwellian politician's partisan account of the English Civil War. He copied into a blank page of his old Harvard copybook a timeline of major political events, from King Charles's accession in 1625 to Archbishop Laud's execution in 1645. Notably, he also transcribed a passage from Trenchard and Gordon's *Cato's Letters* on the proposal during Charles's reign to introduce the Inquisition to England. Most probably, Mayhew further prepared by reviewing *Cato's Letters*, *The Independent Whig*, John Locke's *Second Treatise of Government*, Algernon Sidney's *Discourses Concerning Government*, Benjmain Hoadly's *Measures of Submission*, and John Milton's *Tenure of Kings and Magistrates*, among other works in the canon of Whig and republican political thought. All of these works have echoes in Mayhew's response to Brockwell. For the West Church pastor, there was a clear continuity of ideas from Parliamentarians like Whitelocke, Milton, and Sidney to Whigs like Locke, Hoadly, and Trenchard and Gordon. These were the principles on which he believed the liberty of Britain and New England depended, and he resolved to defend them from attack by his Episcopal adversaries on both sides of the Atlantic.[16]

Mayhew agreed with Brockwell that the principles at stake in 1641 were the same ones at stake in 1749. By vindicating the right of resistance in general and Parliamentarian resistance to Charles I in particular, he proposed to clear Protestant dissent and Real Whiggism of high-church smears. On the approach of the one-hundredth anniversary of the king's execution, Mayhew gave two sermons on the subject of the regicide. On the Sunday following January 30, 1750, he gave his West Church congregation the sermon soon after printed as *A Discourse Concerning Unlimited Submission and Non-Resistance to the Higher Powers; With Some Reflections on the Resistance Made to King Charles I. And on the Anniversary of His Death: In Which the Mysterious Doctrine of That Prince's Saintship and Martyrdom Is Unriddled*. The pamphlet reconciled the natural right of resistance with the Christian duty of obedience in light of Scripture, history, and Real Whig political philosophy. It amounted to a defense of the Parliamentarian cause, including the execution of Charles I.[17]

It might seem odd for a colonial minister to assert the right of the people to resist—and even kill—their king, at a time when Britain was complacently secure in its liberty and prosperity under the benign rule of King George II, whom Mayhew warmly acknowledged as a friend to Protestant dissenters and colonial rights. As Mayhew explained in the preface to his *Discourse*, though, a "spirit of domination is always to be guarded against, both in church and state, even in times of the greatest security." Nations that have fallen under "the iron sceptre of tyranny" could have remained free had they remained sensitive to and watchful against "despotic measures." "Civil tyranny is usually small in its beginning," he observed, "like 'the drop of a bucket,' till at length, like mighty torrent, or the raging waves of the sea, it bears down all before it, and deluges whole countries and empires." Mayhew's political activism was based on the Real Whig principle of *obsta principiis* (resist first beginnings). He believed that power, by its nature, expands through small steps, and tyranny triumphs only when it is not opposed from the start. He acted on this principle from his first political sermon to his last one. "It will always be necessary," he wrote in *The Snare Broken* sixteen years later, "for those who would preserve and perpetuate their liberties, to guard them with a wakeful attention; and in all righteous, just and prudent ways, to oppose the first encroachments on them. 'Obsta principiis.' After a while it will be too late."[18]

Mayhew acted on *obsta principiis* as a general principle, but the increasingly strident memorial sermons of high-churchmen suggested to him a specific and growing threat to the rights of Protestant dissenters. "It was the near approach of the *thirtieth* of *January*," he explained in the *Discourse*'s preface, "that turned my thoughts to this subject: on which solemnity, the *slavish* doctrine of passive obedience and non-resistance, is often warmly asserted; and the dissenters from the established church, represented not only as schismatics ... but also as persons of seditious, traitorous and rebellious principles." Using language very similar to Trenchard and Gordon's *Independent Whig*, he characterized "ecclesiastical tyranny" as "the most cruel, intolerable and impious, of any." Mayhew urged vigilance against "these reverend *jockies*" who lust for the chance to mount and ride the people as if they were animals. "People have no security against being unmercifully *priest-ridden*," he growled, "but by keeping all imperious BISHOPS and other CLERGYMEN who loved to 'lord it over God's heritage,' from getting their *foot* into the *stirrup* at all." Once people fall under tyranny, they find their spirits crushed, and they lose their will to resist. It is therefore critical for the friends of liberty to speak up in its behalf, he declaimed, while they are still free to speak. Mayhew's warnings should be understood in a specific historic context: the aggressive revival of high-church Episcopal Toryism in the wake of the Jacobite Rebellion of 1745. His intentions in writing the *Discourse* were paradoxically conservative—to reaffirm the principles of the Glorious Revolution and prevent the loss of British liberties secured by the Revolution Settlement.[19]

Mayhew insisted that it is appropriate for a Christian minister to address political questions from the pulpit since even the apostles discussed them. He began the *Discourse* as an exegesis of Romans 13:1–8, one of the New Testament's most influential statements on government. In this passage, the apostle Paul proclaimed to Rome's Christians, "Let every soul be subject unto the higher powers." Anyone who resists the higher powers will be damned because they resist "the ordinance of God." One can see that the powers are ordained by God, the apostle explained, because "rulers are not a terror to good works, but to the evil." The ruler is "the minister of God to thee for good," and evildoers should fear him, because "he beareth not the sword in vain." Consequently, God expects Christians to obey their rulers "not only for wrath, but also for conscience sake," and to pay their rulers the "tribute," "fear," and "honor" which they are due. High-church clergy had long interpreted this passage to mean that the only response to tyranny in keeping with Christian duty is nonresistance and "passive obedience" (known today as "passive resistance" or "civil disobedience"). According to Tory obedience principles, armed resistance to one's king is never right, even in defense of life, liberty, and property. The dutiful Christian subject can only endure punishment at the tyrant's hands and await divine intervention with "tears and prayers," as with England's providential deliverance by William of Orange in 1688. Mayhew's *Discourse* aimed to explode the doctrine of passive obedience and nonresistance—and with it, the Tory interpretation of the English Civil War and the Glorious Revolution.[20]

Mayhew's *Discourse* sought to prove that the duty of obedience explained in Paul's letter to the Romans was fully compatible with the active resistance of Parliamentarians to Charles I in 1641 and of Whigs to James II in 1688. Borrowing heavily from a 1705 sermon on Romans by Bishop Benjamin Hoadly, he devoted most of his *Discourse* to the question of "the *extent* of that subjection *to the higher powers*, which is here enjoined as a duty upon all christians." He noted that, throughout history, some "have thought it warrantable and glorious, to disobey the civil powers" in defense of "their natural and legal rights," as in the case of the assassination of Julius Caesar, the execution of Charles I, and the overthrow of James II. Some commentators have interpreted Romans as forbidding resistance under any circumstances, Mayhew observed, because they erred in addressing the clause about obeying rulers separately from the clause about the benefits of rulership to society. When Paul told the Roman Christians to obey the "higher powers" as the ordinance of God, he did not mean all rulers.[21]

Mayhew took the epistle's injunction of obedience as conditional rather than absolute. In commanding Christians to obey the higher powers as the ordinance of God, he meant only those rulers who serve the ends for which God ordained them, specifically, to be "a terror . . . to the evil" and a "minister of God to thee for good." When the apostle refers to "power," then, he could not mean "lawless *strength* and brutal *force*," but only "just *authority*." Paul clearly meant that rulers are the ordinance of God "only so far as they perform God's will, by acting up to their office and character, and so by being benefactors to society." If a magistrate becomes a terror to good subjects, then "the main end of civil government will be frustrated. And what reason is there for submitting to that government, which does by no means answer the design of government?" Magistrates who "rob and ruin the public, instead of being guardians of its peace and welfare," he explained, "immediately cease to be the *ordinance* and *ministers of God*; and no more deserve that glorious character than common *pirates* and *highwaymen*." If a ruler's commands require the violation of divine law, "disobedience to them is a duty, not a crime." Bearing in mind the rights of Protestant dissenters, Mayhew added that "if persons refuse to comply with any legal establishment of religion," then "such obedience is lawful and glorious."[22]

Mayhew's Hoadlyian interpretation explained why Christian duty does not require active obedience to tyrants, but the Tory doctrine of passive obedience and nonresistance already admitted that much. The Boston divine proceeded to contend that, so far from *prohibiting* resistance to tyrants, Paul's letter implicitly *requires* the people to resist those rulers who thwart God's will. Since Christians must obey a king only because he rules for the good of his subjects, Mayhew proposed, then "it follows, by a parity of reason, that when he turns tyrant, and makes his subjects his prey to devour and to destroy, instead of his charge to defend and cherish, we are bound to throw off our allegiance to him, and to resist." The pastor conceded that Paul's epistles never addressed the question of resistance to tyrants. But, "by his grounding his argument for submission wholly upon the good of civil society," the apostle "implicitly authorises, and even requires us to make resistance, whenever this shall be necessary to the public safety and happiness." Having taken for granted that Paul's words should be interpreted logically and contextually, Mayhew was free to deduce from those words, "by a parity of reason," a theory of active resistance "implicitly authorize[d]" by Romans.[23]

By this train of arguments Mayhew arrived at what historian Bernard Bailyn wryly called "the Lockeanism of St. Paul." In terms owing much more to Locke and Hoadly than the apostle, Mayhew described political authority as "originally a *trust*, committed by the people to those who are vested with it," such that no government possesses authority "independently of that society's approbation and consent to be governed by him." Building the political arguments of his *Discourse* on the moral philosophy of *Seven Sermons*, he took for granted that the people have the natural capacity and natural right to judge for themselves whether their rulers have become despotic and must be resisted.[24] Challenging the view of human nature on which Toryism was based, Mayhew declaimed:

To say that subjects in general are not proper judges when their governors oppress them, and play the tyrant; and when they defend their rights, administer justice impartially, and promote the public welfare, is as great *treason* as ever man uttered;—'tis treason,—not against one *single* man, but the state—against the whole body politic; —'tis treason against mankind;—'tis treason against common sense;—'tis treason against GOD. And this impious principle lays the foundation for justifying all the tyranny and oppression that ever any prince was guilty of. The people know for what end they set up, and maintain, their governors; and they are the proper judges when they execute their *trust* as they ought to do it;—when their prince exercises an equitable and paternal authority over them;—when from a prince and common father, he exalts himself into a tyrant—when from subjects and children, he degrades them into the class of slaves;—plunders them, makes them his prey, and unnaturally sports himself with their lives and fortunes.[25]

Armed resistance by the people to a despotic prince is not treasonous or un-Christian, as high-church Tories would have it. So far from it being criminal for a nation to oppose a tyrant, it "would be highly criminal in them, not to make use of this means." Bringing his exegesis of Romans to a stirring climax, Mayhew found it more likely that "they that did NOT resist, than that they who did, would *receive to themselves damnation.*"[26]

Having dismantled Tory obedience theory to his own satisfaction and offered scriptural and philosophic arguments for resistance in general, Mayhew then turned to the specific historical questions that prompted this sermon: the causes for resistance to King Charles I, the matter of who made this resistance, the question of its legitimacy, and the motives of high-church clergy for commemorating Charles's death as that of "a great SAINT and MARTYR." While most Hanoverian Whigs did not want the Glorious Revolution to be associated with the English Civil War, the American clergyman proudly and confidently defended Parliamentarian resistance in 1641.[27]

Against the high-church Tory view that the English people had no objective grievances against King Charles I, Mayhew maintained that Parliament resorted to arms only after years and years of cruel abuses. Drawing upon Whitelocke's *Memorials,* Mayhew claimed that Charles had "governed in a perfectly wild and arbitrary manner, paying no regard to the constitution and laws of the kingdom, by which the power of the crown was limited." He listed the king's violations of English liberty, from levying taxes without parliamentary consent to supporting Archbishop Laud's "church tyranny." Mayhew insisted that "there was no rational hope of redress in any other way," so armed resistance "was absolutely necessary, in order to preserve the nation from slavery, misery and ruin." It was entirely Charles's despotic conduct that provoked the armed resistance "which, at length, issued in the loss of his crown, and of *that head* which was unworthy to wear it." Understood in historic context, parliamentary resistance in the 1640s was not a criminal act of rebellion but rather "a most righteous and glorious stand, made in defence of the righteous and legal rights of the people."[28]

Although Mayhew affirmed the people's natural right of resistance, he emphasized that the Lords and Commons—not an anarchic mob—initiated and directed resistance to the king. Since, in matters of legislation, Parliament has "an equal co-ordinate power, with that of the crown," the war was a defense of the British constitution made by two branches of the government against the third branch. He found it outrageous that Charles invoked the divine right to rule without constitutional limits, since even God "is *limited by law*; not indeed, by *acts of Parliament*, but by the eternal *laws* of truth, wisdom and equity; and the everlasting *tables* of right reason." Mayhew characterized Parliament's resistance as a conservative struggle to prevent England's constitutional monarchy from becoming absolute, but he described the British constitution in terms of the radical Whigs' principles of 1688. He claimed that British sovereigns "hold their title to the throne, solely by the grant of parliament; i.e. in other words, by the voluntary consent of the people." The people consent to be ruled by kings on condition that "the prerogative and rights of the crown are stated, defined and limited by law." A prince who violates the law "loses the king in the tyrant: he does to all intents and purposes, unking himself, by acting out of, and beyond, that sphere which the constitution allows him to move in." Mayhew held that rebellion is force against a lawful ruler, while resistance is "a just and reasonable self-defence" to a ruler who violates the law. Since Charles's reign was "illegal" and "very oppressive," "to resist him, was no more rebellion, than to oppose any foreign invader, or any other domestic oppressor." Parliamentarian resistance was a clear example of national self-defense against a tyrant.[29]

Having validated the right of resistance and vindicated its exercise by the Parliamentarians against Charles I, Mayhew claimed that the Glorious Revolution was another appropriate application of the same right. Against moderate Tory contentions that the Glorious Revolution was a providential deliverance that did not involve popular or parliamentary resistance to King James II, the Boston minister posited:

Upon the same principles that the proceedings of this parliament [the Long Parliament of 1640] may be censured as wicked and rebellious; the proceedings of those, who since opposed king *James II*. and brought the Prince of *Orange* to the throne, may be censured as wicked and rebellious also. The cases are parallel.—But whatever some men may *think*, it is to be hoped that for their own sakes, they will not dare to *speak* against the REVOLUTION, upon the justice and legality of which, depends (in part) his present MAJESTY'S right to the throne.[30]

Mayhew struck an intellectual coup here. Any attack on Parliament for overthrowing Charles I imputed wrongdoing to Parliament for overthrowing James II. And any attack on the Glorious Revolution in turn undermined the Protestant Succession and George II's legitimacy. While high-churchmen like Pickering and Brockwell tried to defame dissenters by associating them with republican disloyalty to Stuart kings, Mayhew retaliated by associating high-churchmen with Jacobite disloyalty to Hanover kings. Despite their efforts at rehabilitating Tory obedience principles since 1746, he would not let high-church clergy shake the old tag of crypto-Jacobitism.

One could object that the Glorious Revolution was essentially different from the Civil War because James II got to keep his head. It was not enough for Mayhew to defend Parliament's right to resist Charles; he also had to address the sensitive subject of regicide. Noting it was not Parliament but the Roundhead army that tried and executed Charles, Mayhew acknowledged that the army trial was "little better than a mere mockery of justice"; those who put him to death *might* have been guilty of murder. He denied, however, that Charles's judges were guilty of regicide, because the Stuart tyrant "had, in fact, *unkinged* himself long before, and had forfeited his title to the allegiance of the people." The army put to death not a king but only a man—and not a good man, at that. Styling him "a man black with guilt and *laden with iniquity*," Mayhew claimed that Charles brought "an immature and violent death upon himself, by being *wicked overmuch*."[31]

The Congregational divine attributed the honors that the Episcopal Church of England heaped upon Charles Stuart—"this *burlesque* upon saintship and martyrdom"—not to the holiness of his life and death but to the arbitrary power he gave the Church during his reign. Charles was "willing that the clergy should do what they would," no matter how oppressive and unchristian it might be. In return, the clergy agreed to "be *tools* to the crown" by preaching the divine right of kings and the doctrine of passive obedience and nonresistance. "In *plain English*," Mayhew proposed, "there seems to have been an impious bargain struck up betwixt the *sceptre* and the *surplice*, for enslaving both the *bodies* and *souls* of men." Even in the eighteenth century, long after the fall of the Stuarts, "all bigotted clergymen, and friends to church-power" continue to praise Charles I in their January 30 sermons as a way of advancing Tory obedience principles and thereby winning royal favor. This is "the true key" to the otherwise inexplicable cult of King Charles I. "He was a saint, not because he was in his life, a good *man*, but a good *churchman*; not because he was a lover of *holiness*, but the *hierarchy*; not because he was a friend to *Christ*, but the *Craft*." Mayhew quipped sardonically, "And he was a martyr to his death . . . , not because he died an enemy to *sin*, but *dissenters*." It may have been this passage that struck John Adams as "seasoned with wit and satire superior to any in Swift or Franklin."[32]

In his closing comments, Mayhew indicated that he attacked the cult of the royal martyr specifically as a menace to the rights of Protestant dissenters. He complained that high-churchmen used their memorial sermons not only to laud Charles I for virtues he did not possess but also to heap dissenters with "that reproach which they do not deserve." The Yankee divine appreciated that the religious liberty of New England Congregationalists and English Protestant dissenters under British law would rise or fall together, and he took up the defense of the transatlantic dissenting interest. "WE are commonly charged (upon the *Thirtieth* of *January*) with the guilt of putting the king to death, under a notion that it was our ancestors that did it," the Congregational pastor protested, "and so we are represented in the blackest colours, not only as schismatics, but also as traitors and rebels, and all that is bad." His vindication of commonwealth principles certainly did little, though, to assuage high-church fears that Protestant dissenters were crypto-republicans and potential regicides. Indeed, Mayhew concurred with his antagonists that January 30, 1649, was a date to be remembered. "It is hoped," he concluded (with allusion to the 1740 anthem "Rule, Britannia!"), that the anniversary "will prove a standing *memento*, that *Britons* will not be *slaves*; and a warning to all corrupt *councellors* and *ministers*, not to go too far in advising to arbitrary, despotic measures."[33]

Charles Brockwell retaliated against Mayhew even before the *Discourse*'s publication at the end of February 1750. On February 19, the *Boston Evening-Post* reprinted on its front page a sermon by the seventeenth-century Royalist Thomas Sprat that eulogized the Christian virtues of King Charles I. Brockwell submitted the sermon with the anonymous lamentation that a certain "wrangling Preacher in this Town" had just "belch'd out a Flood of Obloquy upon the pious Memory of King Charles the first," and he hoped Sprat's testimony on the king's character would "serve as an Antidote against the ill Effects that Wrangler's Railing Accusation may have on the unthinking Multitude." On February 26, the *Boston Evening-Post* carried another front-page testament to Charles's virtue, in which Brockwell condemned Mayhew (again, anonymously) for expressing such contempt for "that good King" who "redressed every Grievance, real or imaginary" before "that infamous Parliament levied War against him." Brockwell wrote the bishop of London that his sermon on January 30, 1748–1749, provoked "this monstrous piece of impudence," and he submitted the February newspaper articles in retaliation. Styling Mayhew an "unlicked Cub of Forty One," he was infuriated that "Treason must be supported by Treason, & in a barbarous & cruel Revenge the Royal Martyr's Character must be Butcher'd a Century after his Sacred Person had been Murther'd." The King's Lecturer denounced the *Discourse* as a "scandalous Libel" against "the Pious Memories of the Royal Martyr," Archbishop Laud, and the Bench of Bishops in the House of Lords, let alone "ye inferiour Clergy." While "a Jury of Fanatics" in Boston would surely clear Mayhew of the charge, Brockwell urged the Bishop to transport Mayhew to England and prosecute him for libel in a London court.[34]

Brockwell was not alone in these sentiments. In his own complaint about the *Discourse*, Dr. James MacSparran, an apostate Congregational pastor and missionary in Rhode Island for the Society for the Propagation of the Gospel in Foreign Parts (SPG), wrote the bishop of London, "I think no Government safe under the Influence of *all* its Principles" and hypothesized that the Boston divine might be a Jacobite spy. Mayhew's pamphlet came under siege in the public prints. From late February to early July, Mayhew's Tory attackers and Whig defenders proceeded to refight the English Civil War on the front pages of the major Boston newspapers. While scholars today tend to view the political culture of provincial New England as uniformly Whiggish, this newspaper debate exposed a vein of true Tory ideology that set the Episcopal clergy in New England at odds with the Congregationalist and Presbyterian majority. Mayhew's outraged high-church antagonists were aggressive and determined in their campaign to scuttle the *Discourse*. On April 17 and 23, one reader of the *Boston Evening-Post* attempted to discredit Mayhew by accusing him of plagiarizing a sermon by Bishop Hoadly and closely imitating Trenchard and Gordon's *Independent Whig*. In the May 8 edition of the *Boston Gazette*, a reader responded to the charge of plagiarism, claiming that the Tory accuser "has alter'd, added to, and omitted Part of the Words of those passages he pretends to quote, both from Bishop Hoadley and Mr. M—w." The newspaper disputants most often expressed their differences in terms of emotional appeals to party principles and old grievances, indicating that

Mayhew was not alone in viewing modern British politics within the framework of the long and bitter conflict between high-church Tories and low-church Whigs.[35]

As for the charge of plagiarism, the West Church reverend seemed amused and even proud that colonial Tories thought his sermon read like Hoadly's. When Dr. Benjamin Avery wrote Mayhew on July 17, 1750, to congratulate him for attaining an honorary doctorate from the University of Aberdeen, the London philanthropist noted that old Bishop Hoadly read Mayhew's *Seven Sermons* and had directed Avery to "join his thankful acknowledgment with my own." On October 17, the gleeful young man wrote Avery of his "profound veneration" for Hoadly and asked him to forward to the Whig prelate a copy of the *Discourse Concerning Unlimited Submission*. In his enclosed letter to Hoadly, Mayhew conveyed—with uncharacteristic humility—his "worthless Thanks to those which all the good Men of three Nations owe, & the best pay, to your Lordship, for your writings, both political & theological." Offering the bishop of Winchester a copy of the *Discourse*, he wrote with a wink that Hoadly had "an undoubted Right to a Copy of it so that I could not omit sending it, without manifest Injustice; if that be true which some here have assented, viz., That the greater Part of it was stolen from your Lordship's Original." To have his own work mistaken for that of his intellectual hero was a source of affirmation rather than embarrassment.[36]

Although Mayhew never retracted any part of the *Discourse*, he did feel, upon reflection, some need to explain the severity of its sardonic attacks upon the high-church clergy. After Dr. George Benson helped secure him a doctorate in recognition for *Seven Sermons*, Mayhew sent him a copy of the *Discourse*. He expected that Benson "will probably, think some of the Expressions too harsh." Mayhew wrote, "I have no other apology to make, than that I was, about this time, much irritated by the sensible Clamors of some Tory-spirited Churchmen; this being the strange Spirit that seems to prevail amongst the Episcopal Clergy here, even to this Day." Some twentieth-century commentators have been less charitable than Mayhew was to himself. Alan Heimert, a scholar of colonial literature, claimed that Mayhew unfairly made his reputation as a political radical "by the easy means of flogging a dead king and inveighing against 'high-church tory-principles and maxims.'" In light of the historic context, though, there was nothing easy about writing the *Discourse*.[37]

Mayhew reaffirmed Real Whig political ideas at a time when those ideas had lost respectability in England. In the wake of the Jacobite Rising of 1745–1746, high-churchmen expressed new confidence in reasserting Tory obedience theory and denigrating Protestant dissenters as potential rebels and regicides and their Puritan ancestors as "rabble" and "vermin." Horrified to hear high-church Toryism preached in his native Boston, Mayhew rose to defend the dissenting interest and Whig revolution principles, upon which he believed the achievements of the Glorious Revolution and the civil and religious liberty of New England depended. He knew that, in attacking Tory principles and the cult of the royal martyr, SPG missionaries could be expected to respond with outrage and threats of prosecution. As he wrote of such high-church bigots in the preface to the *Discourse*, "*Their* censure is praise: *their* praise is infamy." While few Whigs rose to his aid, New England Tories savaged him in the press for half a year, and the pamphlet's notoriety returned to bite him years later in clashes with such well-placed antagonists as the royal governor of Massachusetts and the archbishop of Canterbury.[38]

Like *Seven Sermons*, though, the *Discourse* won him new admirers in England among a small circle of theologically heterodox Protestant dissenters who still upheld the old revolution principles. The New England Tory who accused Mayhew of copying Hoadly also accused him of imitating John Trenchard and Thomas Gordon's *The Independent Whig*. Mayhew was honored to have his pamphlet received not only by Hoadly but by Richard Baron, the friend and heir of Gordon, who had died in 1750. Determined to sustain England's Whig revolution principles, Baron reprinted Mayhew's *Discourse* in London in 1752 as part of *The Pillars of Priestcraft and Orthodoxy Shaken*, a collection of anti-high-church tracts in the idiom of *The Independent Whig*. Baron saw the fading spirit of Trenchard and Gordon alive and well in Mayhew's sermon. The twenty-nine-year-old American pastor picked up the Real Whig tradition of revolutionary politics in the mid-eighteenth century where Gordon and Hoadly left off.[39]

Some New Englanders of the rising generation picked up that tradition, in turn, from Mayhew. On July 18, 1818, John Adams mailed a new edition of the sixty-eight-year-old *Discourse* to his fellow retired US president, Thomas Jefferson. In the cover letter he enclosed with the pamphlet, Adams asked his Virginian friend, "Will you accept a curious Piece of New England Antiquities? It was a tolerable Chatechism for The Education of a

Boy of 14 Years of Age, who was destined in the future Course of his Life to dabble in so many Revolutions in America, in Holland and in France." He explained to Jefferson that he often heard Mayhew preach from the pulpit of the Braintree meetinghouse. "This discourse was printed, a Year before I entered Harvard Colledge," Adams related, "and I read it, till the Substance of it was incorporated into my Nature and indelibly engraved on my Memory." Mayhew was not the progenitor of new ideas in political thought. His *Discourse* and later political sermons served to advance the ideas of Milton, Sidney, Locke, Hoadly, and other English opposition writers within New England's political culture at a time when those ideas were under siege in Britain. As many scholars have argued, one reason why the ideas of the great Whig philosophers resonated so intensely with the rising generation of New England leaders is that they, like Adams, had first encountered these ideas as boys and teenagers in the written and spoken sermons of Mayhew and like-minded Congregational ministers over the decade preceding the constitutional crisis with Britain.[40]

Although eager to defend the revolt of his Puritan ancestors in 1641, Mayhew's goal was not so much a radical justification of Charles I's execution and the English Commonwealth as a conservative justification of the deposition of James II and the Revolution Settlement. He understood the Glorious Revolution as based upon the Whig revolution principles of natural rights, popular sovereignty, consensual government, religious liberty, and the right of resistance. In defending these ideas against Tory criticism, he championed Britain's Revolution Settlement and the rights of English Protestant dissenters, which that settlement imperfectly secured against high-church and Catholic persecution. In their January 30 memorial sermons, high-churchmen readily extended their denigration of seventeenth-century Puritans and commonwealth principles to eighteenth-century dissenters and revolution principles, so Mayhew felt compelled to offer a comprehensive response. His intentions were conservative and Anglophilic, but the *Discourse*'s implications were radical and potentially subversive of British Crown rule, as his Tory critics attested. While New England Congregational clergy took the right of resistance for granted, Mayhew's justification of the regicide was the first one argued publicly by a Yankee minister for a century.[41]

It would not be the last. Over the following three decades, more Congregational clergymen—like Andrew Eliot, Gad Hitchcock, Samuel West, Charles

Chauncy, and Samuel Cooper—followed him in preaching Whig revolution principles with increasing boldness and frequency, thereby contributing to the political radicalization of the New England laity. The ideas of popular sovereignty and armed resistance that appeared marginal, subversive, and even treasonous to many Englishmen (and all high-churchmen in America) seemed self-evidently true to New Englanders who had grown up hearing them from hometown pulpits. By reconciling the Christian duty of obedience with the natural right of resistance in the minds of New Englanders, Mayhew and the Congregational clergy who followed his example contributed critically to that "change in their religious sentiments of their duties and obligations," which Adams considered "*the real American Revolution.*"[42]

Considered by historian Bernard Bailyn as "the most famous sermon preached in pre-revolutionary America," Mayhew's *Discourse* provided one important conduit for the transmission of English Real Whig political thought to the minds of young New Englanders like John Adams. "With the publication of the *Discourse*," Bailyn has written, "Mayhew's reputation was complete, and he stood out thereafter as a pre-eminent spokesman in the colonies for everything that was new, bold, and radically nonconformist in matters of church and state." It was eighteenth-century New England's first great presentation of the political principles that guided Yankee opposition to British authority in the 1760s and early 1770s, ultimately providing justification for national independence in 1776. "If the orators on the 4th of July really wish to investigate the principles and feelings which produced the Revolution," Adams wrote in 1818, "they ought to study . . . Dr. Mayhew's sermon on passive obedience and non-resistance." Indeed, Bailyn concluded that "the American Revolution itself" was "the fulfillment and application of his *Discourse Concerning Unlimited Submission.*" In this sense, Mayhew's *Discourse* marked the modest beginning of the cultural change in New England that culminated in war twenty-five years later.[43]

3

Virtue and Liberty

"The purpose of the divine mission of Jesus Christ and the divine admonitions," Mayhew began one of his undated sermon manuscripts, "is the happiness of man: but that happiness can only result from Virtue, and virtue is inseparable from Civil Liberty." He could hardly have summarized his worldview more succinctly. In his first book, *Seven Sermons*, the West Church pastor propounded the natural religion of the British Enlightenment, largely reducing Protestant Christianity to the practice of classical moral virtue from pious motives, with happiness—both worldly and heavenly, private and public—as the goal and reward of a virtuous life. Mayhew believed that humans are born with a "moral sense," an innate faculty for intuiting good and evil, but it must be guided by reason. Each individual has a natural right and duty to exercise his rational faculty in acquiring moral and religious knowledge and to live by the guidance of moral virtue in the pursuit of happiness. To think for themselves and act accordingly, humans must be free from coercion and intimidation. Since the identification, pursuit, and attainment of happiness require moral knowledge and moral action, faith and works, humans must be free in both mind and body. Religious liberty, therefore, is "of no less importance even to the present happiness of human society, than that of civil liberty, in opposition to arbitrary power." For Mayhew, happiness, reason, virtue, and liberty are all interconnected and inseparable values, and ministers of the Christian Gospel have a duty to defend civil as well as religious liberty.[1]

In his second published work, the 1749 *Discourse Concerning Un-*

limited Submission and Non-Resistance to the Higher Powers, Mayhew affirmed the basic political principles of English Country Whiggism: individual natural rights, popular sovereignty, consensual and contractual government, religious liberty, and the right of resistance to tyranny. Mayhew erected his political philosophy upon his moral philosophy; the political assertions of the *Discourse Concerning Unlimited Submission* presupposed the religious and philosophic premises of *Seven Sermons*, principally, that man is the rational creature of a benevolent Creator, deriving from his God-given nature a right and duty of private judgment. In the *Discourse*, he claimed that the people hold sovereign political authority, they create civil governments and subject themselves to law for their own good, their governments enjoy authority only through the consent of the governed, and the people may judge for themselves when their government has violated the public trust and must be "*discarded*" and replaced. His confidence in the people's capacity for civil self-government followed from his belief in their capacity for rational deliberation and moral agency—that is, for *personal* self-government.[2]

The moral and religious principles of British Enlightenment natural religion and the political principles of British Country Whiggism provided the framework and set the parameters for Mayhew's political writings and political activism in the 1750s and 1760s. Over the decade following publication of *Seven Sermons* and *A Discourse Concerning Unlimited Submission*, he emerged as New England's most politically active and influential clergyman. Mayhew regularly felt compelled to justify his political activism as appropriate for a Christian minister, but his "practical religion" required action in accordance with belief and engagement with the world of practical affairs. While his first two published works addressed such broad philosophic subjects as the nature of God and man and the purpose and limits of political authority, his political sermons in the 1750s frequently applied general principles to more specific political issues and controversies.

The overarching crisis of the era was Britain's struggle with France for imperial domination of North America, a contest in which New England provided the front line against French expansion from Canada. Approaching the French and Indian War from a religious perspective, though, Mayhew saw it fundamentally as a moral contest. France clearly represented the forces of darkness for Mayhew as it had for his Puritan forebears. In addition to the external military struggle between Catholic absolutist France and Protestant constitutionalist Britain, his sermons also addressed another moral contest—an internal spiritual struggle for the soul of the British Empire which would ultimately decide the outcome of war with France. As a heterodox Protestant influenced by British rationalist theology, Mayhew felt embarrassment for the religious bigotry and intellectual backwardness of New England and looked to Britain admiringly as the beacon of the Enlightenment and the stronghold of international Protestantism. As a New England Congregationalist minister, Mayhew felt reverence for his Puritan ancestors and their heritage of civil and religious liberty and resented Britain for its moral corruption and curtailment of dissenters' rights.

At the beginning of the 1750s, Mayhew was alienated from his fellow Boston clergymen for his theological heterodoxy, and he escaped intellectual loneliness in his correspondence with like-minded Englishmen. Over the course of the decade, that transatlantic correspondence and the unfolding of military events increased his suspicion of Britain as well as his appreciation for America as an asylum of liberty. By the end of the decade, British victory at Quebec revived his confidence in the mother country, his hope that its moral virtue was not lost, and his excitement for the prospects of the American colonies under British Crown rule. His political writings over this period, then, demonstrate his emergence as a leading political activist as well as his ambivalence about being simultaneously a New Englander and a British subject. The decade ended with Mayhew hopeful for the future of the Empire but wary and watchful for signs of New England's corruption and oppression by the British Crown.

On October 17, 1750, a week after his thirtieth birthday, Mayhew received a letter from Dr. Benjamin Avery informing him that Aberdeen University had awarded him an honorary doctorate on the recommendation of Avery and three London Presbyterian ministers, James Foster, George Benson, and Benson's assistant pastor, Nathaniel Lardner. A former Presbyterian minister, physician, and treasurer of a London charity hospital, Avery was secretary for the Committee of Dissenting Deputies and as such the principal spokesman for England's Protestant dissenters. He secured approval for the doctorate from Massachusetts governor William Shirley on Shirley's condition that Avery "was satisfied about your Orthodoxy, which I readily assur'd him I had no Reason to suspect." All four of Mayhew's recommenders were Arian (anti-Trinitarian), so Avery's own understanding of "Orthodoxy" might well have differed from that of the Episcopalian governor.[3]

Britain's heterodox Protestant dissenters expressed delighted astonishment that a New England Congregational clergyman produced *Seven Sermons*, a book in the literary and theological mode of the British Enlightenment. "It was a great Suprize, as well as Pleasure, to us both, to receive such a Present from New England," Dr. Avery wrote of himself and Bishop Hoadly, the Church of England's foremost champion of Protestant dissenters' rights. "We could not but consider it as a manifest Sign that our Brethren there were greatly improved in their Taste," as well as proof that "just & rational Principles & Sentiments are gaining ground among you." In his own letter congratulating Mayhew for *Seven Sermons*, Dr. Benson remarked that the book gave them "a pleasing prospect of such a spirit's being diffused in N. England." A few months later, the Yankee pastor received another letter from a London dissenting minister. Benson's friend, Rev. Edward Sandercock, took the Boston publication of *Seven Sermons* as "a sort of pledge, that liberty & charity will spread in the Churches of New England." Long embarrassed by the bigotry and repressiveness of New England's orthodox Calvinist Congregationalists, Britain's Arian Presbyterians welcomed Mayhew's book as evidence of the Enlightenment's arrival on Massachusetts Bay.[4]

The embarrassed young Boston divine could not disagree with the contempt these Englishmen expressed for his native land. "It is no little mortification to me to find what a mean Opinion Gentlemen abroad entertain of my Country's Taste," he responded, "But it is a much greater [mortification], to know that this opinion is just & well grounded." Mayhew conceded that "the general Taste of N.E. and the manner of writing here" were "but just tolerable." Moreover, a "catholic [ecumenical] Spirit, is what this Country has hitherto been almost a Stranger to." He could personally testify that the "Clergy are generally very contracted in their Principles; and the Laiety, if possible, more so: But there are so little Symptoms of an Alteration for the better: And, indeed, (I am sorry to say) an Alteration for the worse, is hardly possible." The scandal over his ordination, his subsequent ostracism by the Boston clergy, the Congregational clergy's cool reception of *Seven Sermons*, and the Episcopalian clergy's ferocious hostility to *A Discourse Concerning Unlimited Submission* left Mayhew feeling embittered against his fellow clergymen and gloomy about the Enlightenment's prospects in New England.[5]

His adoption into the English dissenters' network of correspondence helped alleviate that intellectual loneliness. Living on the periphery of British civilization, he already felt isolated "in so remote & obscure a Part of the world as N. England." The London divines sought him out, in part, because the young man's audacious expression of heterodox ideas and unpopular sentiments won him their admiration and affection. In his first letter, Benson told Mayhew "I love you, tho' unknown," while another English minister, Rev. Robert Cornthwaite, ended his second letter: "Thus, my dear friend, you see, I have open'd my heart to you, with all the freedom of a long & intimate acquaintance, judging you (& I think I shall not be mistaken) a man after my own heart." Throughout his life, Mayhew's openness with his thoughts and feelings either infuriated strangers or won their hearts completely.[6]

The English dissenters reached out to Mayhew in part because they felt intellectually lonely themselves, even in enlightened London. "We are ground, as it were, between Enthusiasm & Infidelity," complained Sandercock, summing up the plight of the heterodox dissenter. "The Cause of Liberty hath suffer'd extremely here in the house of its friends: So many instances are there of those, who taking out upon principles of rational & [Christ]ian freedom have degenerated into mere Deism & Scepticism." Believing in "the reasonableness of the Christian religion," heterodox dissenters were a small minority held in contempt by both the orthodox and the unbelieving, and their numbers dwindled as the eighteenth century wore on. A few years later, Benson expressed dismay that "so few stand by you, in America, in promoting truth & liberty." He urged Mayhew to persevere as Christ and his apostles did. "The name of Dr. Mayhew may be precious in New England, when he is in the grave; & the names of his opposers are buried in oblivion," Benson wrote, boosting the young minister's morale. "Truth & liberty may make a slower progress than we'd wish. But they will spread. They will prevail." Over many years to come, Mayhew and his English admirers found mutual benefit in exchanging letters, books, and ideas, drawing moral support from one another in their common struggle for a seemingly lost cause.[7]

Mayhew's theologically heterodox Congregationalism was the key to his respect for Britain as the stronghold of the Enlightenment and the House of

Hanover as the champion of international Protestantism and the dissenting interest. In *A Discourse Concerning Unlimited Submission*, the Boston divine celebrated the Glorious Revolution and praised the Toleration Act and Protestant Succession for saving dissenters from Roman Catholic or high-church Episcopal persecution. His admiration for the British constitution as "originally and essentially *free*" was based on the Real Whig principles that the people are sovereign and kings "hold their title to the throne, solely by grant of parliament," which means, "by the voluntary consent of the people." Mayhew's Anglophilia was always conditional upon the British state's respect for individual natural rights in general and the rights of Protestant dissenters in particular.[8]

As a *heterodox* Congregationalist, Mayhew was embarrassed by New England's narrow orthodoxy and impressed by England's liberal, tolerant, and cosmopolitan spirit. As a heterodox *Congregationalist*, though, he admired New England's civil and religious liberty and resented the curtailment of English dissenters' rights under British law. The Yankee divine remained wary of Britain's legal and political system, which vested executive power in a hereditary crown, deprived some loyal subjects of representation due to their religious beliefs, established a church whose officers were royally appointed bishops, and provided unelected seats in Parliament to bishops as well as nobles. Warning his West Church congregation in principle against arbitrary power and its corrupting influence, Mayhew was anxious that so many English institutions remained unaccountable to popular consent.

In *Christian Sobriety*, an ethical treatise he wrote later in his career, Mayhew sought to provide moral instruction to New England's young men in terms owing something to John Locke's *Thoughts on Education* and *Essay Concerning Human Understanding*. Mayhew described man as "a free, moral agent" with the power to accept or reject moral law. He took "Christian sobriety" as the fundamental characteristic of the virtuous man, describing "sobriety" as synonymous with the Greek concept *sophrosyne*: rational self-mastery, the regulation and direction of one's will and actions by reason. He cited as examples of sobriety the Jewish king Solomon, the Greek philosopher Socrates, and the Roman statesman Cicero, but he considered Christian piety the most reliable source of morality. When correctly interpreted, Christianity was "a most reasonable religion" that taught morality in rationalistic terms very similar to classical philosophy. Mayhew saw the teachings of Judaism and Christianity, of Cicero and Locke, as sharing this understanding of rational self-mastery as man's ethical ideal. On this conception of moral virtue Mayhew believed man's civil and religious liberty depended.[9]

Mayhew's second published political sermon conveyed anxieties about the capacity of arbitrary power within the British monarchical system to corrupt moral virtue and thereby subvert civil and religious liberty. Originally preached on May 26, 1751, the sermon addressed the untimely death of Prince Frederick, son of King George II and heir to the British Crown. In the wake of his first political sermon, which provoked cries of treason and sedition a year before, one might expect the pastor to use this opportunity to reaffirm his respect for the House of Hanover by heaping praise on the late Prince of Wales.

On the contrary, *A Sermon . . . Occasioned by the Much-Lamented Death of His Royal Highness Frederick, Prince of Wales* preached the corruptibility of princes and the conditionality of allegiance. In his *Discourse Concerning Unlimited Submission*, Mayhew acknowledged that "a great deal of *implicit confidence*, must unavoidably be placed in those that bear rule: This is implied in the very notion of authority's being originally a *trust*, committed by the people, to those who are vested with it." In *The Death of Prince Frederick*, he returned to this fiduciary conception of political authority, emphasizing that there are limits to the trust that the governed should put in their government. "Trust in any person or being, if it be a reasonable trust," he told his congregation, "presupposes in him certain qualities and powers as the proper ground of it." It would be as rational to put one's trust in a ruler of bad character as it would be "to put confidence in a bear or a tyger." The attributes of goodness, wisdom, and power are "the foundation of a rational trust," he taught. Trust in any prince must be conditional upon his character and conduct.[10]

Unlike God, Mayhew reminded his congregation, earthly rulers cannot be trusted to be perfect in goodness. Since man has free will, and even a virtuous prince can become bad over time, the pastor observed, "subjects can never have an absolute security, that even the best of kings will not alter their measures; and oppress and devour, instead of defending, them." He denied that "any state of earthly power and greatness, can make a man *independent*; exalt him above the reach of temptation, or remove him beyond a possibility of doing the most cruel, unjust and shameful things." So far from being true that the king can do no wrong, Mayhew found that corruption tends to increase with power. "As men rise to wealth and power and grandeur," he observed, "their old passions often rise with them; or some new and unnatural ones start up in their breasts, to lead them astray." As the pastor had also preached in his *Discourse Concerning Unlimited Submission*, Britain had not too long ago suffered under corrupt and tyrannical princes, or "do you not remember there was once a royal House of *Stewart!*" Mayhew's theme echoed both traditional Puritan sermons and *Cato's Letters*. "The common People generally think that great Men have great Minds, and scorn base Actions," John Trenchard and Thomas Gordon had warned, "which Judgment is so false, that the basest and worst of all Actions have been done by great Men."[11]

While kings are not perfectly good, Mayhew argued in *The Death of Frederick*, neither are they perfectly wise or powerful. Having contended in *Seven Sermons* that all humans have the natural capacity and right of private judgment, he was not prepared to defer to the judgment of hereditary monarchs as superior to his own or anyone else's. "Good sense is not entailed with the crown, on the elder branch of the male line," he maintained. "Human laws cannot make wisdom hereditary, tho' they may things of inferior value—thrones and scepters. And what great degree of trust is there to be placed in a weak, short-sighted prince, whose head has nothing but a crown to *adorn* it?" For him, the power of kings was no more an object of awe than their wisdom. Even at best, princes are "but frail, weak creatures, being frequently unable to accomplish their well-meant designs for their subjects." Indeed, rulers often lack the power to save themselves from disaster, as evidenced by royal deaths through war, assassination, accident, and sickness. As Prince Frederick's untimely demise demonstrated, great monarchs are no more invulnerable to death than the humblest peasant.[12]

On the contrary, the minister told his flock, humble and obscure men are often of greater virtue and more deserving of praise than the great and famous. Similarly, *Cato's Letters* had praised the "natural honesty of the people" and contrasted it with the vices of the powerful. Mayhew claimed that one would have to be ignorant of the state of the world not to see "how small a stock of real merit will usually go a great ways in persons of high birth and distinction; especially in those who have that great merit of having a crown in possession or reversion." Mayhew disdained the sycophantic practice of extolling the minor virtues of great men while ignoring the great virtues of ordinary men. He explained that, for this reason, he was hesitant to say anything favorable at all about the deceased Prince of Wales. Concerned that his silence on this point might be taken as an indication of ill will toward Frederick, though, the pastor then found it safe to praise him as a good man who would have made a good king. He extolled Frederick for his firm attachment to "the *protestant* interest, and a limited monarchy" and his "due abhorrence of popery and arbitrary government." Whatever the prince's virtues and promise, Mayhew wanted his readers to learn from his sudden death the fundamental lesson that we are "not to place our great security and happiness, in the governors and princes of the world, whose *life is a vapor*, like that of other men," but to rely on God.[13]

As the West Church pastor exhorted his hearers and readers to withhold unconditional obedience from any human authority, he implied that the people ought to have confidence in their own judgment and virtue. Mayhew had argued in *Seven Sermons* that all humans are capable of rational deliberation and moral agency, and he maintained in *A Discourse Concerning Unlimited Submission* that the people are the source of sovereign authority, lawful government requires their consent, and they are fully competent to judge for themselves when rulers have violated the law and must be deposed. Mayhew conceded the need to delegate political power to representatives and to give them a measure of "implicit confidence." He made clear in *The Death of Frederick*, though, that rulers are even more susceptible to corruption than ordinary people, because the opportunities for temptation increase as one's power over others increases. Although Mayhew focused on the subject of power and corruption in *The Death of Frederick*, his sermon implied that the people are the repository of moral virtue as well as political sovereignty, and that civil liberty depends upon their lack of corruption and their vigilance against abuses of power.

Like most New Englanders and many Britons in the eighteenth century, Mayhew believed that the Protestant religion and constitutional government were based on the common premise that political authority originates with God, God vests authority in the people, and the people in turn delegate specific powers to religious and political leaders while retaining their God-given sovereignty over church and state. Mayhew maintained that—as the negation of liberty, of popular consent, in both church and state—Roman Catholicism and divine-right monarchy were the world's two greatest evils. According to his reasoning as both a Congregationalist and a Real Whig, "popery" and "arbitrary government" are inseparable, as both exalt one unelected and unaccountable man as absolute in authority (the pope over the Church, the king over the state) and demand the people's unquestioning faith and unconditional obedience.

Britons and New Englanders despised Bourbon France as the great champion of royal and papal absolutism. King James II, secretly in league with French king Louis XIV, had tried to reintroduce Catholicism and absolutism in the 1680s, but William and Mary rescued Britain from both in the Glorious Revolution of 1688. Under King William and then the House of Hanover, Britain emerged as the defender of international Protestantism and constitutional monarchy, fighting a long series of wars in Europe and the Americas to check French imperialism. New Englanders, long suffering on the front line of the Anglo-French wars, understood them as a continuation of the old wars of religion, a struggle between liberty and tyranny, "true religion" and "superstition," light and darkness.

In 1753, the French Crown began building a chain of forts south from Lake Erie along the Allegheny Mountains with the objective of monopolizing the Ohio River Valley, a rich and strategically important region claimed by France, Britain, and the Iroquois Confederation. In April 1754, French troops expelled Virginians from the crude palisade they had erected at the Forks of the Ohio River (present-day Pittsburgh) and began building a permanent stronghold, Fort Duquesne. The royal governor of Virginia directed Lieutenant Colonel George Washington to lead a small force to Fort Duquesne and issue an ultimatum to the French requiring their withdrawal from the Forks. As Virginia mobilized for war, it remained an open question whether Britain's other American colonies, let alone the British Crown itself, would rally behind Virginia in confronting French aggression.

The specter of another war with France loomed as the Massachusetts General Court assembled on May 29, 1754. Under the charter of 1691, granted to Massachusetts by William and Mary, the province was governed by a General Court, consisting of a royally appointed governor, a popularly elected assembly (the House of Representatives), and the king's council, whose members were nominated by the House and confirmed by the governor. Elections for the House of Representatives occurred annually in March. At the end of each

May, upon the election of a new council, the governor, council, and assembly would meet ceremoniously for the first session of that year's General Court. Since 1634, Massachusetts had upheld the tradition of marking the opening day of the General Court with an election sermon, in which one member of the Congregational clergy reminded the assembled officers of their divinely ordained duties. On the recommendation of Governor William Shirley, Dr. Jonathan Mayhew gave the 1754 election sermon.[14]

Considering Mayhew's notoriety among both orthodox Congregationalists and high-church Episcopalians, it was a curious choice. While on a leave of absence in London, Governor Shirley had recommended Mayhew for his Aberdeen University doctorate but only with Benjamin Avery's assurance of the young pastor's "Orthodoxy." Since the governor was an English-born member of the Episcopal Church, Mayhew was surprised to learn of Shirley's role in his award. He wrote the governor in October 1750 that he thought "my profession, as a non-conforming minister, sufficient to exclude me" from the governor's favor, but "I find your Excellency is of too generous and catholic a Spirit, to confine your good Offices within the Pale of any religious Establishment; even one, for which you have always expressed the highest Regard, consistent with proper Candor & Moderation towards those of a different Persuasion." When Shirley returned from London in 1753, he was apparently unmoved by anything he might have learned—as a member of King's Chapel, for instance—about Mayhew's distinct lack of "Moderation" toward the high-church Episcopal clergy in *A Discourse Concerning Unlimited Submission*.[15]

Mayhew had made many foes, but he did have friends among the governor's advisors, including Stephen Sewall, king's councilor and chief justice of Massachusetts, as well as provincial treasurer Harrison Gray, both of whom were full members of the West Church and Mayhew's close confidants. As conflict with France loomed upon his return from London, Shirley acknowledged the need to rebuild the province's neglected frontier defenses and provide military support for Virginia, and he wanted the new House of Representatives to raise funds for mobilization. Perhaps Gray informed the governor that, if chosen to give the election sermon, the West Church pastor would speak in favor of preparations for war against France. For Mayhew, any war between Britain and France would be a contest between good and evil, Christ and Antichrist. With God on their side, Britain and the American colonies would surely win. The outcome of the war, then, would ultimately depend upon whether British subjects on both sides of the Atlantic could secure God's favor by practicing the classical moral virtues required of rational Christians.[16]

Still banned from the Boston Association of Ministers for his heterodox views and combative personality, the thirty-three-year-old heretic entered the Massachusetts Town House on King Street on May 29, 1754, and addressed the governor, council, and House of Representatives as spokesman for the Congregational establishment. In keeping with both Protestant and Whig premises, Mayhew stated that God is the original source of "civil power," but "this power is derived from God not immediately, but mediately." Contrary to "the divine right of monarchy" taught by "lawned parasites" (that is, high-church bishops), God does not grant dominion to kings—nor indeed to any other specific form of government. All civil governments are "the creatures of man's making; so from man, from common consent, it is that lawful rulers immediately derive their power." Those who exercise civil power not based on the consent of the governed possess it "only as the thief or the robber has the spoil, which fraud or violence has put into his hands." Sweeping aside royal absolutism, either high-church Tory or Catholic Bourbon, he established the Real Whig principles of popular sovereignty and consensual, contractual government as the proper moral grounding for government.[17]

Mayhew reminded the General Court that government exists not to advance their own ambitions but to serve "the good of man, the common benefit of society." Breaking with the Calvinistic assumptions of previous election sermons, he described that "common good" in distinctly secular and individualistic terms. Man's benevolent Creator, "who is good unto all, and whose tender mercies are over all his works," ordained civil government "for the preservation of men's persons, properties & various rights, against fraud and lawless violence; and that, by means of it, we may both procure, and quietly enjoy, those numerous blessings and advantages, which are unattainable out of society." In the Old Testament, God founded "the commonwealth of *Israel*" so "his chosen people" would be "delivered from oppression and slavery" in Egypt, "conducted into a good land, flowing with milk & honey," and "there possess property, enjoy the blessing of equal laws, and be happy."

For all peoples, as for the Israelites, the end of government is "the happiness of men." Mayhew accordingly understood government, "as it is a divine ordinance," as serving God's will by securing individuals in their rights to life, liberty, property, and the pursuit of happiness.[18]

Thanks to his rationalist reading of Scripture, the pastor found it easy to move seamlessly from an argument based on the Book of Exodus to one based on John Locke's *Second Treatise of Government*. He contended, as the English philosopher had, that specific governments could only be based upon "common consent," "since we cannot suppose that men would voluntarily enter into society, and set up and maintain a common authority, upon any other principles than those of mutual security and common good." While most rulers did not have the consent of the governed, Mayhew said that one must not take one's model for the proper end of government "from the views of banditti, and robbers," but from "what reason suggests must be the motive with reasonable and honest men to unite together in the bonds of society." Both reason and Scripture point to the conclusion that "the end of government must be the common good of all, and of every individual, so far as is consistent therewith." Further elaboration upon the nature of civil government, however, "would be to deliver a system of politicks, rather than a sermon."[19]

The clergyman turned to a theme perhaps more befitting an annual election sermon, namely the relation of government to morality. Mayhew had argued in *Seven Sermons* that the goal of moral virtue is the attainment of happiness. Since "the happiness of men in society depends greatly upon the goodness of their morals," and "morals have a close connection with religion," he posited in his election sermon, the magistrate should encourage both virtue and religion by his own good example, as well as "by his laws, as far as is consistent with the natural, unalienable rights of every man's conscience." How can government make laws promoting religion without violating the individual liberty of conscience? His election sermon did not try to answer this conundrum except to add that the government's protection is "due to all persons indifferently, whose religion does not manifestly, and very directly, tend to the subversion of the government." "Persecution and intolerance," he added, are "not only unjust, and criminal in the sight of God," but impractical for promotion of national wealth and power, in decimating populations and driving human talent into exile. He did not take violence to be inherent in religion but only in the entanglement of religion with government that "has so generally prevailed in Christendom from the days of Constantine." Since princes have styled themselves the "nursing fathers" of the Catholic Church, they have "suckled her with human blood, and fed her with the flesh of those, whom angry Ecclesiasticks are pleased to stigmatize with the names of heretic, schismatic and infidel." As if to highlight his own reputation for heterodoxy, Mayhew added to the sermon's printed edition a footnote to *The Age of Louis XIV* by the noted French "infidel," Voltaire.[20]

While civil officers should serve from sincere commitment to "the public good," Mayhew lamented that "patriotism is indeed become a jest with some men." But, he told the assembled statesmen, a "generous mind" will find "the public good" to be such a "noble and excellent" goal that "the prospect of attaining it will animate the pursuit, and being attained, it will reward the pains" of pursuing it. Since patriotic concern for "the good of the public" seems wanting in the present day, "shall we go to the pagans to learn this god-like virtue? Even they can teach it." But Christianity, as "a religion of charity and beneficence," can also provide motives for public service. Since Mayhew's natural religion largely conflated Christian godliness with the classical moral virtues, he found pagan philosophy and Christian religion teaching essentially the same virtues—patriotism, charity, beneficence, justice—to those who would wield civil power. Magistrates who practice such virtues have an additional, self-serving motive, as they can expect the public to reward and honor them. While Mayhew emphasized in his *Discourse* that the people can judge for themselves when their rulers have wronged them, his election sermon noted that "people are not usually either so blind and insensible as not to know when they are well governed; or so ungrateful as not to acknowledge it, and to require their benefactors suitably to their merits."[21]

With the gratitude becoming a well-governed subject, Mayhew conveyed his admiration for the British constitution and the reigning House of Hanover. While his *Discourse* impressed some critics as subversive of all government, the pastor's election sermon emphasized "how great a blessing good government is," as "the great guard and security of mens property, peace, religion, lives; of every thing here, for which it is worth while to live." He added that "this is a blessing which British subjects enjoy, in as high a degree, perhaps, as any other people," as they are "governed by such men, and by such laws, as themselves approve; without which their boasted liberty wou'd indeed, be but a name." Mayhew praised Britain's constitutional, parliamentary monarchy as "the envy of most other nations" and the Hanoverian kings as "Princes too just & good to encroach upon the rights of their subjects, and too wise to think that Britons can endure a chain."[22]

The West Church pastor did not fail, however, to visit the darker theme of his *Death of Frederick*: the conditionality of allegiance. In Hoadlyian terms, Mayhew reminded the assembled officers that, as "law, and not will, is the measure of the executive Magistrate's power; so it is the measure of the subject's obedience and submission." The notorious author of the *Discourse* could not help but vent spleen at those who preach "that loyalty and slavery mean the same thing" and "even now, have the forehead to ventilate, in order to bring a reproach upon the *Revolution*, upon the present happy settlement of the crown, and to prepare us for the dutiful reception of an *hereditary Tyrant*." Again presenting himself as the conservative champion of the Revolution Settlement, this was about as close as he would come to accusing the high-church Episcopal clergy publicly of Jacobite sympathy for the Young Pretender, the Stuart grandson of King James II who conspired in the 1750s to depose the Hanoverians.[23]

Having expressed both admiration for the British constitution and the limits of allegiance to the British Crown, Mayhew then pressed his concerns about the rampant practice of buying votes in British parliamentary elections. True to his theme of the importance of virtue to liberty, the minister noted "how much care and integrity should be exercis'd in the choice of those, who are to have a share in government; that they may not be unworthy of it." It is not enough for the people to have the liberty of electing their own representatives if they have only "weak or dishonest men" to elect. The Yankee pastor said that people, "in some countries," have been "so regardless of their own welfare" as to "make an infamous merchandize of their hands and voices to the highest bidder, without any consideration of merit, of capacity or inclination to serve the public." Mayhew could not say "who are the most criminal, they who would make their way to places of power and trust, by indirect means, or they who have so little concern for the welfare of their country, as to hearken to them, and to become the tools of their ambition and covetousness." One could hardly expect faithful public service from those who acquire public office "by bribing the avaricious, by flattering the foolish, and making fine promises to the credulous." When the only way of attaining public office is "to beg or to buy" it from a corrupted populace, then "the men of the greatest merit" who "do the most distain those arts and practices" will not seek public office, leaving only unscrupulous men to take their places. Mayhew never stated plainly that he was describing political corruption in Britain. Since continental Europe had no monarchies with popularly elected parliaments, though, his criticism of the mother country must have been clear enough.[24]

Rather than lamenting the moral declension of New England from its original purity, as Congregational preachers traditionally had, Mayhew instead praised New England for its comparative virtue. "God forbid," he said of the buying and begging of votes, "that ever such things should become fashionable and reputable amongst us; or that any Son of *New-England*, should prove such a profane *Esau*, as to sell his birthright!" Although he had repudiated the Calvinist theology of New England Congregationalism in *Seven Sermons*, Mayhew expressed reverence for his Puritan fathers and for the free institutions of his native New England. "Our ancestors, tho' not perfect and infallible in many respects," he said, "were a religious, brave and vertuous set of men, whose love of liberty, civil and religious, brought them from their native land, into the American deserts." It was thanks to God and the Puritan fathers, he claimed, that eighteenth-century New Englanders enjoyed "a goodly heritage" and "many invaluable privileges." "Nor can I think we are so far degenerated from the laudible spirit of our Ancestors," he observed, "as to despise and abuse what they procured for us at so dear a rate."[25]

Mayhew found much to praise in Yankee virtue by contrast with British corruption. "I am not willing to believe we are running so fast into the evil practices and customs of other places," he told the General Court, "or so fond of imitating the fashionable follies and vices of any, even of those whom decency may perhaps require us to call *our betters*, as some would insinuate that we are; and from hence prognosticate our destruction." The pastor believed that New Englanders in the 1750s "fear God, reverence the memory of our fore-fathers, love our country and ourselves, more than to do thus." He did not specify the "other places" that had been corrupted by "evil practices and customs," but his criticism of Britain was evident from the exhortation for Yankees to reject the decadent fashions and manners of their social "*betters*," the English aristocracy. He obliquely warned that New England's commercial and political connection with Britain could eventually provide the conduit for its moral corruption and loss of liberty. "Tho' we are not an independant state," he remarked, "yet, Heaven be thanked! we are a free people."[26]

In May 1754, the threat of French imperialism was much more immediate than the threat of British corruption. After discussing the nature of government and the importance of virtue to liberty, Mayhew again broke with the election sermon tradition by turning to a laundry list of policy proposals, from agricultural improvement to the encouragement of immigration by European Protestants. As the son of a missionary to the Indians, Mayhew considered the Christianization of the Indians a high priority, and he seized this opportunity to carp at the high-church Society for the Propagation of the Gospel in Foreign Parts (SPG) for failing to do so. The pastor argued that Protestant New England had a moral duty to save the Indians from conversion to Roman Catholicism by French Jesuit missionaries. Converting the Indians to Protestantism would also serve the practical end "of attaching them to the British interest" rather than the French interest. Otherwise, one could expect the Jesuits to "inculcate upon their savage converts" the virtues of "butchering and scalping Protestants." The interest of the British Empire and the security of New England as well as Christian morality pointed to the need for government patronage of aggressive proselytization.[27]

The issue of Indian mission work provided the segue to his principal policy recommendation: preparation for war against the French Empire and their Indian allies. Mayhew argued that "whoever has the friendship of most, or all, of these natives, may probably, in time, become masters of this part of the Continent." With the French push into western Pennsylvania, it was clear that a showdown between Britain and France would soon be at hand, and the stakes were nothing less than control of North America from the Mississippi to the Atlantic. "The continent is not wide enough for us both," he grimly concluded, "and they are resolved to have the whole." French offers of a diplomatic settlement were not to be trusted, since their imperialistic ambitions and record of "perfidy" were well known. "We are peaceably extending our settlements upon our own territories," he claimed, while "they are extending theirs beyond their own, by force of arms. We must meet at length; which cannot be without a violent concussion: and the time seems not to be far off." Although he did not know that only one day earlier George

Washington's Virginian militia had a bloody clash with French troops, Mayhew urged Massachusetts to join Virginia in preparing for the war that was clearly inevitable.[28]

Mayhew's election sermon became a war speech with the object of stirring the General Court to moral action. "I am sure there is not a true New-England-Man, whose heart is not already engaged in the contest," the pastor declaimed, "and whose purse, and his arm also, if need be, is not ready to be employed in it." In the coming war, "our liberties, our religion, our lives, our bodies, our souls" are at stake, and any man who refuses to support the cause "is so far from being worthy the privileges of a *citizen of Heaven*, that he is not worthy to enjoy the rights of an *Englishman*." Mayhew dramatized for the assembled officers the catastrophic consequences of French victory for New Englanders. He imagined "the slaves of *Lewis* with their Indian allies, dispossessing the free-born subjects of King GEORGE" of the liberty and property they inherited from their Puritan ancestors. Appealing to fear of forcible conversion to Catholicism, he cried, "Do I see Christianity banished for popery! the bible, for the mass-book!" He imagined the invasion of New England by a "herd of lazy Monks, and Jesuits, and Exorcists, and Inquisitors" criminalizing Protestant worship. "Do I see all liberty, property, religion, happiness, changed, or rather transubstantiated, into slavery, poverty, superstition, wretchedness!" He brought his philippic against the French to a climax with the prediction that, in the event of such catastrophe, the wretched survivors of invasion and conquest would curse "the negligence of the public Guardians!"[29]

Having raised his voice to a fevered pitch, he drew back, expressing the hope that his predictions would not prove a "prophetic vision." He described another scenario, with "liberty" and "virtue" victorious over "slavery" and "pride," Christianity triumphant over Catholic superstition, and "another Great Britain rising in America!" To win the war, Massachusetts must not "presume on God's protection" but rather take vigorous action for "timely and effectual opposition" to the French and Indians. As Governor Shirley no doubt had hoped, he urged the House of Representatives to respond to the threat with "the granting of monies" so that "no necessary supplies will be wanting." "Shall the sword rust? Shall our gold and silver lye cankering in our coffers?" he asked the legislators. In December 1753, the House rejected Shirley's plan to rebuild frontier defenses. Mayhew said that surely now it was unimaginable they would be "parsimonious" in support of a war on which God's glory and the king's honor, "the protestant interest" and "the liberties of Europe," the memory of their Puritan ancestors and the freedom of future generations, all depended. The General Court had an immediate and personal stake in resisting French aggression. "It is even uncertain, Gentlemen," he concluded dramatically, "how long you will have an *House* to sit in, unless a speedy and vigorous opposition is made to the present encroachments, and to the farther designs, of our enemies!" The preservation of New England's civil and religious liberty required the moral virtues of not thrift but "liberality," not prudence but courage and resolution in the face of evil.[30]

Mayhew's use of the annual election sermon to issue such specific proposals on secular issues of policy was unprecedented, and he ended it by offering an "apology" for lingering too long on "our temporal and worldly concernments" and saying anything "too near to politics" with inappropriate "liberty of speech." Whether or not the minister's blandishments lent greater urgency to the cause of mobilization, the House did appropriate funds and support the governor's proposals for military preparations. The pastor's election sermon pressed one other action for the General Court to take to secure victory, and that was the pursuit of unity. He urged the governor, council, and assembly to repudiate "party disputes and factions" and seek "unanimity and harmony" in the name of the common interest. "A public spirit, is a spirit of union," he preached, "and union is the source of public happiness: and public happiness is the great end which you should have in view."[31]

Not only must the Massachusetts government be internally unified but all of the American colonies must unite against the French threat. While French Canada was unified under one absolutist government, Mayhew explained, British America was divided into bickering provinces, and the French Crown had always followed the maxim of "divide and conquer" in its ambitions for North American domination. He believed that "whenever all our scattered rays shall be drawn to a point and proper focus, they can scarce fail to consume and burn up these enemies of our peace." The pastor seemed to envision nothing less than a constitutional union of the American colonies. "What UNION can do," he noted, "we need only look towards those Provinces, which are distinguished by the name of the UNITED, to know." British Protestants like Mayhew had always been impressed by the United Provinces of the Netherlands in their David-and-Goliath stand against the Spanish and

French Empires, and he held up the Dutch confederation as an example for America.[32]

Here again, Mayhew threw his support behind Governor Shirley, the architect of the Albany Congress. At Shirley's prompting, the British Board of Trade called for a congress of delegates from all thirteen colonies to prepare a common plan for defense and Indian policy. The governor of New York announced his decision to host such a congress at Albany in June 1754. In April 1754, the House of Representatives approved Shirley's request to send delegates to the Albany Congress. Three weeks after Mayhew's election sermon, colonial delegates convened in Albany to develop the constitution for a continental government that would provide a common policy for all colonies on matters of defense and Indian relations. Thomas Hutchinson of Massachusetts and Benjamin Franklin of Pennsylvania collaborated in framing the Albany Plan of Union, which the Congress adopted. Mayhew evidently took great interest in these proceedings. His personal papers still include one of only four original copies of the Albany Plan still in existence. He may have acquired it from the merchant James Bowdoin, a friend who served in the Massachusetts delegation. Massachusetts displayed the greatest support for the Albany Plan of Union. Even there, though, the legislature did not approve it. Even with the press of events behind it, Mayhew's plea for union failed to sway the Massachusetts General Court.[33]

Believing that divine providence directs the operations of nature and the fortunes of man, Mayhew took for granted that God would decide the outcome of the French and Indian War. Like many Protestants, he thought that the "Antichrist" described in the Book of Revelation must be the Papacy. By enforcing and spreading Catholicism and absolutism, Bourbon France was the principal agent of Antichrist and so the enemy of God. Just as God rewarded the Israelites with victory only so long as they honored their covenant with him, the pastor believed that God would favor Britain with victory only so long as it practiced moral virtue and served the Protestant interest. For Mayhew, then, every victory or defeat had religious implications, and his attitude toward Britain shifted accordingly. Early military setbacks prompted him to question, as he had previously in the election sermon, whether Britain entirely shared New England's commitment to virtue and liberty.

On July 9, 1755, French soldiers and Indian warriors ambushed and decimated British and American troops along the Monongahela River, south of Fort Duquesne. General William Braddock, commander in chief of British forces in North America, perished from his battle wounds, as did his secretary, William Shirley, Jr., son of the Massachusetts governor. Replacing Braddock as commander in chief, Governor Shirley directed a disastrous expedition against the French fort at Crown Point on Lake Champlain. By the fall of 1755, there was growing fear in Britain and America that the war would end in the destruction of the British Empire and the loss of the thirteen American colonies to France. It looked to some as if Mayhew's lurid predictions in his election sermon might well come true after all.[34]

In November 1755, Boston experienced earthquakes that caused no deaths and only minor damage. On December 18, Mayhew gave a sermon in the West Church on the Book of Revelation interpreting the tremors as a sign from God—communicated by secondary, natural causes rather than supernatural miracles—that the British Empire was losing the war due to the neglect of moral virtue. He accused Americans of rebelling against God by acts of "flagrant immorality, profaneness, irreligion, throughout these colonies." While New England was partly at fault for provoking divine punishment, the Boston pastor suggested that another part of the Empire was responsible for the major part of the sinning.[35] He lamented:

I TREMBLE not only for my dear native country, when I consider the sins of it; but also for a *certain European nation*, which I will not mention by name: A nation blest with some peculiar advantages, civil and religious: A nation not much "exalted by righteousness," for a long time past: A nation often admonished by providence, and sorely scourged: A nation often threatened even with utter ruin and destruction: A nation often almost miraculously preserved from ruin and destruction by her enemies, both foreign and domestic: And yet a nation where infidelity, irreligion, corruption and venality, and almost every kind of vice, seems to have been increasing all the time!—Will not almighty God, who "only is holy," sooner or later "visit for these things?" and will not "his soul be avenged on SUCH A NATION AS THIS!"[36]

Mayhew expressed his dismay at the corruption of British virtue in 1755 as he had in the election sermon a year and half earlier. The implication stood, clear enough though unstated, that God was punishing New England for the sins of Old England, and that the corruption of the mother country could prove to be the doom of the child.

Correspondence from England bolstered the Yankee minister's opinion of Britain as declining in reason, happiness, virtue, and liberty. One member of George Benson's Presbyterian congregation in London, a politically active draper named Jasper Mauduit, began corresponding with Mayhew in the mid-1750s. Mauduit wrote in July 1756 that public affairs in London "have but a gloomy prospect," including anticipation of an imminent French invasion of England, allegedly supported by Catholic Jacobites. Mauduit hoped God would "deliver both Countrys from such base spirited Rascalls." Mayhew's anti-Trinitarian *Sermons* of 1755 had drawn fire from orthodox Congregationalist clergy, and Benson wrote him in February 1757 complaining of similarly rough treatment from English ministers for his own anti-Trinitarian tract. "But such an inquiry can't pass, even with ye friends of liberty, here; much less with ye sons of orthodoxy," he grumbled. "They rail ag't me, in private. They preach ag't me. They write ag't me." Benson continued to believe, though, that a few such men like himself and Mayhew, "in every country, firm & faithful to one another, w'd shake ye foundations of orthodoxy, & make primitive [Christianity] to arise, in it's primitive purity." Mayhew and Benson could commiserate with one another's injuries and isolation but also take hope from one another's endeavors that the cause of heterodox Protestantism was not yet lost either in Britain or America.[37]

While the defeats of 1755 prompted Mayhew to wonder if God was punishing the British Empire for its vices, a series of signal victories in 1758 restored his confidence in Britain as a virtuous and enlightened nation. On November 23, 1758, he gave two discourses in thanksgiving to God for the victories of King George II and his ally, the Prussian king, Frederick the Great. Mayhew took this opportunity to laud "the British government and laws, by which the subject's life and liberty, his property and religion, are all so well secured to him." He praised the British king as "a steady defender" of British liberty, "a true protestant," and "a friend to the natural rights of mankind, especially of his own subjects." By contrast, a Catholic prince like the Stuart Pretender would have no respect for the "most fundamental laws of the kingdom" or the civil and religious liberty of his Protestant subjects. He might try to reconvert the English nation to Catholicism, as James II had. The pastor described Catholicism as "a superstition, falsely called religion" and "a horrid superstition, the reverse of all rational piety," which prepares people for tyranny by teaching them to renounce the right of private judgment and obey papal authority without question. Indeed, had God not used William of Orange to deliver Britain from James II in 1688, "we might at this very time have groaned under the iron scepter of a confirmed, lawless despotism, and the antichristian yoke of religious persecution." The Papacy recognized the Pretender as Britain's lawful sovereign, and French king Louis XV had threatened to restore him to the British throne in the event of French victory. That horrifying prospect renewed Mayhew's fear of the Stuarts and devotion to the Hanoverians as champions of the Protestant interest.[38]

While offering unconvincing apologies for preaching politics, Mayhew continued to use the West Church pulpit for political activism during the French and Indian War. On October 25, 1759, he gave two discourses in thanksgiving for the British capture of Quebec City, which effectively ended the war in North America. In the first discourse, he offered a detailed narrative of the major events of the war, making a vivid, excited, almost ecstatic description of the British commander, General James Wolfe, as a military "genius" who infused "courage enough into each breast, to make every man a hero." "He was one of those, whose courage nothing could abate," the pastor said worshipfully of Wolfe, "whose ardor, regulated by prudence, nothing could damp; whose resolution no difficulties, however great, could shake or alter, so long as a possibility remained of carrying his design into execution; and in fine, one of those, whose wisdom and address at a critical juncture, were not inferior to his other great military accomplishments." For the Yankee pastor who had repeatedly despaired of British corruption over the 1750s, Wolfe incarnated classical moral virtue, and his triumph over French forces reassured Mayhew that Britons retained the attributes necessary for the manly defense of liberty.[39]

Mayhew contrasted Wolfe—the virtuous son of a free nation and a rational religion—with the Marquis de Montcalm, commander of French forces at Quebec. He asked rhetorically why Montcalm took his army out on the Plains of Abraham to meet Wolfe rather than withstanding a siege inside the city's protective walls. "Dost thou not know, that those who fight for a Tyrant, will not fight like free-born Britons?" Mayhew sardonically attributed Montcalm's decision to Catholic superstition. "Or, perhaps thou thinkest thy relicks, thy crosses, and thy saints, either St. Peter, or thy great *Lady*, whom thou profanely stilest 'The Mother of God,'" he growled, "will now befriend and make thee victorious. . . . Cross thyself speedily, if thou thinkest it will be of any advantage to thee!" Apparently in response to criticism of this uncharitable treatment of the slain French general, Mayhew ended the printed version of the first discourse with a footnote explaining that, "tho' the dead are not to be inhumanly insulted," Montcalm was responsible for "the perfidious and horrid massacre of our troops at Fort William Henry" in August 1757, for which there could be no forgiveness.[40]

The confrontation between Wolfe and Montcalm on the Plains of Abraham summed up Mayhew's conception of the war as a moral struggle between liberty and despotism, virtue and mendacity, reason and superstition, good and evil. His first discourse rose to an ecstatic climax in which he announced that British victory at Quebec was "the Lord's doing." God heard New England's prayers and saw fit to send "deliverance to his servants that hoped in his mercy." He heard "the cry of so much blood, unrighteously and inhumanly shed; the blood of helpless women, tender children, and infants at the breast." Mayhew described the French as "cruel and perfidious," having "long dealt most treacherously and unrighteously with us," seeking nothing less than "our utter extirpation and ruin!" While the French Catholic forces were clearly evil, God granted victory to British Protestant forces only because they demonstrated courage and humility. They won the external moral contest with France only after winning the internal moral contest against their own vice and infidelity.[41]

In his second discourse on *The Reduction of Quebec*, Mayhew reflected on the implications of the victory, and he saw nothing less than the approach of the Millennium—the thousand-year rule of Christ on earth. French defeat at Quebec meant the loss of Canada to British possession, "saving the right of the natives." It meant an end to Indian attacks upon New England, which Mayhew blamed on French agitation, and the realignment of Indian loyalties with the British interest. It meant security for civil and religious liberty and rescue from persecution by "blind and furious zealots for the religion of Rome." These threats had dogged New England since its founding, and Mayhew imagined their Puritan forefathers rejoicing in heaven. "We, I mean New England, and all the British American plantations, had never so much cause for general joy as we have at present." He reiterated that "without any degree of superstition or enthusiasm," one could interpret British victory over the French in Quebec and setbacks for Catholicism in Europe as signs that the coming of the Kingdom of God foretold in the Book of Revolution "is at no very great distance from the present."[42]

In an early example of the "manifest destiny" doctrine, Mayhew argued that the British Empire, by expanding north and west, would advance God's will by extending its free institutions, particularly by converting the Indians to Protestantism. The opening of the West to American settlers and Protestant missionaries raised astonishing new prospects for British America. He imagined that, through western expansion, America would "in another century or two become a mighty empire (I do not mean an independent one) in numbers little inferior perhaps to the greatest in Europe, and in felicity to none."[43] As his election sermon had predicted the destruction of New England in the event of French victory, British victory inspired in Mayhew an ecstatic vision of America's future greatness. He intoned:

I cannot forbear fancying that I see a great and flourishing kingdom in these parts of America, peopled by our posterity. Methinks I see mighty cities rising on every hill, and by the side of every commodious port; mighty fleets alternately sailing out and returning, laden with the produce of this, and every other country under heaven; happy fields and villages wherever I turn my eyes, thro' a vastly extended territory; there the pastures cloathed with flocks, and here the vallies cover'd with corn, while the little hills rejoice on every side! And do I not there behold the savage nations, no longer our enemies, bowing the knee to Jesus Christ, and with joy confessing him to be "Lord, to the glory of God the Father!" Methinks I see religion professed and practiced throughout this spacious kingdom, in far greater purity and perfection, than since the times of the apostles; the Lord being still as a wall of fire round about, and the glory in the midst of her! O happy country! happy kingdom![44]

The West Church minister was not the first New Englander to see transcontinental expansion as the outcome of British victory over France. In October 1755, Mayhew's young admirer John Adams had written in a private letter to a friend that, if the French were removed and European immigration continued, one might see the "transfer [of] the great seat of empire into America." Adams warned that this process could be thwarted if the colonies remained disunited. In Mayhew's mind, as in Adams's, the cause of American union once promised by the Albany Plan—combined with conquest of the trans-Appalachian West—pointed toward the dazzling prospect of an American empire.[45]

Mayhew had been quick to add parenthetically in *The Reduction of Quebec* that this American empire would not be "an independent one." He had once implied that New England's constitutional connection with the British Crown might hamper its liberty and that its commercial connection with the British nation might compromise its virtue. In the wake of the Battle of Quebec, however, the Yankee minister was flush with admiration for Britain's commitment to virtue and liberty, as embodied in General James Wolfe and his heroic death on the battlefield. He regretted ending the triumphant second discourse on a note of "gloom," but he could not leave the subject of the Battle of Quebec without offering a long and grandiloquent apostrophe to "Immortal WOLFE." Mayhew concluded with the reflection that, while Wolfe's death was a great loss to Britain, "the nation has other wise, brave, and magnanimous commanders." Britain's capacity to produce military geniuses and heroes suggested something about the relation of virtue and liberty. Since "superior merit is so early observed and so gloriously distinguished" under the administration of Prime Minister William Pitt and the reign of King George II, Mayhew claimed that Britain would never be "destitute of such commanders, till either her happy government is subverted, and her liberties lost." A nation's liberty enables virtue to flourish; the exercise of virtue, in turn, enables the nation to defend and preserve its liberty. This is at least partly what Mayhew meant when he remarked that "virtue is inseparable from Civil Liberty."[46]

A year after he preached *The Reduction of Quebec*, the hopes he had expressed then were beginning to materialize. Britain had completed its annexation of French Canada, territory extending from Hudson's Bay south to the Gulf of Mexico and from the Appalachian Mountains west to the Mississippi River. There seemed hardly any limit now to the expansion of British America's religious and political institutions, and Mayhew conveyed his euphoria in two more thanksgiving discourses on October 9, 1760. He rejoiced that the British victory over France had enormously advanced God's plan for the world by undermining the cause of international Catholicism. As historian Nathan O. Hatch has observed, the outcome of the French and Indian War raised the hopes of New England Congregational clergy that the Millennium was close at hand. In Mayhew's case, though, his excitement was tempered by his heterodox connection of Christianity with the classical moral virtues. He did not believe that arrival of the Millennium was guaranteed or imminent—it depended upon human choice.[47]

The expansion of Protestant Christianity in America and Europe required man's own voluntary commitment to virtue. While echoing the triumphant strains of *The Reduction of Quebec*, his 1760 thanksgiving discourses urged the West Church congregation not to fall into complacency. Victory had dramatically expanded the British Empire in North America, but previous empires—like Persia, Greece, and Rome—fell into decadence after great victories. In terms owing more to *Cato's Letters* than the Book of Revelation, he reminded his fellow Bostonians that ancient Rome's victory over Carthage resulted in "extravagant luxury, venality, and a total depravation of manners." A fate "not wholly unlike this" could "possibly befall us in time, the American Carthage being subdued, unless God should give us the wisdom to avoid those rocks and shelves on which so many have split, and suffered a wretched shipwreck." Not just the defense of liberty in wartime but the preservation of liberty in peacetime required rigorous commitment to moral virtue.[48]

News of the death of King George II and the coronation of his young grandson as King George III followed only months after Mayhew's 1760 thanksgiving discourses. On January 4, 1761, with the interior of the West Church draped in black, the pastor gave his *Discourse Occasioned by the Death of King George II*. This sermon summed up the major themes of his political sermons over the last decade. As in his *Discourse Concerning Unlimited Submission*, Mayhew blamed Charles I for starting the English Civil War and cursed James II for trying to impose on Britain "the two-fold curse of popery and slavery; which have indeed a close connexion one with the other." He reiterated his Real Whig interpretation of the Glorious Revolution, by which "the prince and princess of Orange were *elected*" to the British throne by Parliament, which grounded future royal claims to power upon "an 'original contract,' in opposition to the notions of an indefeasable hereditary right," securing "the public liberty" by limited hereditary succession to Protestant heirs. Elevated by parliamentary law and popular consent, the Hanoverians acquired the British throne by the "best and most indisputable right, that any king can possibly reign by." Through this review of modern British history,

Mayhew argued that such Real Whig principles as popular sovereignty, consensual and contractual government, and the right of resistance were "the fundamental principles, on which the present government is established."[49]

The glory of George II's reign, Mayhew contended, lay in his commitment to Whig principles and his respect for liberty of conscience. Like George I, George II was "a constitutional king" who "well knew both the extent to his own prerogative, and the rights of the people." During his entire reign, the prince never did or even attempted to do "an arbitrary, illegal thing," taking the British constitution as his rule of action. He executed the law impartially, such that never before "were private property, the life and rights of the subject, ever more secure perhaps, than under his administration." The minister also praised the Protestant prince as "a friend to toleration and religious liberty; which cannot indeed be violated without violating the natural rights of mankind." Although supreme head of the Episcopal Church of England, George II never tried "to make his own private judgment and conscience the ruler to his subjects, or to tyrannize over their consciences." Mayhew imagined that the king would have preferred to abolish the Test and Corporation Acts, laws limiting the civil rights of English Protestant dissenters, though he never took action against them. The pastor took heart from Hanoverian rule that the time would come "when all good protestants, and loyal subjects shall have their share in the honors and emoluments of the state, without being subjected to any narrow-spirited, and injurious *tests*."[50]

Despite Britain's shortcomings, George II's reign had given English Protestant dissenters and New England Congregationalists cause for joy and gratitude. "There has not, perhaps, been greater harmony in the nation," Mayhew observed, "since the last days of queen Elizabeth, if then, than during some of the last years of his majesty's reign." Had the peace with France been signed before the king's death, one could say unequivocally that "the reign of king George II [was] the most glorious period in the British annals." The pastor expressed hope that the new prince would follow his grandfather's example in ruling according to law. In return for respecting the people's rights, George III could expect their loyalty and obedience. Mayhew remarked that the "Northern American colonies have indeed ever distinguished themselves by their loyalty, and their zeal for the protestant succession in the house of Hanover," and that George's father, the late Prince Frederick, had been a friend to Protestant dissenters and the American colonies. "We have no reason to doubt, but that his present majesty will have the same gracious regard for us," Mayhew wrote, "and, perhaps, perfect that deliverance so happily begun, and carried on so far, for his American subjects, within these few years past." He thought the American colonists could expect to enjoy from George III the "favour" they derived from his Hanoverian predecessors, "if we persevere in our accustomed loyalty; and still conduct ourselves as dutiful subjects."[51]

Much had happened since the darkest years of the war to brighten Mayhew's view of the mother country. Britain's military victory, and the moral example of James Wolfe, had restored his confidence in British virtue and liberty. He greeted the coronation of George III with optimism. Indeed, his hopes for the security of New England's free institutions, the rights of Protestant dissenters, and the progress of British America had never been higher than they were in 1761. A Real Whig committed to "the principles of true British liberty," he took heart that Britain's reigning House of Hanover shared that commitment. A Congregational pastor devoted to New England's civil and religious liberty, Mayhew honored Hanoverian Britain as champion of the Protestant interest and New England's defender against French aggression. A heterodox Protestant critical of New England's theological orthodoxy, he was attracted to the British Enlightenment and found solace in correspondence with like-minded English friends.

The same principles and values that attached Mayhew to Britain, however, were also the source of his ambivalence toward the mother country. As a Real Whig, he maintained that the American people's loyalty to the British king was conditional, wholly contingent upon his respect for their rights. As a Congregational pastor, Mayhew was galled by the Test and Corporation Acts and high-church attacks upon Protestant dissent. As a heterodox Protestant, he began to fear that Britain's own commitment to Enlightenment ideas and religious tolerance was fading. In George Benson's final letter to Mayhew, written April 16, 1761, the old minister sighed, "Ye spirit of freedom (which decays here very much, & which, I apprehend, will be succeeded by bigotry & enthusiasm) will, I hope, spread, in America." In 1750, Benjamin Avery had expressed a low opinion of New England thought and culture, and Mayhew escaped intellectual loneliness through his correspondence with heterodox English Protestant dissenters. By 1761, though, Mayhew's correspondents were deeply pessimistic about the prospects of heterodox Protestantism in

England and looked increasingly toward America as the cradle of their hopes for reason, happiness, virtue, and liberty.[52]

Mayhew emerged from the French and Indian War with strong attachments to both Britain and New England. In the 1760s, his commitment to the Protestant dissenting interest and New England's free institutions grew only stronger. His commitment to Hanoverian Britain, however, was strained by renewed concerns about the corrupting influence of arbitrary power. His expression of cautious optimism for the reign of George III came only one month before James Otis's speech in the Massachusetts Superior Court, denouncing general search warrants as unconstitutional. The West Church minister soon had reason to fear that the forces of civil and religious tyranny were again on the rise in Old England, threatening to destroy New England's cherished self-government in church and state.

4

Power and Corruption

On the night of August 14, 1765, a crowd of hundreds of Bostonians clamored for Andrew Oliver, provincial secretary of Massachusetts, to renounce his royal commission as a distributor of Parliament's new stamp tax. Eleven days later, Jonathan Mayhew addressed the Stamp Act Crisis from his West Church pulpit, offering implicit approval of the mob's protests in a sermon on the nature and value of liberty. According to a memorandum he composed days after the sermon, Mayhew told his congregation that a nation "actually abused by their rulers to a great degree" had the right of "opposing such rulers, and the execution of unrighteous & oppressive laws." The following evening, the mob ransacked the homes of two customs commissioners, William Story and Benjamin Hallowell, as well as Lieutenant Governor Thomas Hutchinson's house. Mayhew offered his condolences to Hutchinson the next day, denying the gossip that his sermon incited the riot. "The D[octor's] venomous arrows were aimed at you," Hutchinson wrote privately to Francis Bernard, royal governor of Massachusetts. "I had the misfortune to be grievously wounded by his random shot." Why did Hutchinson not only accept the rumors against Mayhew as true but further conclude that Bernard had been the clergyman's intended victim?[1]

In assuming the worst of Mayhew on the basis of gossip and supposition, the lieutenant governor was hardly alone. Over the previous several years, ecclesiastical tensions had roiled public life in Massachusetts, and the West Church pastor had been deeply involved in them. From 1762 to 1764, he had conducted a one-man campaign to derail the archbishop of Canterbury's plan to introduce bishops to the American colonies. In April 1762, the pastor wrote his influential English friend, Thomas Hollis of Lincoln's Inn, "We are apprehensive, Sir, that there is a scheme forming for sending a Bishop into these parts, and that our Governor, Mr. Bernard, a true church-man, is deep in the *plot*." Like Hutchinson in 1765, Mayhew failed to provide Hollis any substantiation for his suspicion. He made this accusation one month after the conclusion of the Indian Affair, a fierce quarrel between the minister and the governor. Before the Bishop Controversy, before the Stamp Act Crisis, the Indian Affair had already embittered Mayhew and Bernard against one another.[2]

Nearly four years earlier, in December 1761, an Indian visitor named James Tallman had remarked to the pastor that he offered the governor a two-dollar gratuity for submitting a petition to the Massachusetts General Court and that the governor accepted the money. When Mayhew had shared the story with high-ranking friends, his accusation of corruption spread quickly, setting the governor on a collision course with a minister well known for preaching vigilance against corruption and resistance to tyranny. It may have struck the lieutenant governor as hardly coincidental that three out of four victims of the Boston riots in August 1765—Andrew Oliver, William Story, and himself—supported Bernard during his 1762 quarrel with the Boston divine. The scandal had poisoned Mayhew's relations with Bernard and his allies. Due to the Indian Affair, Mayhew had decided that Bernard would be a tyrant if he could, while Hutchinson concluded that Mayhew's hatred of Bernard made him capable of the rankest demagoguery.

The Indian Affair turned the highest royal official in Massachusetts and eighteenth-century America's most politically active clergyman into enemies. Immediately following his clash with the governor, Mayhew went into opposition against Bernard's administration, working with his friend James Otis, Jr. to confound government policies at every step. Accelerating with the Bishop Controversy in 1762–1764 and climaxing with his sermon against the Stamp Act on August 25, 1765, Mayhew's political war against Bernard helped mobilize New England's Congregational clergy for political opposition to royal authority, transforming them into "Mr. Otis's black regiment." Although ephemeral in its own time and now forgotten, the Indian Affair had long-range consequences for Mayhew and Massachusetts, contributing indirectly to the downward spiral in political relations between the royal government and the popular opposition in Massachusetts.[3]

This confrontation between Mayhew and Bernard has wider implications for our understanding of the American Revolution's origins. Their clash of egos resulted from a clash of principles. Both men interpreted this private dispute in the contexts of the contemporary political struggle between the popular party and the government party in 1760s Massachusetts—as well as the savage civil war between Parliamentarians and Royalists in 1640s England. Combined with the spur of violated honor, conflicting religious and political principles prevented each man from admitting his share of fault and backing down. The Indian Affair is suggestive, then, of the ideological conflict that rendered political compromise between the royal government and the Sons of Liberty all but impossible in the years following the riots of August 1765.

An Englishman born into the communion of the Church of England and the son and stepson of Episcopal clergymen, Francis Bernard received his education at Christ Church, Oxford—the intellectual stronghold of high-church Episcopalian religion and Tory politics—and trained in canon law at London's Inns of Court. Over the 1740s and 1750s, he aggressively advanced himself from office to office within the hierarchy of the Church of England. The canon lawyer was presiding as lay judge over an ecclesiastical court when he secured appointment as governor of New Jersey in 1758. In 1760, he gladly accepted the Massachusetts governorship, a far more lucrative and influential office, thanks to its control over the customs duties and patronage of the Port of Boston. Father to nine children, Bernard strove to keep his large family in good stead by augmenting his income however possible. An archetypal courtier, he owed his advancements in the colonies less to demonstrated merit than to devotion to king and Church and the influence of his wife's cousin, the second Viscount Barrington, who then served as Britain's secretary-at-war. Historians have not been kind to the governor. Edward Channing found Bernard "an English gentleman of third-rate abilities," while Hiller Zobel styled him "a roast beef of a man" unprepared for the subtleties of colonial administration.[4]

The new governor arrived in Boston on August 2, 1760, with instructions from the king's Privy Council to begin aggressively prosecuting violators of parliamentary regulations on colonial trade. Bernard was only too eager to comply. If a ship were seized for smuggling and its cargo confiscated, one-third of the proceeds went to the Crown, one-third to the customs officers, and one-third to the governor. Unlike Thomas Pownall, his immediate predecessor in the Massachusetts governorship, Bernard was quite willing to alienate the local merchants if it meant he could fulfill his duties and at the same time double his yearly income. That fall, the customs service took four ships, including one belonging to a member of the Massachusetts Council. Exploiting every legal loophole to claim ships and their freight, Bernard initiated—in collusion with Charles Paxton, surveyor of customs for the Port of Boston—what one historian called the "era of customs racketeering."[5]

The principal weapon Bernard needed to bring smugglers to heel was the writ of assistance, a search warrant that did not specify the person or place to be searched or the items to be seized. In Britain, courts of exchequer issued writs of assistance. During the French and Indian War, Governor William Shirley issued these general search warrants himself until Lieutenant Governor Thomas Hutchinson advised him privately that only the Massachusetts Superior Court should have such authority. As the legality of such writs became the foremost political controversy of the day, all eyes turned to the province's highest court. In a twist of fate, Stephen Sewall—the fifty-eight-year-old chief justice of the Superior Court—died unexpectedly of natural causes on September 11, 1760.

For Jonathan Mayhew, the death of the chief justice was a personal rather than a political tragedy. The Mayhews had long enjoyed friendship with the Sewalls. Stephen's famous uncle, Judge Samuel Sewall, helped Jonathan's father Experience Mayhew to attain grants for his mission work among the Pokanauket Indians of Martha's Vineyard. Stephen Sewall was likely responsible for securing scholarships for both Jonathan and his older brother Nathan to attend Harvard College. The chief justice was a full member of Mayhew's congregation and the pastor's close friend. On the Sunday following Sewall's death, Mayhew gave a heartfelt sermon praising his many virtues. The service was a public event, as the surviving four justices of the Superior Court and other government dignitaries assembled in the West Church to pay final respects to their colleague. Mayhew expressed the sentiments of many in the province when he said, "There are, to be sure, but very few persons, equally qualified in all respects to fill that important station, which is now left vacant by the death of judge SEWALL."[6]

The governor's choice of a replacement for Sewall would necessarily bear enormous consequences for the legal and political struggle between Bernard and the merchants over enforcement of British trade regulations in Massachusetts. Shortly before his demise, Sewall expressed "great doubts" about the constitutionality of writs of assistance, and he approached James Otis, Jr.—the acting advocate general of the vice-admiralty court—to inquire whether it was possible to harmonize such writs with Magna Charta. Indeed, Mayhew praised Sewall in his funeral sermon as one who zealously upheld "the just rights and liberties of the people." In the chief justice, Boston's merchants lost a promising ally against the royal customs service.[7]

Immediately after Sewall's death, Otis reminded Bernard that his predecessors, William Shirley and Thomas Pownall, had both promised to promote his father to the high court in the event of a vacancy. Jeremiah Gridley, doyen of the Massachusetts Bar, recommended Lieutenant Governor Hutchinson for the chief justiceship. Bernard, Paxton, and Provincial Secretary Andrew Oliver—Hutchinson's brother-in-law—all gave Otis reason to think that his father would receive serious consideration as a candidate. Privately, though, Oliver and Paxton urged Bernard to act on Gridley's recommendation. Although a merchant by trade with no legal training, Hutchinson had the coolly deliberative temperament well suited to the bench, and he was a steadfast friend to royal authority. Paxton thought Hutchinson could be trusted to support the legality of writs and the crackdown on smuggling. On November 13, the governor named the lieutenant governor as chief justice.[8]

Stunned and furious, James Otis, Jr., resigned his royal commission and declared political war on Bernard, Hutchinson, Oliver, and Paxton, characterizing them in the Boston press as a corrupt and self-serving "junto" that sought to monopolize all civil offices in the province. He observed that Hutchinson—as councilor, lieutenant governor, and chief justice—had combined in his own person legislative, executive, and judicial powers, a clear threat to liberty according to such philosophers as the Baron de Montesquieu. During his service as acting advocate general, Otis witnessed the institutionalized corruption of the royal customs service. While one-third of the proceeds of vice-admiralty court convictions were supposed to go to the

Crown for public use in the province, Otis observed that customs officers used royal funds illegally to pay informers and line their own purses. On December 17, 1760, he petitioned the Massachusetts House of Representatives to authorize the provincial treasurer, Harrison Gray, to sue Paxton for misappropriation of funds. The House agreed. Otis represented Gray in the case of *Gray v. Paxton*. Twice the Inferior Court decided in favor of Gray. Twice Hutchinson's Superior Court reversed the decision in Paxton's favor.[9]

In February 1761, Otis represented sixty-four Boston merchants—four of them members of Mayhew's congregation—in a suit to stop the customs service from acquiring new writs of assistance. Invoking the principles of radical Whig political philosophy, Otis denounced the writs as a violation of each person's right, under natural law and the British Constitution, to be secure in his home, property, and person from unlawful search and seizure. He framed the conflict with his rivals for power in ideological terms—as a clash between the liberty of a virtuous people and the tyranny of a corrupt faction. Otis's Real Whig rhetoric failed to move the court, but it succeeded in moving the people. In March 1761, the Boston Town Meeting gave Otis and his supporters a firm majority in the House of Representatives. Relentlessly hammering Bernard in the legislature, press, and courts of law throughout that year, Otis emerged as the leader of a popular opposition party aligned against the policies of the governor and his "junto."[10]

In December 1761, after Hutchinson gave formal approval of the legality of writs of assistance, Paxton resumed his crackdown on smuggling. The "friends of government" were ready to strike back against Otis's opposition movement. The governor saw New England's political institutions as the root cause of popular insolence toward royal authority. On December 15, Bernard mailed Lord Barrington his proposal for "a new establishment of the governments in N. America upon a true English-constitutional bottom." He recommended that "New England is the proper place to begin" such radical reforms. Under his proposed form of government for the New England colonies, a royally appointed council would balance the power of the popularly elected assembly, balancing Yankee democracy with an element of imported English aristocracy. Bernard drafted his plan to revoke the semirepublican charter of Massachusetts four days after an infuriating encounter with Dr. Mayhew, a nasty confrontation that confirmed his opinion of Bostonians as ungovernable rabble.[11]

❖ ❖ ❖

The only surviving record of the quarrel between Bernard and Mayhew was a long memorandum that the West Church minister drafted, at the urging of an unnamed confidant, as a way "to vindicate my own conduct & character with relation to this affair, of which some persons, I know, have very wrong conceptions." Probably writing in February 1762, he recorded the facts as he remembered them from mid-November 1761 through mid January 1762. Entitled "A circumstantial Narrative of what passed betwixt the Author and an Indian, relating to a certain Petition and two dollars," the memorandum took the form of thirteen letters bound as booklets in two volumes. Although written in the pastor's hand, he did not sign the memorandum or identify the friend to whom he addressed it. Since "A circumstantial Narrative" is the only account of the Indian Affair, it is well that Mayhew had a firmly established reputation for ingenuousness.[12]

Although a lightning rod for controversy since his ordination in 1747, Mayhew had secured a respectable place in Massachusetts society by 1761. Despite the controversies his sermons provoked in the 1750s, the West Church congregation remained firmly behind him. While he had won several enemies, he had well-placed friends like Harrison Gray, and some of his parishioners were among the city's wealthiest merchants. In 1756, Mayhew married Elizabeth Clarke, one of the most beautiful women in the city, and the daughter of the well-to-do physician, Dr. John Clarke. Noted for her charity work among the West End poor, Elizabeth Clarke was, in Gray's words, "a Fine accomplished lady, admired and almost adored by the whole parish." Although it is a glum and corpulent man who stares back from Paul Revere's crude engraving of the pastor, Mayhew had a happy family life and an affectionate marriage. In one undated letter, he wrote his absent wife, "My Dear Betsy," that their little daughter was not the only one who missed her, concluding, "I . . . desire you would believe me your ever loving and TENDER Husband, who longs to see you." Gray later said of their marriage that "there never was a more happy Match upon Earth." Thanks to his nouveau riche mercantile congregation, Mayhew was among the best-paid ministers in Boston. The family's income was sufficient to rent a comfortable, well-furnished townhouse in the West End and keep a maid and an indentured servant for household chores.[13]

On November 17, 1761, Mayhew received two unexpected guests at his home. They were James Tallman and Judah Ossoit, a pair of Pokanauket Indians from Martha's Vineyard. The minister was unacquainted with Ossoit, but his indentured servant was Tallman's teenaged son. Tallman explained that they came to Boston with a petition to present to the General Court, and they gave it to the governor at his home. Since Bernard was "a great man," they judged that it would be "honourable" to offer him money. So the Indians handed the governor a gratuity of two dollars—their last two dollars. They asked Mayhew if he would spot them two more dollars to cover their expenses for the long journey back to the Vineyard. The clergyman agreed and let them sleep overnight in his home. In the morning, Mayhew questioned them about the curious matter of the gratuity. Tallman reaffirmed that the governor accepted the money and put it in his pocket. Musing that it must be customary for a governor to receive a fee on such occasions, he let the Indians go on their way. They returned to the governor's residence, discussed the petition with him "to their satisfaction," and then went home to Martha's Vineyard.[14]

It was against the pastor's open nature to keep this story to himself for long. His close colleague, Dr. Charles Chauncy of Boston's First Church, once remarked to their mutual friend, Dr. Ebenezer Gay of the Congregational church in Hingham, that Mayhew could not "keep a secret." Chauncy dared not entrust a confidence to Mayhew, since "such is his frankness that all the world will soon know it." Mayhew remained true to form in the Indian Affair. Sensitive to signs of corruption in high places, he began to wonder if Bernard had behaved properly in accepting the gratuity. After three weeks, on December 8, the pastor confided in two unnamed friends. He related Tallman's story about a certain "great man" in the government who took money in return for accepting a petition. When one confidant asked if the person in question was the provincial secretary, Andrew Oliver, Mayhew corrected him, acknowledging that it was Francis Bernard. The confidant explained to Mayhew that the provincial secretary charged a fee for bringing a petition to the General Court. The governor could not accept money for himself, but they concluded that Bernard likely accepted the dollars on Oliver's behalf. A third gentleman came within range of hearing, so they dropped the subject.[15]

When Mayhew related this conversation in the Indian Affair memorandum, he did not reveal the identities of his two confidants. He later described them to the governor as his "intimate friends: One of them a worthy member of his Majesty's council; the other a deacon of my church, a person of as unexceptionable a character, and as generally esteemed, as any one of his rank & degree." One of these friends might have been James Bowdoin, a member of the Massachusetts Council, or Thomas Flucker, who was both a councilor and a member of the West Church congregation. The other confidant almost certainly was Harrison Gray. After Stephen Sewall's death in September 1760, Gray filled his empty council seat. He was Mayhew's closest friend and a deacon in the West Church. As provincial treasurer, he would have been the most appropriate person for Mayhew to address a question about fees and bribes. It was also his duty to investigate any claim of corruption, and he joined James Otis in suing Charles Paxton for misappropriation of funds. If Gray then made tentative inquiries to substantiate Tallman's story about Governor Bernard, that would explain how Mayhew's confidence was broken.[16]

Whoever his two friends were, and however the story spread, spread it did, and quickly. On December 11, William Story, the Town of Boston's auditor and the deputy registrar of the vice-admiralty court, came to call at Mayhew's home in the West End. Story said he had overheard someone talking about Mayhew's accusation that a certain great man of the town accepted payment from Indian petitioners. This gossip made Bernard nervous, and Story laid a wager of ten guineas that Mayhew would retract it once challenged. The pastor informed Story that he could count the wager lost. He further confirmed that the governor was indeed the great man in question and called in his maidservant as a witness to confirm that he repeated the story just as Tallman had originally told it. Story departed to report this exchange to Bernard.[17]

At nine the following morning, Mayhew received yet another unexpected guest at his home: Andrew Oliver. The provincial secretary announced that the governor wanted to see him within one hour to give an accounting for his accusation. At ten o'clock, Mayhew walked up the front steps of Province House, the official gubernatorial residence. Today, only those stone steps remain to mark the site. In 1761, however, Province House was, at three stories, one of the grandest homes in Massachusetts. The third story was topped with an attic, the attic was topped with a cupola, and the cupola was topped with a weather vane, hammered in the form of an Indian. The gilded Indian glowed in the morning sun—a beacon of warning to the approaching divine.[18]

Mayhew assumed that Bernard desired a private interview, but the governor kept him waiting until Hutchinson and Oliver could join them as witnesses. By bringing this matter before the province's lieutenant governor and secretary, Bernard charged their private affair with legal and political implications to which the pastor was keenly sensitive. Mayhew later wrote that this interview felt like an "extraordinary *trial*" before "a court, if I may call it such, which was unprecedented amongst us, at least no legal and constitutional one, to the jurisdiction of which I had therefore a good right to object." The governor indignantly presented his own side of the case. He expressed shock "that any one could possibly have so *mean* an opinion of *him*, as to give the least credit to such a story from an Indian," considering that "he had not been reckoned a lover of money." Mayhew's accusation "convinced him more fully of the diabolical spirits of slander & defamation in the town [or province]; of which he had had great experience since his coming to this government." Bernard called Tallman's story a lie and declaimed, "the spreader of *a lye* was equally obnoxious in law, with the *Author* of it; and that he expected *satisfaction* of me." He said he could prove it was a lie and then summoned his house servant. The young man explained that it was he, not Bernard, who received the Indians' petition, but that he did not receive any money from them. The governor was fully satisfied by his servant's version of events.[19]

While much of Boston abhorred the governor for the rapacity of his customs racketeering, this strange interview indicates that Bernard viewed himself in quite a different light. After the servant completed his testimony, the governor added that he was astonished that "any one could believe such a story about *him*; who had never, since he came here, taken money in any dishonourable way." Bernard asked Mayhew how he "could possibly believe *him* guilty of so mean a thing." The pastor answered—in light of the servant's testimony—that he was now inclined to disbelieve Tallman's account of the incident, but he was not willing to beg the governor's pardon. Infuriated by the pastor's stubbornness, Bernard said he had never been angrier with anyone in Massachusetts than he was with Mayhew at that moment—quite a claim, considering how James Otis had hounded him doggedly for a year.[20]

Bernard told Mayhew he should have kept the Indian's allegation a secret. The minister answered defiantly that, "in speaking of it in the manner I had done, I had taken no liberty unbecoming a Christian, or British subject," as "the English government allow'd of great freedom of speech & writing."

While the freedom of speech and of the press could and had been abused, he said, it "was found, and acknowledged to be, of the utmost importance to the public welfare, & liberty; and that our free constitution of government could not be secured without it." Losing his last shred of patience, the governor furiously accused Mayhew of breaking the law by spreading a lie. He claimed that the pastor "did not understand, but abused British liberty," and that liberties of speech of the sort he had taken "were never allowed, 'even in the Oliverian times, which I so much adored.'" Bernard added that he could imagine no reason why Mayhew might resent him, "except perhaps some remarks he might have occasionally made upon some of my writings." This remark and the allusion to Mayhew's love for "the Oliverian times" suggest Bernard's disapproving familiarity with the pastor's vindication of the Parliamentarian cause in *A Discourse Concerning Unlimited Submission*.[21]

Denying that he adored Oliver Cromwell, Mayhew further rejected the claim that he had broken the law or his duty. While Tallman might have told a lie, the doctor wrote in his memorandum, "I had myself told no more than truth; and such truth as, I apprehended, I had a right to tell." As such his conscience was clear. Mayhew wrote, "His E[xcellency] answered to this purpose, (you may conclude, not very calmly) that *some folks* had a way of appeasing their 'consciences,' and making them easy, however criminal their conduct might be." The governor told Mayhew that he did not understand the nature of British law, and that "if any person in London had spoken in the like manner of a minister of state, [or, of a member of the privy council] he would have been *sent for*, or *taken up*." Bernard demanded satisfaction for this insult to his honor. Asked what amends the governor required, Bernard responded that he would decide after seeking further advice and would notify the pastor if he intended to take additional action against him. After an hour and a half, the ordeal finally ended. Mayhew observed that he left Bernard, "if possible, more dissatisfied and perplexed than I found him."[22]

Assuming that the advice and action Bernard had in mind were of a legal nature, the clergyman took immediate care to feel out the legal soundness of his own position. He sought counsel from two unnamed "gentlemen of the law." He most likely went to the firm of Gridley and Otis. Jeremiah Gridley was not only the province's most respected lawyer but a full member of Mayhew's congregation. Gridley's junior partner, James Otis, had been a friend of his at Harvard in the 1740s, and his younger brother Samuel Alleyne Otis was a member of the West Church and an admirer of the pastor who later named one of his sons Jonathan Mayhew Otis. As Bernard's political nemesis and Harrison Gray's partner in the campaign against Paxton, Otis was uniquely equipped and motivated to defend Mayhew against Bernard in court. The attorneys concurred that he had violated no law. Mayhew reported that "one of them"—probably the hot-tempered Otis—"blamed me very much for submitting to such an extrajudicial & unfair examination." His consultation with the lawyers only sharpened his initial sense of victimization by a budding tyrant. Mayhew began to see his legal dispute with Bernard as part of the wider political conflict between the governor and Otis's opposition party. The same principles—personal liberty versus royal authority—appeared to be at stake in his case as in the larger constitutional struggle.[23]

Taking pains to get the facts straight in the event of a judicial hearing and trial, Mayhew wrote a letter on December 14 to his brother Zachariah, who worked with their aged father in the Indian mission on Martha's Vineyard, and asked him to inquire into the truth of "the Indian Story." While the Boston minister braced for a civil lawsuit or criminal indictment, Hutchinson tried to defuse the explosive situation. On December 16, the lieutenant governor dropped by Mayhew's home, acting as the governor's second in their as-yet-bloodless affair of honor. Hutchinson "express'd his desire, that the affair might be compromised; and intimated, if I rightly understood his Honor, that his E[xcellency] would be willing to drop it, upon my making an acknowledgment, or asking his pardon." Mayhew replied that he was sorry to see Bernard so disturbed, but that "in sincerity" he could not beg the governor's pardon when he had done nothing wrong. Hutchinson duly reported their exchange to Bernard. To redeem his besmirched honor in the eyes of the colonial elite, the outraged governor considered presenting the case before the Massachusetts Council. Determined to keep a private quarrel from escalating into a political crisis, Hutchinson talked him out of it. The following day, Harrison Gray—serving as Mayhew's second in this affair of honor—related Bernard's proposal that they instead submit their dispute to private arbitration by five council members.[24]

The night of Friday, December 18, was "remarkably cold." Galled by the governor's threats, Mayhew's mind raced, and he could not sleep. What he had to do could not wait until the light and warmth of daytime. Despite the bitter chill in his house, the minister left behind the warmth of his bed and his wife and drew a chair up to his desk. With frosty breath and trembling hand, he composed the governor a fifteen-page letter by candlelight. Expressing himself better in written than in spoken words, Mayhew preferred to commit his side of the dispute to paper. The pastor reiterated his position that he could not ask pardon in good conscience. "I beg leave to assure you, Sir," he wrote, "that this proceeds not from any contumacy, or obstinacy of temper in me, but from *principle*; I mean, from the conceptions which I have of what is *right & equitable* in the case."[25]

Gossip then circulating in town alleged that Mayhew had accused Bernard of pocketing the Indian's two dollars. The minister said he had never made such a claim but merely repeated Tallman's account. He told the Indian story privately to two friends and never intended for it to become public and cause the governor any distress. Even if he had told the story in public, Mayhew insisted, "it would not have been defamatory in the eye of the law." He believed he was not obligated—legally or morally—to give Bernard the "satisfaction" he had demanded. Just as Bernard was unwilling to acknowledge that Mayhew had good reason to think him a "lover of money," so Mayhew refused to concede that Bernard had good reason to think him a rumor monger.[26]

Persuaded that his motives were pure and his cause was just, the West Church minister stood his ground in defense of both his personal honor and his civil liberty. He believed that the governor's veiled threat of a suit under the law of slander was an attempt to destroy his freedom of speech. In terms reminiscent of Trenchard and Gordon's essay on freedom of speech and of the press in *Cato's Letters*, Mayhew wrote Bernard:

In my humble opinion, Sir, no person deserves to enjoy the rights & privileges of a British subject, which has not the spirit to defend them to the last: Of which rights & privileges, freedom of speech & writing, within the limits of law & decency, is not the least valuable, or important in its consequences. And I hope I might indeed say, am *confident*, you have no desire to obtain and establish such a universal influence over the tongues or pens of his Majesty's loyal subjects, as is not warranted by law; such an one, as is not consistent with the genius of the British government; in short, such an one as true Britons neither will nor ought to be under, so long as they enjoy both tongues & pens, and their liberties.[27]

The private dispute turned into a matter of principle for both men—the same principles of royal authority and personal liberty that were at stake in the very public struggle between the governor and the popular opposition.

Weeks went by, and Mayhew's defiant letter received no response from Bernard. The pastor made conciliatory visits to Hutchinson and Oliver and expected some peace offering from the governor. He received only contemptuous silence, and their dispute continued to fester. It became a favorite subject for loose talk in Boston, with different versions of the Indian Affair that reflected badly on both Bernard and Mayhew. The minister imagined that the anti-Mayhew gossip was "spread abroad chiefly thro' the indiscretion of some of the G[overno]r's over-zealous & officious friends; those 'gentlemen of so much spirit & honor'"—that is, William Story. Bandied about "even in *barbers' shops*," these rumors claimed, among other unflattering things, that Bernard was preparing a criminal indictment against Mayhew for slander.[28]

When the "grossly misrepresented" stories began to spread "amongst the good people of my pastoral charge," Mayhew knew that he had to take action to rescue his declining reputation. As he had written in the letter to Bernard, "My own moral character, especially as a minister of the gospel, is very dear, and of great importance to me." Mayhew considered clearing his name with the publication in a newspaper of a statement on the Indian Affair. He confined his efforts at self-vindication to the drafting of his sixty-four-page memorandum, which he thought should be a sufficient explanation for all inquirers, "excepting with those persons who were either prejudiced against *me*, or were *dependent* on his E[xcellency], and in *servile* fear of him."[29]

It was critical that he stop the hemorrhaging of his reputation in Boston. Mayhew's pastorate depended upon a good name for moral character and Christian conduct. As a Congregational clergyman, he was elected by his parishioners and ordained by his fellow ministers, and a controversy could prompt a formal inquiry into his behavior by an ecclesiastical council and even removal from the pulpit of the West Church. Disgrace in this affair of honor could destroy not only his livelihood but also the great influence he wielded as a champion of civil and religious liberty on both sides of the Atlantic. His young friend Rev. Lemuel Briant of the Braintree church sank into an early grave in 1753 due to shattered health after the disgrace of removal from his pulpit, thanks in part to rumors of immoral behavior. Mayhew did not compose his lengthy memorandum until gossip about the Indian Affair spread among his own congregation. To preserve his honor, his pulpit, his fortune, and his station in society, he had to vindicate himself at least in the eyes of his own flock. Mayhew seems to have succeeded. There is no indication that the minister lost any member of his church over the Indian Affair.[30]

Unlike Mayhew, Francis Bernard was officially accountable to the Crown rather than the people. The real powers of his office, however, derived largely from his influence over the people of Massachusetts, and that influence in turn depended upon his reputation. Considering the rancorousness of the governor's relations with the Massachusetts House of Representatives and the tenuousness of his influence over the electorate, Bernard's violent reaction to the Indian story should not have shocked Mayhew. He saw in the pastor's stubborn refusal to admit his error a particularly infuriating example of the "diabolical spirits of slander & defamation in the town [or province]; of which he had had great experience since his coming to this government." Over the preceding year, Bernard's opponents in the House and the press had snapped at his heels like hounds. Mayhew's friends James Otis and Harrison Gray had persecuted the governor's closest political ally, Charles Paxton, on charges of corruption. Bernard had already endured anonymous accusations of political gangsterism in the public papers—most of them the work of Otis's hand. Mayhew's accusation came at the worst possible time, and his stubbornness conveyed everything Bernard had learned to hate about New Englanders. Only four days after his clash with the obstinate Yankee pastor, Bernard began plotting the replacement of the Massachusetts Charter with a new one under which the people would have less power within the General Court.

Under the Massachusetts Charter of 1691, the king of England—not the provincial populace—vested governors with their office and authority. There was, however, no executive apparatus financially independent of the House of Representatives with which a governor could compel the people's submission to his will. A chief executive could exercise direct influence on the handful of persons who derived offices from him—those who, as Mayhew uncharitably put it, "were *dependent* on his E[xcellency], and in *servile* fear of him." But governors in the American colonies had not yet developed an elaborate and expansive system of patronage of the sort with which the king's ministers controlled Parliament. To work his will on the people and their elected representatives, a Massachusetts governor had to rely upon their voluntary cooperation. A governor without status, without a reputation for sincere commitment to the public interest, would lose the consent of the governed and with it all control of the province. "It would be hard to overstate the importance of personal honor to an eighteenth-century gentleman," historian Joanne Freeman has observed, "let alone to a besieged leader whose status is under attack."[31]

Badly weakened by the challenge of Otis and the popular opposition, Bernard evidently feared letting Mayhew's accusation of corruption go unchallenged, lest he risk the loss of all influence and suffer recall to Britain and the ruin of his political and financial prospects. Mayhew and Bernard were able to drop the Indian Affair once they had cemented the support of their respective factions. Hutchinson, Oliver, and Story stood firmly behind the governor, and Mayhew's memorandum stopped the spread of unflattering gossip within the West Church. By the end of February 1762, the controversy had burned itself out.

Mayhew ultimately resolved the mystery of the two-dollar gratuity to his own satisfaction. He had initially been inclined to believe Tallman's story, as the Indian gave it "with an air of simplicity, not with any design to reflect upon the G[overno]r, nor as having the least suspicion that any ill construction could be put upon it." After hearing from Bernard and the servant in the Province House interview, he remarked to the governor that perhaps Tallman had indeed lied to him. In his memorandum, the pastor concluded that he "went *too far*" in making that statement. Mayhew felt embarrassed for casting aspersion on Tallman's honor and wished "to give him any reasonable satisfaction that he shall desire. For all men have a right to justice, and none, to moreso." He saw nothing odd in taking the word of a poor Indian over that of a royal governor.[32]

Mayhew eventually heard from his brother Zachariah, who wrote him from Martha's Vineyard on January 14, 1762. At his request, Zachariah questioned James Tallman. The Pokanauket Christian confidently explained that he gave two dollars to the governor's liveried servant, whom he and Judah Ossoit mistook for the governor himself. When they subsequently met with Bernard, the governor made no mention of their gratuity; Tallman implied that the servant kept the money for himself. Persuaded by Zachariah's letter, the Boston minister thought it most likely that neither the Indian nor the governor were lying. Tallman made "a very pardonable mistake" in thinking the liveried servant was the governor. "And then, if there be any blame in the case," he wrote, "you perceive it will fall wholly upon the G[overno]r's young man: first, in taking the dollars of the Indians, and then in denying it, the latter of which were without doubt, far the greatest." On the last page of his memorandum, though, the pastor added a notation in a different ink, apparently after the passage of some time: "The author of the foregoing letters has great reason to suspect that the Indian's story was false, after taking much pains to examine into the affair." Mayhew ultimately concluded that Tallman and Ossoit had invented the whole story as a means of defrauding him of two dollars. He did not, however, provide any explanation for this conclusion.[33]

For Mayhew and Bernard, the Indian Affair had long since ceased to be a matter of who told the truth about giving or taking two dollars. For the pastor, the question at issue was whether a man had the right to speak freely on matters of public interest. For the governor, the question was whether the king's American subjects could abuse "British liberty" with impunity. Both men viewed their dispute as part of the political war between the government party and the opposition party in Massachusetts. That conflict originated as a legal controversy over writs of assistance but quickly became a constitutional struggle over the balance between the people's liberty and the king's authority—the same issue that had been at stake in the English Civil War.

In the confrontation between Bernard and Mayhew over the Indian story, one can see how easily this incendiary analogy leapt to the minds of political elites in Massachusetts in the 1760s. Mayhew's bold manner of addressing men in authority reminded the governor of the "Oliverian times," which he alleged the pastor "adored." Similarly, Mayhew wrote his unnamed confidant that Bernard's ambush in Province House "often brought to my mind the violent & extrajudicial proceedings in the reign of Charles I, to the fatal consequences of which, you are no stranger." Mayhew and Bernard interpreted their private grievances in light of their political convictions. This identification proved dangerous because their ideologies were so radically opposed.[34]

While the two men compared their dispute with the English Civil War, both shared a firm commitment to the constitutional settlement that Englishmen produced after the Glorious Revolution of 1688. Mayhew was no more a Commonwealthman than Bernard was a Jacobite. In his letter to the governor, the pastor disavowed the cause of Oliver Cromwell and the English Republic. "I am as far from 'adoring' those times of confusion & religious madness," he wrote, "as yr. Excellency is from 'adoring' the times of the *Jameses* & *Charleses*; when arbitrary power was carried to such enormous lengths; and hardly any wise & honest man could, with freedom & safety, speak his thoughts." The pastor insisted that "if I 'adored' any *times*, they would be those of the glorious *revolution*." He added that, in this "one respect, I flatter myself that I have the honor of being of the same mind with yr. Excellency." In "A circumstantial Narrative," Mayhew acknowledged that Bernard was loyal to the House of Hanover and "as little disposed as almost any man living, to follow the ruin'd fortunes of that out-law'd family, in which there is still a Pr[e]t[e]nd[e]r to his Majesty's throne." Shared commitment to the Revolution Settlement seemed to provide some room for mutual understanding.[35]

If there was indeed such room, it must have been a narrow and crooked space. While Mayhew did not accuse Bernard of Jacobite disloyalty, he privately believed that the governor reserved "strong affection to the *ancient* family of the Stewarts, and particularly to Ch[arles] I and his measures." The minister offered "facts" in support of his "suspicions," among them Bernard's order that portraits of Charles II and James II be removed from storage and displayed in the council chamber of the Massachusetts State House. Finding this memorial to Stuart tyranny most distasteful, Mayhew offered his confidant a tongue-in-cheek proposal: "Either that some proper means ought to be used to make James II *abdicate* the council chamber; of which the best that I can think of, is to *introduce* William III. Or else if the said James must continue then, that a *painter* should be speedily employed *to clap a good halter about his neck*." All joking aside, the ideological tension between Mayhew and Bernard was very real and very deep.[36]

While both men identified with the Glorious Revolution, their interpretations of the Revolution and the resulting constitutional settlement remained starkly opposed. In the early eighteenth century, Real Whigs—such as Mayhew's intellectual heroes Benjamin Hoadly, John Trenchard, and Thomas Gordon—maintained that sovereignty lies in the people. They held that, in 1688, the English people resumed their sovereign power after deposing James II and consented to be ruled by William and Mary. The radical Whig interpretation remained marginal to political discourse in eighteenth-century England, finding widespread acceptance only among Britain's American colonists. The interpretation of the Revolution Settlement that prevailed in England, as moderate Whigs such as James Tyrrell and Gilbert Burnet propounded it, held that sovereignty in Britain was shared jointly by king, House of Lords, and House of Commons, while high-church Episcopal clergymen continued to question the legitimacy of the Glorious Revolution and the Protestant Succession, reviving Tory obedience principles in the late 1740s and 1750s. By the mid-eighteenth century, however, most Tories had renounced Stuart absolutism and sided with moderate Whigs in their view of the Glorious Revolution in particular and the British constitution in general. This consensus on principles provided the ideological foundation for Britain's vaunted political stability over the first half of the eighteenth century. But the moderate Whig consensus that united most eighteenth-century Britons conflicted sharply with the radical Whig consensus that united most eighteenth-century Americans.[37]

The Glorious Revolution meant something very different for a moderate Tory like Bernard than it did for the radical Whig Mayhew. According to the governor's biographer Colin Nicolson, Bernard "lauded the Glorious Revolution for establishing a balanced constitution with a limited monarchy." For him as for most Britons, the Revolution Settlement secured the sovereignty of king-in-Parliament, and the constitutional balance of power among king, Lords, and Commons was the best security for liberty and property. Bernard viewed the Revolution, as Nicolson put it, in light of "a neo-Tory interpretation of the Lockean concept of contractual government, which stressed the obligations of subjects and deference to entrenched authority over any revolutionary right to make and unmake governments." By contrast, Mayhew claimed in his sermon on the death of George II that Parliament—acting on behalf of the people—"invited" William and Mary to Britain and "*elected*" them king and queen, thereby grounding the British monarchy on "an 'original contract,' in opposition to the notions of an indefeasable hereditary right." For him, the Revolution Settlement anchored sovereignty in the consent of the governed. The sovereign people in turn delegated power to king-in-Parliament, which they might revoke upon breach of the "original contract." The best security for liberty and property was to keep power accountable to a sovereign people jealous of their rights and vigilant against abuses of power. Bernard and Mayhew could have reached agreement on many political points, had they wished. In a conflict between doctrines as clearly opposed as parliamentary sovereignty and popular sovereignty, however, there was little chance for compromise and reconciliation.[38]

Their differences in constitutional theory were indicative of a gulf separating their broader philosophies of society and government. According to the pastor's memorandum on the Indian Affair, he told the governor during the interview on December 12, 1761:

> I doubted not but that some men in as high stations as his E[xcellency] had really been guilty of as *little* & *mean* things as taking those dollars would have been. So that the thing was not absolutely, or in its own nature, incredible. His E[xcellency] then asked me, with a seeming surprize, whether I could suppose that any Governor of a British province or colony ever did so mean a thing? To which I replied, that I did not in the least doubt it. Then his E[xcellency] said, that he could not possibly suppose it, no, not *even* of the G[overno]r of _____. Afterwards, making an apology for speaking of that particular gentleman, whom I shall not name.[39]

Implicit in this tangent from their discussion of the bribery allegation are two essentially different understandings of the locus of authority within civil society.

As a native-born Englishman, an Episcopalian, an Oxford graduate, a moderate Tory, a canon lawyer who built his career within the church hierarchy, and a Crown appointee to colonial governorships, Bernard believed that authority originated with king-in-Parliament and flowed downward. For the governor, it was a given that common folk should humbly defer to men of high station as their social and moral betters, and that the Empire was administered by gentlemen in whom subjects should have an implicit trust. True to his Episcopal and moderate Tory view of society, Bernard assumed the best of those who govern—"*even* of the G[overno]r of _____"—while remaining suspicious of his colonial subjects.

As a son of semirepublican Massachusetts, a dissenter from the Church of England, a Harvard graduate, a radical Whig, and a pastor elected by and accountable to his congregation, Mayhew believed that authority originated with the people and flowed upward. By contrast with Bernard's assumptions, the minister had preached that the people must never put blind trust in any ruler, including the king. In his 1751 sermon on *The Death of Frederick*, he denied that "any state of earthly power and greatness, can make a man *independent*; exalt him above the reach of temptation, or remove him beyond a possibility of doing the most cruel, unjust and shameful things." So far from being true that the king can do no wrong, Mayhew found that corruption tends to increase with power. "As men rise to wealth and power and grandeur," he observed, "their old passions often rise with them; or some new and unnatural ones start up in their breasts, to lead them astray." True to his Congregational and radical Whig view of society, Mayhew assumed the best of the governed—even a poor, humble Indian like James Tallman—and remained watchful against any sign of corruption or tyranny in his imperial overlords.[40]

While Mayhew wrote that "all men have a right to justice, and none, to moreso," he failed to offer Bernard the same benefit of the doubt that he gave Tallman. The West Church pastor initially believed Tallman's story because he expected corruption and self-aggrandizement from someone in the royal governor's station. Meanwhile, Mayhew's refusal to retract the story drove Bernard to distraction because he expected deference and humility from someone in the provincial minister's social station. Their emotional responses followed from their basic philosophic premises. Mayhew and Bernard became political enemies because they associated their clash of egos in the Indian Affair with a clash of principles—*fundamental* principles. They differed not only in their understanding of the Glorious Revolution and the British constitution but also in their basic philosophies of government and society.

Mayhew himself interpreted his affair of honor with Bernard in these terms—as ultimately the result of ideological conflict. Mystified by Bernard's fury during the Province House interview, he attributed the governor's "disproportionate" response to an ideologically grounded animosity that must have been building for some months prior to the Indian Affair. Mayhew concluded plausibly that Bernard disliked him due to their fundamental differences of opinion on religion and politics. The pastor remarked in his memorandum that the governor "considers me as a man of *bad* principles, relative to civil government." In that regard the feeling was mutual. He found it natural that Bernard "should have a particular aversion to me, on account of my notions of civil liberty; which he might possibly think incompatible with his own, respecting power & prerogative; not to say, *with some of his practices upon them.*" By this, he likely meant the governor's campaign of customs racketeering.[41]

As for Mayhew's motive in recounting James Tallman's story to his friends, gossip around town attributed his behavior to personal resentment of Bernard on two grounds. The first rumor alleged that the governor angered Mayhew with ungenerous comments in the past about the minister's political writings. During the Province House interview, Bernard himself confirmed that he made such derogatory remarks. In his memorandum Mayhew wrote that, before the Indian Affair, he was unaware of any such statements; had he known them, he would have borne them with "*mirth* or *good humor*." Mayhew could not write down the second rumor without "smiling." It alleged that the pastor resented the governor for never extending to him an invitation to dine at Province House. "I may be pretty confident," he quipped, "that if I have any real disaffection to him, it does not proceed from *hunger*."[42]

While resentment toward Mayhew for his religious and political principles likely contributed to Bernard's infuriated response to Mayhew's allegation, Mayhew remarked that no Boston wag need indulge "odd conjectures" about his motive for making the allegation in the first place. "Methinks, he needed only to reflect, in one word, that I was an *Englishman*." Although the pastor claimed to have no personal animosity toward the governor before the Indian Affair, he clearly harbored such feelings afterward. On this point, however, he exercised uncharacteristic discretion. Mayhew jested that his personal opinion of the governor's character was "more closely concealed than prohibited merchandize; And if Mr. P[axto]n himself came with his *Wr[i]t* of *As[sista]nce*, he would make no discovery."[43]

While Bernard made no explicit allusion to the Indian Affair in his own papers, his treatment of Mayhew during and after the interview proved a transformative experience for the West Church minister. After writing many political sermons about liberty and tyranny in an abstract sense, Mayhew felt for the first time that his own rights and those of his fellow New Englanders were in real danger of abridgment by their own government. Framed in the wider context of Bernard's despotic "practices" against the Boston merchants, the governor's high-handed, bullying conduct during the Indian Affair convinced Mayhew that he would be a despot if he could. In "A circumstantial Narrative," the clergyman balked at Bernard's claim that he should have kept the Indian story a secret. "People must be reduced to an abject state of slavery indeed," he wrote, "before they can think themselves obliged to be silent on such occasions; which, I pray God may never be the case amongst ourselves."[44]

Mayhew privately promised to render Bernard the respect all subjects owed him as governor, but he vowed not forget his own "civil rights"—nor let the people forget theirs. He wrote in "A circumstantial Narrative":

> I should be heartily glad indeed to see more of a truly British spirit amongst us, than seems at present to prevail. Which is opposed, on one hand, to a *servile* fear of those in authority, and an implicit acquiescence in all measures, however arbitrary or oppressive; and, on the other, to a spirit of faction & licentiousness; or which, in other words, consists in a warm zeal for our *constitution* & *laws*; the only centre of union in a free state.[45]

While Mayhew hoped that the governor's tenure would be short, his brush with tyranny in Province House set him in permanent opposition to the Bernard administration. After the Indian Affair, Mayhew resisted any of the governor's policies in which he discerned the thorny sprouts of arbitrary power, true to the Real Whig principle of *obsta principiis*. Within a month of the scandal's conclusion, he emitted the first low growl of his dogged campaign to quash the archbishop of Canterbury's plan of introducing an English bishop to the American colonies. On April 6, 1762, Mayhew warned Thomas Hollis that "our Governor, Mr. Bernard, a true church-man, is deep in the *plot*." Detecting a conspiracy by the governor to curtail New England's civil and religious liberties, Mayhew appears to have formed with James Otis, Jr. a loose political partnership to frustrate his ambitions at every turn.[46]

On March 8, 1762, at a meeting of the Harvard Board of Overseers, Mayhew faced Bernard for the first time since their Province House interview. It was the setting for the first of several political battles to follow. One of Bernard's allies in the Massachusetts Council, the magnate Israel Williams, promoted his plan for a new college in western Massachusetts. The House of Representatives approved the college bill, but the council rejected it. When Bernard then decided to approve the college's charter upon his own prerogative, Otis and Mayhew went on the attack. In the House of Representatives, Otis denounced Bernard's decision as an unconstitutional extension of executive power. Meanwhile, Mayhew, as a member of the Harvard Board of Overseers, composed its remonstrance against the proposed college as a threat to Harvard. Hutchinson pleaded Williams's case in meetings of the overseers, but the governor backed down in the face of organized opposition. Otis and Mayhew scored a victory in their first collaboration against the Bernard administration.[47]

Later in April, the pastor and the attorney infuriated Bernard and Hutchinson by persuading the House of Representatives to replace William Bollan as the province's London agent with Jasper Mauduit. Since Benjamin Avery's death, Mauduit had emerged as the leading activist on behalf of London's Protestant dissenters, and he had corresponded with Mayhew since the mid-1750s. On April 23, Otis informed Mauduit that members of the Church of England in Massachusetts were "very high in their religious and political principles" and were united with "a few dissenters" in "a party whose plans of power were diametrically opposite to the rights of mankind." Three days later Mayhew echoed Otis, warning the new agent against "the Ch[urc]h Party here, and perhaps *some Persons of distinguished Eminence*," by whom he meant Bernard, Hutchinson, and Oliver. As the pastor explained in his April 26 letter, the "most steady friends of Liberty amongst us, and all the Friends to the dissenting Interest" considered Mauduit "much more likely to serve the Province in its most essential Interests, than a Gentleman of the Ch[urc]h of England" like Bollan. In the fall of 1762, Mayhew and Otis worked together in trying to secure Jasper Mauduit's brother Israel as co-agent, but the Bernard faction foiled their machinations.[48]

The spring of 1762 saw another of Mayhew's political initiatives—the establishment of the Society for Propagating Christian Knowledge among the Indians of North America (SPCK), a private society to advance missionary work. His plan was backed by his friends Harrison Gray, James Bowdoin, Charles Chauncy, and Andrew Eliot. "We are not without apprehensions," Mayhew wrote Thomas Hollis, on April 6, "that our *good Friends* of the Church of England will endeavour to obstruct this scheme; but hope, to no purpose." A year later, the Massachusetts General Court approved the incorporation of the SPCK. Eager to avoid another fight with the province's Congregational majority, Bernard signed the bill and sent it to the Privy Council. Viewing the SPCK as a threat to the Society for the Propagation of the Gospel, Episcopal missionaries such as Bernard's friend Rev. Henry Caner lobbied the archbishop of Canterbury for a veto of the charter. In May 1763, the Privy Council voided the Massachusetts General Court's incorporation of the proposed missionary society. By then, however, Mayhew was embroiled in his crusade against an episcopate for the American colonies.[49]

Mayhew published pamphlet after pamphlet exposing the bishop plan as a threat to New England dissent, while Otis's *Rights of the British Colonies Asserted and Proved* attacked Parliament's Sugar Act and proposed Stamp Act. Their loose political partnership thrived on a division of labor in which the pastor responded to encroachments on religious liberty while the attorney addressed threats to civil liberty. Over the course of 1763 and 1764, they successfully mobilized the New England public against further constitutional innovations. When news of the Stamp Act arrived in the spring of 1765, Massachusetts was ready to boil over. Mayhew's notorious sermon of August 25, 1765, was the culmination of years of political activism in opposition to Bernard and his allies among the Church of England clergy. The minister's political war had its start in the otherwise forgettable Indian Affair.

The quarrel between Mayhew and Bernard over James Tallman's story is little marked or remembered, and their affair of honor proved a transient matter even at the time. At the beginning of the second letter of "A circumstantial Narrative," Mayhew wrote, "The Indian affair hinted at in my last, of which I am now to enter on a more particular account, has been a kind of *war*, tho' hitherto an un-bloody one." Their dispute remained bloodless. The governor never did seek his "satisfaction" in a court of law, let alone on the field of honor. Thanks to the grudging forbearance of the two disputants and the moderating influence of Thomas Hutchinson and Harrison Gray, their quarrel did not turn into a political controversy or legal contest. Bernard decided against bringing his case before the Massachusetts Council, and Mayhew declined to submit his version of their dispute to the newspapers. The public press took little notice of their quarrel. Fading from public discussion by the end of February 1762, the Indian Affair remained the ephemeral stuff of barbershop gossip. If not for Mayhew's written account, the scandal would have been wholly lost to history. The consequences of this trivial episode, though, were long-term—its implications wide in scope.[50]

Both men interpreted their private misunderstanding in political terms, as an extension of the struggle between the royal government and the popular opposition for control of Massachusetts. Not only did they conclude that their conflict was a matter of principle, but the particular doctrines in question were fundamental and irreconcilable. For Mayhew, Bernard's behavior threatened the right of an English subject to speak on matters of public interest. For Bernard, Mayhew's behavior challenged the right of a royal official to receive the due deference and obedience upon which government depended. Implicit for both men was the question of whether authority flowed from the people to the Crown or from the Crown to the people. The principles at stake, then, were those that distinguished radical Whigs from moderate Tories in eighteenth-century British politics and, more frightfully, those that set Parliamentarians and Royalists at one another's throats in the English Civil War.

So long as Bernard and Mayhew—and, by extension, other partisans of Massachusetts politics, such as Hutchinson and Otis—viewed their personal clashes in such stark ideological terms, mutual understanding, compromise, and reconciliation had to remain difficult if not unattainable. If royal officials and native elites could not reach a consensus on the fundamental nature of government, the political process in Massachusetts could not be sustained. It ultimately gave way to extralegal violence in August 1765, collapsing altogether by 1774. Like the political conflict between Crown government and its popular opposition in the 1760s, the private quarrel between Bernard and Mayhew in 1761–1762 was "a kind of *war*, tho' hitherto an un-bloody one." So long as American colonists framed their dispute in the same ideological terms as the English Civil War, it could hardly remain bloodless for long.

The Indian Affair provides an example of the ideologically driven politics that led to the constitutional crises of 1765–1775. But the scandal itself contributed indirectly to those crises by propelling Mayhew into the popular opposition aligned against Bernard's administration. After the climax of his quarrel with the governor in January 1762, the pastor clashed repeatedly with Bernard and Hutchinson in political controversies. He emerged as the foremost defender of New England's religious liberty against the royal administration and the Church of England—the sacerdotal analogue to his secular friend and colleague James Otis. Their spirited campaign to expose Britain's allegedly despotic designs agitated New Englanders against further encroachments on colonial liberties. Mayhew and Otis sowed the wind, but

Hutchinson and Bernard reaped the whirlwind. The riot against Hutchinson in 1765—allegedly incited by Mayhew's "venomous arrows"—was in part the escalation of a political war that five years later sent Bernard back across the ocean, drew British soldiers into Boston, and bloodied the cobbles of King Street.

5

Sceptre and Surplice

Following quickly on the heels of the Indian Affair, the Bishop Controversy embroiled Jonathan Mayhew from the spring of 1762 until the eve of the Stamp Act Crisis. His tenacious opposition to the archbishop of Canterbury's plan to appoint bishops to the American colonies should be understood in light of the pastor's commitment to New England Congregationalism and Real Whiggism. As a New England Congregationalist devoted to the transatlantic Protestant dissenting interest, he resented the confinement of full civil rights to those Englishmen who took communion in the Church of England, the enjoyment of special civil privileges by English bishops as "lords spiritual," and the accountability of bishops to the Crown rather than their congregations. As a Real Whig devoted to the people's civil and religious liberty, Mayhew despised the Tory obedience principles preached from high-church Episcopal pulpits and feared the oppression of dissenters that followed logically from such principles. He shared the conviction of John Trenchard and Thomas Gordon, expressed in *The Independent Whig*, that one must "oppose all Claims of Dominion in the Clergy" because priests with political power never fail to use it to persecute their denominational rivals.[1]

Guided by these religious and political principles, Mayhew sniped at high-church Episcopal Toryism throughout his career. "People have no security against being unmercifully *priest-ridden*," Mayhew growled in his 1750 preface to *A Discourse Concerning Unlimited Submission*, "but by keeping all imperious BISHOPS and other CLERGYMEN who love to 'lord it over God's heritage,' from getting their foot into the stirrup at all. Let them be once fairly *mounted*, and their 'beasts, the laity,' may prance and flounce about to no purpose: and they will at length, be so *jaded* and *hack'd* by these reverend *jockies*, that they will not even have spirits enough to complain that their backs are galled." Like civil tyranny, ecclesiastical tyranny must be opposed from its first beginnings, Mayhew taught, lest it grow too powerful to stop by any means short of armed resistance. Indeed, civil and ecclesiastical tyranny seemed to run hand in hand. Denouncing the Episcopal clergy's service to King Charles I in his drive toward absolute monarchy, Mayhew wrote in the *Discourse* that "there seems to have been an impious bargain struck up betwixt the *sceptre* and the *surplice*, for enslaving both the *bodies* and *souls* of men."[2]

The eighteenth-century controversy over a colonial bishop flared brightest in the public press in 1763 and 1764, reigniting in the late 1760s. While it is easy to dismiss the First Bishop Controversy of 1763–1764 as a denominational squabble over matters of strictly religious significance, Jonathan Mayhew—and the American and British Episcopalians who answered him—viewed it primarily in political terms. Their debate over whether England's state church establishment extended to New England raised the broader constitutional questions of the proper relation of church and state and the limits of parliamentary jurisdiction over the American colonies. While Mayhew broadly construed America's religious and civil liberty under the Hanoverian Crown, his adversaries insisted upon America's complete subjection to Church and Parliament. Mayhew's agitation of the episcopate issue helped to unite New England Congregationalists of different theological views against a common threat, alienate America's Congregational and Presbyterian clergy from Britain, and draw the ideological lines between Whig and Tory, between the champions of liberty and the champions of order.

Eighteenth-century New Englanders hated both tyranny and licentiousness, but some abhorred licentiousness more than tyranny and valued order more than liberty. Prominent among these conservatively inclined Yankees—Tories by natural disposition—was Samuel Johnson. As a student at Yale College in New Haven, Connecticut, he blamed the colony's tradition of religious self-government for what he considered its religious and political disorder. With the encouragement of a missionary from the Society for the Propagation of the Gospel in Foreign Parts (SPG), Johnson converted to the Episcopal Church of England and left the Presbyterian clergy. He hoped to find in the Church of England the unity, harmony, and deference to authority he could not find among his native Connecticut's hard-headed, rock-ribbed, independent-minded nonconformists. After announcing his apostasy in 1722, Johnson sailed to England to receive Episcopal ordination, as the Church of England had no bishops in America. Johnson then returned to Connecticut as an SPG missionary and in 1754 became the first president of King's College, a public institution of higher learning in New York City that he brought under Episcopal control, over the strident objections of Presbyterian New Yorkers.[3]

Dr. Johnson's goal of teaching Yankees a humble submission to royal authority proved frustratingly elusive over the decades to follow. The Great Awakening's religious turmoil disgusted him. In response to a debate among English bishops and ministers of state in 1750 over whether to plant an episcopate in America, Johnson wrote to England that the colonies desperately needed a bishop, not simply to provide pastoral and administrative functions among Episcopalians but also to prop up royal authority. He thought that "the awe of a bishop" would bring New England's nonconformists "to a better state of unity" and thereby promote "the political interest of the [British] nation." While colonial Episcopal clergymen assured their Presbyterian and Congregationalist critics that they desired a bishop for solely religious purposes, some privately confessed their hope for one with coercive power to discipline "dissenters" from the king's Church under canon law in ecclesiastical courts. In 1751, the Episcopal clergy of Connecticut—under Johnson's guidance—wrote the SPG that they "would like an episcopate with full power as in England but will accept a limited one as better than none."[4]

Among English prelates in the 1750s, Thomas Secker, bishop of Oxford, was the most eager and determined proponent of a colonial episcopate, having made the case for one as early as February 1741. Like Johnson, Secker was an apostate from Protestant dissent, committed to theological orthodoxy and fired with all the proselytizing zeal typical of the convert. Unlike Johnson, he did not desire a colonial bishop with disciplinary power over American nonconformists. Nevertheless, when King George II appointed Secker the archbishop of Canterbury in 1758, Johnson took heart that his vision for new-modeling New England might finally be at hand.[5]

In July 1760, the college president drew up a plan for reform of the colonies and sent it to Secker for submission to the London papers. On the side of ecclesiastical reform, he proposed that Parliament endow the Church of England in America with two or three bishops. On the side of civil reform, Johnson's plan called for the Crown to revoke the charters of Rhode Island and Connecticut and merge them with the royal government of Massachusetts. Secker wrote back that he largely agreed with the proposals but prudence required a delay. He would first need to make quiet preparations "to facilitate what we must ever pray and labor for, till we obtain it, the establishment of bishops of our church in America." Secker vowed that he would never "abandon the scheme as long as I live, but pushing it openly at present would certainly prove both fruitless and detrimental." Johnson continually badgered the archbishop to advance their secret plan. Secker explained that, once Britain and France made peace, the British ministry would begin revamping colonial policy. That would be the best time to press Parliament for an American bishop.[6]

Until the peace, though, Secker and Johnson had the hard work of tilling New England's stony ground for the foreign plant of episcopacy. In 1759, Rev. Henry Caner—an SPG missionary and rector of King's Chapel, Boston's first Anglican church—pleaded with the new primate to establish a mission in Cambridge, Massachusetts. After consulting with several English bishops, Secker authorized the project. Wealthy Episcopalians from Braintree, Boston, and Cambridge formed a commission to erect Christ Church on a site only three hundred feet from the gates of Harvard College, Congregationalism's intellectual stronghold. The archbishop handpicked Dr. East Apthorp to head the mission.[7]

A recent graduate of Oxford, he was the son of Charles Apthorp, one of the wealthiest merchants in Massachusetts and a generous benefactor to King's Chapel. In the spring of 1760, East Apthorp returned to Massachusetts to settle his late father's estate and begin his mission work. Dr. Johnson hinted privately that the twenty-nine-year-old heir was "reserved for yet higher and better things"—the ideal candidate for the first American bishop. He certainly fit the social profile. Peter Harrison, the Rhode Island architect selected to build Christ Church, also built a magnificent mansion for Apthorp on

Cambridge Common. In August, Apthorp moved into the house with his new bride, the daughter of Judge Eliakim Hutchinson, a warden and vestryman of King's Chapel and a relative of the lieutenant governor. The young missionary's place in the provincial aristocracy was secure.[8]

Dr. Apthorp felt secure enough in his status and future prospects to lecture Massachusetts nonconformists about their backwardness and the wisdom of conformity to the Anglican confession. He was the likely author of an anonymous letter from Cambridge that ran in the *Boston Gazette* on January 12, 1761. Apthorp greeted the founding of Christ Church in Cambridge as the sign of a new era in New England's religious progress. "Hail, my happy Countrymen!" he exulted, "upon the hopeful Prospect of being freed from the Shackles of Bigotry, which their Fathers brought into this Land, and with which their Posterity have been so long fetter'd." The missionary expressed his hope that the time would "soon come" when all denominational distinctions would be dropped in favor of "*one Way* (and if it be not inconsistent with my Character, I would speak in Time for the *Established Way*)."

In preparation for the conversion of all Yankees to the Episcopal confession, he proposed that one of the two Harvard commencement services be held in Christ Church, and that Episcopalians be added to Harvard's Board of Overseers. Such concessions would be only fair, considering the "unlimited Charity" which the Church of England had "always expressed toward dissenters from the beginning, even unto this Day." Considering Congregationalists' keen awareness of the persecution of their Puritan fathers and the ongoing exclusion of British dissenters from public office by the Test and Corporation Acts, this letter was ill crafted to win Yankee converts.[9]

It was well crafted, though, to irritate Dr. Jonathan Mayhew. For years, Mayhew angrily criticized the Society for the Propagation of the Gospel. Like many of his fellow dissenters, he thought the nonsectarian society should convert Indians and slaves to Christianity rather than convert Congregationalists and Presbyterians to Episcopalianism. SPG missionaries based in thriving cities like Boston and New York struck a poor contrast to the doctor's father, Rev. Experience Mayhew, who had labored for half a century in isolation and poverty as missionary to the Indians of Martha's Vineyard. Dr. Mayhew attacked the SPG in his sermons and discourses throughout the 1750s and early 1760s. After Secker approved the mission at Cambridge, Mayhew started preparing a systematic critique of the SPG, as indicated by his attempts in April 1760 to acquire copies of the society's charter and annual meeting sermons.[10]

In early 1762, Mayhew joined forces with Dr. Charles Chauncy, Rev. Andrew Eliot, the merchant James Bowdoin, and other Boston Congregationalists to provide a non-Episcopalian alternative to the SPG that would actively christianize the Indians. They drafted a charter and secured an endowment for the SPCK. On February 11, the Massachusetts General Court approved the SPCK charter. Although an Anglican canon lawyer and member of the SPG, Governor Francis Bernard approved the bill and sent it to the Privy Council for royal approval. "We are not without apprehensions," Mayhew wrote his English friend Thomas Hollis on April 6, "that our *good Friends* of the Church of England will endeavour to obstruct this scheme; but hope, to no purpose." He was right to worry.[11]

On the question of the SPCK, Henry Caner wrote Thomas Secker that the "real design of it is to frustrate the pious designs" of the SPG. In October 1762, the archbishop wrote privately of the SPCK's officers, "nor do I imagine, that there is one Member of the Church of England amongst them, but there is a considerable number of Dissenting ministers; amongst them one Dr. Mayhew, who hath been a most foul-mouthed Bespatterer of our Church & our Missionaries in print." Secker appreciated that it would be politically damaging to the Anglican cause in the colonies if any of his bishops voted against the society's charter in the Privy Council. So, behind the scenes, Secker lobbied aggressively to prevent royal approval of the society's charter. On May 20, 1763, the Privy Council voided the Massachusetts General Court's incorporation of the SPCK. Mayhew received a letter from Israel Mauduit, the province's London agent. Mauduit reported that "from the beginning there was a strong prejudice conceived against this New Society. The word had been given, that it was set up in opposition to the Society here for propagating the Gospel, & nothing could stand against it." Rev. Eliot wrote bitterly to Jasper Mauduit, Israel's brother and co-agent in London, "It is strange that Gentlemen who profess Christianity will not send the Gospel to the Heathen themselves, nor permit it to be sent by others."[12]

Mayhew's fears of Episcopalian intrigues against New England's religious and political interests were well founded. On June 28, 1762, the well-connected Thomas Hollis assured him that, while the Church had long planned a colonial episcopate, he detected no signs that the plan's introduction to Parliament was imminent. The politically savvy archbishop of Canterbury knew that his plan would founder if released too early, and he kept his cards close to his surplice. Secker told his American ally, Dr. Johnson, that he would not push for a colonial episcopate until the war was over and Britain's ministers of state turned their thoughts toward reform of colonial policy. On February 10, 1763, Britain signed the Peace of Paris with Spain. On March 30, Secker wrote Johnson that, with the next Parliament, the time to push for an American bishop would finally be at hand.[13]

By then, Mayhew had already launched a preemptive strike against the Anglican Church in general and the SPG in particular. On February 21, 1763, an anonymous letter appeared in the *Boston Gazette* that bore the marks of Mayhew's ruthless wit. Rev. Ebenezer Miller, an SPG missionary, had just died in a suburb of Boston. The letter sardonically honored Miller for "traveling about the rugged Wildernesses, and Lakes of Braintree, from Cottage to Cottage, with Incredible Toil; endeavouring to turn the miserable Barbarians 'from Darkness to Light and from the Power of Satan.'" Outraged by this uncharitable abuse, East Apthorp composed a formal defense of the SPG.[14]

On March 14, 1763, two Boston printers issued Apthorp's *Considerations on the Institution and Conduct of the Society for the Propagation of the Gospel in Foreign Parts*. Dedicated to Archbishop Secker and the SPG, the twenty-four-page pamphlet lamented the "insult offered to the late Dr. MILLER of Braintree" and aimed to establish "*once for all*" that the society had not misapplied its funds by building churches in New England's towns rather than converting slaves and Indians to Christianity. According to *Considerations*, the society's royal charter directed it to provide worship to the king's subjects by "orthodox clergy," and Apthorp took this to mean none other than Episcopal clergy.[15]

Thanks to the SPG's moderating influence, the rector of Christ Church claimed, New England's religion had been "manifestly improved" since its founding. "Religion no longer wears among us the savage and gloomy appearance, with which Superstition had terribly arrayed her," Apthorp piously intoned. "Its speculative doctrines are freed from those senseless horrors with which Fanaticism had perverted them." He expressed relief that the "exterminating monster Persecution, is itself exterminated both from the temper and practice of the age"—attributing religious persecution to Puritans rather than churchmen. By impugning the memory of New England's revered founders yet again, Apthorp unintentionally provoked dissenters throughout the region, including the influential Rev. Ezra Stiles of Newport, Rhode Island, who urged Mayhew to respond in the public press.[16]

The West Church pastor hardly needed encouragement. A little over one month from the publication of Apthorp's *Considerations*, three Boston presses simultaneously printed Mayhew's 176-page pamphlet, *Observations on the Charter and Conduct of the Society for the Propagation of the Gospel in Foreign Parts: Designed to Shew Their Non-Conformity to Each Other*. Apthorp's Episcopal triumphalism provided the final spur for Mayhew to write his systematic critique of the SPG, contemplated at least since 1760. Through devastating use of logic, textual evidence, and historic citation, Mayhew amply demonstrated that the SPG's royal charter authorized it to convert American Indians and African slaves to Protestantism, not to advance the Episcopal confession to the detriment of low-church Protestant denominations. Much more was at stake, though, than whether the society had misappropriated its funds. In the introduction to *Observations*, Mayhew claimed that the SPG had implicitly challenged New Englanders' liberty of conscience and the continued existence of Congregational churches.[17]

The majority of *Observations* defended New England Congregationalism against Apthorp's *Considerations*. Mayhew reminded his adversary that the Puritans originally came to New England fleeing "Episcopal persecution, seconded by royal power; which often condescended to be subservient to the views of domineering prelates, before the glorious revolution." They were "a sober, virtuous and religious set of people in general" who separated from the Church of England and left their homeland for conscience's sake. In New England, the Puritans made ample provision for Protestant worship and education, including publicly funding an "orthodox" clergy and a university in which to train them. Unlike Old England, New England had always been free of infidelity and Roman Catholicism. "The common people in New-England," Mayhew contended, were "philosophers and divines in comparison of the common people in England, of the communion of the church there established." New Englanders were hardly fit objects of charity for Episcopal missionaries.[18]

Mayhew charged that the Society for the Propagation of the Gospel was concerned not with propagating the Gospel but with propagating episcopacy. This, he noted, was why the Society set up its missions in rich and populous New England towns rather than amidst the Indians of the frontier or the blacks of the south. Apthorp founded Christ Church "about half a quarter of a mile from the College, and from the meeting-house there. What is this but setting up altar against altar?" The missionaries sought to expand the Episcopal communion, Mayhew alleged, by encouraging factions to separate from Congregational churches. They carried on a "spiritual siege of our churches, with the hope that they will one day submit to an episcopal sovereign." The Boston divine accused the SPG of having "long had a formal design to dissolve and root out all our New-England churches," of sparing no effort or expense "in order to effect their grand design of *episcopizing* (if I may use the term) all New-England, as well as the other colonies." One could see this design in the plans to introduce a bishop to New England. Mayhew slyly insinuated that Apthorp's grand mansion in Cambridge was built to serve as nothing less than a prelate's palace.[19]

Mayhew's *Observations* expressed his Congregationalist contempt for episcopacy as unscriptural and his Whiggish fear of episcopacy as tyrannical. He offered a searing critique of the Church of England for its resemblance to the Church of Rome, particularly with respect to its "enormous hierarchy, ascending by various gradations from the dirt to the skies," for its persecution of Protestant dissenters before the Glorious Revolution and for continuing curtailment of their civil rights after the Revolution. He warned, "if this growing party should once get the upper hand here, and a major vote in our houses of *Assembly*," then "the church of England might become the established religion here; *tests* be ordained, as in England, to exclude all but conformists from posts of honor and emolument; and all of us be taxed for the support of *bishops* and their *underlings*."[20]

After two centuries of inflicting persecution, abuse, and discrimination on nonconformists, the Church of England threatened to introduce prelacy to America, the last refuge of religious liberty. Mayhew's indictment of Anglican militancy rose to a fierce climax. He declaimed:

Will they never let us rest in peace, except *where all the weary are at rest?* Is it not enough, that they persecuted us out of the old world? Will they pursue us into the new to convert us here? . . . What other new world remains as a sanctuary for us from their oppressions, in case of need? Where is the COLUMBUS to explore one for, and pilot us to it, before we are consumed by the flames, or deluged in a flood of episcopacy?"[21]

Mayhew reminded Episcopalians that King Charles I provoked Presbyterian Scotland to armed resistance by trying to impose on them the Anglican liturgy, "at the instigation of the furious episcopal zealots of that day; by which he was wheedled and duped to his destruction." He added that neither George III nor modern bishops would advocate such oppression, but he offered the veiled threat of armed resistance nonetheless. In closing, Mayhew exhorted "the people of New-England to stand fast in the liberty wherewith CHRIST made them free; and not to return under that yoke of episcopal bondage, which so miserably galled the necks of our Forefathers."[22]

Mayhew's *Observations* was a call to arms, and he was eager to carry the fight to the enemy's home ground. A week after the pamphlet's publication, he sent his influential English friend Thomas Hollis a copy with the recommendation of a London reprint. "I hope all who regard interests of religion and liberty in New England," Mayhew wrote Hollis, "will do all that in them lies, both to prevent the establishing of Bishops here, and to get our Society's charter confirmed by the crown. These things seem to me to be of great importance both to our civil and religious welfare." The pastor also sent *Observations* to Jasper Mauduit, provincial agent for Massachusetts in London. Harrison Gray—the provincial treasurer, Mayhew's closest friend, and a deacon of the West Church—wrote Mauduit on May 3. Gray urged him to advance "the dissenting interest" by getting *Observations* reprinted in London. "I think I never knew any performance of a Controversial nature," Gray reported, "meet with so general approbation & applause, excepting among some bigoted high-churchmen, who most sincerely curse it." He observed that "Gentlemen of the best sence & learning here, think that the Doc[tor]'s Arguments are conclusive."[23]

While Congregationalists and Presbyterians toasted Mayhew for his passionate attack against the Church of England, many colonial Episcopalians despised him for it. In June 1763, the *Newport Mercury* published *Verses on*

Doctor Mayhew's Book of Observations, submitted anonymously by an Episcopalian lawyer named John Aplin. Aplin did not attempt to answer Mayhew's accusations against the SPG but merely to "shew, that this blind Bigot is for setting up an Inquisition against the Religion of the Nation, within his Majesty's own Dominions," as Oliver Cromwell had during the English Civil War. Among the doggerels that Aplin aimed at Mayhew was the prediction that "Th'Unborn shall curse thy sland'ring Pen, / And scorn thy narrow Soul." Later that summer, Rev. Arthur Browne, an Episcopal minister in New Hampshire, applauded Aplin and heaped more anonymous abuse on Mayhew in *Remarks on Dr. Mayhew's Incidental Reflections*. Browne appealed to New Englanders to repudiate Mayhew as a heretical "outcast" and compared his attack on episcopacy with "the fanatic ravings of his predecessors the Oliverian holders-forth, whose spittle he hath lick'd up, and cough'd it out again, with some addition of his own filth and phlegm."[24]

Aplin and Browne did not rely entirely on ad hominem smears. Their more cogent responses to *Observations* followed from Tory obedience principles. In response to Mayhew's concern that Episcopalians would monopolize political power if they achieved a majority in New England, both Aplin and Browne unabashedly concurred. Aplin wrote that the legal establishment of the Episcopal Church in New England would be "consistent with a State of Liberty" so long as the majority favored it. For Browne as well, "liberty" meant the consent of the majority, without consideration of individual and minority rights. With a majority in the lower houses of colonial legislatures, the reverend maintained, Episcopalians could and should establish the Church of England, bar "dissenters" from the Church from civil office by a test act, tax them for the support of Episcopal clergy, and introduce a bishop with "a right to enjoy the fulness of our ecclesiastical government." The naked Toryism of such high-church controversialists confirmed Yankees' worst fears about Episcopalian plots against civil and religious liberty.[25]

Despite the rebukes of Aplin and Browne, Mayhew's *Observations* mobilized public opinion against the SPG, compelling the archbishop of Canterbury to revise his plans for the Anglican Church's future in America. On August 8, Israel Mauduit, Jasper Mauduit's brother, informed Mayhew by letter that, at the previous month's meeting of the SPG, Archbishop Secker spoke largely about *Observations*. At the meeting, Mauduit reported, two or three American applicants for Episcopal ordination requested assignments in New England. The "Archbishop observ'd, that New England had already more than their proportion of Missions establish'd in it," so the SPG should stay away from areas where other Protestants had already established places of worship. The popularity of Mayhew's *Observations* indicated that the presence of so many missionaries in New England had "created prejudices there," which Secker feared would discourage Parliament from approving a colonial episcopate. While he hoped the accusations Mayhew leveled against Episcopal missionaries in the colonies were incorrect, the Church should do nothing more to provoke such criticism. "You cannot expect that he sh[oul]d have openly prais'd your book," Mauduit told Mayhew of the primate's remarks, "but he s[ai]d nothing in dispraise of it, & tacitly stamp on it the highest mark of his approbation, by adopting the Principles & recommending the Practice of it."[26]

The response of Boston's leading Episcopal clergyman to Mayhew's dazzling victory was rather less conciliatory. On October 13, 1763, three Boston printers simultaneously issued editions of an eighty-page pamphlet called *A Candid Examination of Dr. Mayhew's Observations*, to which was appended *A Letter to a Friend, Containing a Short Vindication of the Said Society*. Henry Caner authored the *Examination* and the letter, though they were published anonymously. Like Aplin and Browne, Caner smeared Mayhew as an anti-Calvinist and anti-Trinitarian. "How is it then that you have complimented the Dr. with your thanks (for so I hear many of you at Boston have done), for his book of observations," Caner asked New England's orthodox Congregationalists, "who by his other writings, has been destroying the fundamentals of your faith?" The missionary did not endear himself to nonconforming readers, though, when he—like Apthorp—denied Mayhew's statement of fact that the Puritans had come to New England feeling Anglican persecution.[27]

Unlike Aplin and Browne, Caner relied less on sectarian smears than on Tory obedience principles. While Mayhew claimed that the Massachusetts General Court had "established" all Protestant denominations by providing them with public funds, Caner insisted that British law recognized the Church of England as America's only religious establishment. He took it as given that all acts of Parliament bound the colonies. Since Parliament established the Episcopal Church in England by statute, he reasoned, it was also established in all American colonies. Massachusetts might well declare another denomination "established," but any colonial law contrary to British law was "ipso facto void." Writing of nonconformity with contempt, Caner maintained that "the churches (as [Mayhew] affects to call them) of New England subsist here as the dissenting congregations do in England, upon no other foot than that of a toleration." In Caner's mind, American Presbyterians and Congregationalists enjoyed religious liberty only by permission, not by right. Moreover, Crown and Parliament could revoke that permission at any time. The king, as head of the Church of England, could appoint a bishop with full disciplinary authority over New England. This he could do by his own prerogative, without parliamentary consent. Against New England's "republican[,] separating and leveling principles," Caner defiantly posed his own royalist, conformist, and hierarchical view of government and society— though with the discretion of anonymity.[28]

The attacks by Johnson, Apthorp, Aplin, Browne, and Caner substantiated Mayhew's long-held fear that many colonial churchmen were Tories in sheep's clothing, determined to destroy American liberty from within. In November 1763, he published a *Defence of the Observations* against "these warriors of the church militant." The controversy between Mayhew and the Church of England raised questions about the constitutional relationship between Britain and the colonies. After a review of the law in consultation with attorneys, Mayhew concluded that English subjects who emigrated to the colonies were bound by "only the *common law* at most, and those statutes that are made in affirmation or explanation of it." England's system of common law "had its origin among heathen nations" and "was compleat as a system long before the reformation," so the Church of England could not have been established by common law. The Crown, Parliament, and Church could not override colonists' rights, which were grounded in natural law and common law and therefore inviolable by statute.[29]

While Caner made the broadest construction of British authority over America, Mayhew made the narrowest. He denied the royal chaplain's claim "that all the laws of England, without exception, or of Great Britain, are, as such, binding on the colonies." British statutes only bound Americans when Parliament expressly applied them to the colonies. More specifically, "the statutes relative to the church of England, should not be supposed to extend to New-England," and "the national church of England is not, and never was supposed, to be established here, by the statutes." If the reach of the Anglican Church extended to America, the West Church pastor reasoned, then the Puritans would never have left their homeland. Mayhew reasserted his original position that Puritan congregations—persecuted by prelates acting in King Charles I's name—seceded peacefully from the Church of England and set up civil governments in New England where "they might enjoy intire liberty of conscience."[30]

In his *Defence of the Observations*, Mayhew reconciled liberty of conscience with the legal establishment of his own church in Massachusetts. "I never supposed," the pastor insisted against his high-church critics, that the government established "*a provincial church*," but only "*protestant churches of various denominations; or rather, of any or all denominations that have been, or shall be set up among us; in conformity to the language and spirit of the charter.*"[31] Alluding to the 1692 act of Parliament that mandated legal provision for "orthodox" ministers in Massachusetts, he wrote:

According to which act, compared with what the charter says of *liberty of conscience*, to all christians except *Papists*, I conceive, protestants of all denominations are considered by the *government* here, as *orthodox*. So that if any particular town in the Province should legally chuse, settle and support a protestant minister of any denomination, whether episcopalian, presbyterian, congregational, baptist, or Lutheran, this would be looked upon as satisfying the said law.[32]

The Yankee divine understood a religious "establishment" to be any church supported by government with tax revenues. By that definition, all Protestant churches were established under current Massachusetts law. Mayhew's theory of multiple religious establishments provided a middle way between the orthodox Congregationalists' view that the Congregational Church alone was established in Massachusetts and the high-churchmens' view that only the Church of England enjoyed that legal status.[33]

Like Europeans on the Continent, Britons on both sides of the Atlantic had traditionally thought of religious establishments in monopolistic rather than pluralistic terms. Mayhew appreciated that some of his readers might "think it an inconsistent supposition, that several distinct churches, of various denominations, and differing very considerably from each other, should, in my sense, be established in the same province, and respectively protected and encouraged by the same legislature." But British subjects should not be confounded by this pluralistic conception of religious establishment, Mayhew insisted, since this was precisely the practice in Great Britain itself. The 1707 Act of Union united the crowns and parliaments of England and Scotland into one British state. But the law recognized, within this political union, two legal establishments of religion: the Episcopal Church of England and the Presbyterian Church of Scotland. Mayhew maintained that a system of multiple religious establishments within the same polity was not merely his own idea but actual legal practice within the Empire.[34]

The balance of eighteenth-century British and provincial law seems to weigh in favor of Mayhew's side of the debate against Caner's. In 1727, the Massachusetts General Court gave Episcopalians the right to have their payments of the church rate go to their own churches. In 1728, it exempted Baptists and Quakers from paying the church rate. One of Mayhew's high-church critics, the SPG missionary James MacSparran, carried on a thirty-year legal battle centering on his claim that only Episcopal clergy should qualify as "orthodox" under law in New England. When Rhode Island decided the case against him, MacSparran appealed to the king's Privy Council in London, which ruled in 1752 that orthodoxy in New England was not synonymous with Episcopalianism. Ecclesiastical pluralism was compatible with loyalty to the Crown and Constitution within the British Empire. In maintaining that the Church of England alone was established by British law in the colonies, Henry Caner was pressing a claim long since conceded by the Crown. For high-church clergymen like Browne and Caner, though, the dream of Episcopal hegemony over New England did not die in 1752.[35]

To preserve New England's religious liberty against such "warriors of the church militant," the West Church minister found it necessary to champion civil liberty in the forum of public opinion. Of the provincial law providing tax support for all Protestant churches in Massachusetts, Caner had insisted that the king did not necessarily approve those colonial laws that he had not yet vetoed. This principle, Mayhew responded, "is manifestly striking at our laws in general." "So that, it seems," he declaimed, "I must first defend our *laws* themselves against his bold attacks, before I defend our *churches* by them." If Caner held Massachusetts law in such contempt, Mayhew asked, one must wonder if "he allows the legality and validity of our charter itself."[36]

A threat to the Massachusetts Charter was a threat to the people's civil and religious liberty. In England, Parliament exempted Protestant Trinitarians from the requirement of attending Anglican worship, but it did not suspend the Act of Uniformity nor recognize liberty of conscience in principle. Moreover, the Test and Corporation Acts prohibited Protestant dissenters from holding public office, voting for Parliament, or attending royally chartered universities. In Massachusetts, though, the charter issued by William and Mary guaranteed liberty of conscience to all Protestants and required conformity to the Anglican Church only for the royally appointive office of governor.

Mayhew noted Caner's irritation at the fact that religious tests were not "universally required" in Massachusetts and that "*schismatics* may be admitted to places of public trust" under the charter. The King's Chaplain had accused Mayhew of seeking to exclude all Episcopalians from civil office. The doctor responded that this claim was "absolutely false." He added, though, that he greatly feared any new order in which civil government would come "*wholly* into the hands of churchmen." If Aplin, Browne, and Caner got their way, New England would be governed by Episcopal "*bigots*" who "contemn and despise all non-conformists thereto, who desire to deprive them of their ancient privileges, to trample and crush them under their feet." The imposition of a bishop by royal fiat or parliamentary statute not only threatened New Englanders' control of their churches but control of their governments as well.[37]

Within only a few months, a denominational controversy over the SPG's missionary activities had metastasized into a constitutional debate over the limits of American liberty under British law. Its ominous rumbles could be heard as far away as London. Shortly after publication of Mayhew's *Defence* in Boston, Thomas Hollis informed the minister that a London press had reprinted his *Observations*. The SPG's official publisher thought so highly of Mayhew's pamphlet that he agreed to reprint it under an assumed name. A keen political operative, Hollis timed the publication to coincide with the beginning of the winter session of Parliament, hoping that Mayhew's arguments would derail Secker's plan for a colonial episcopate. "You are in no real danger, at present, in respect to the creation of Bishops in America, if I am rightly informed," Hollis wrote his colonial friend, "though a matter extreamly desired by our Clergy and Prelates, and even talked of greatly, at this time, among themselves. You cannot however be too much on your guard, in this so very important an affair." The archbishop of Canterbury was as determined as ever to plant bishops in the American colonies, but he decided to wait until he could reverse Mayhew's damage. Having discontinued further expansion of the SPG's mission work in New England, Thomas Secker next extended an olive branch to the nonconformists, to soothe their fears.[38]

In January 1764, Secker completed an *Answer to Dr. Mayhew's Observations* to calm America and reassure Parliament. Although he published the fifty-nine-page pamphlet anonymously, the archbishop addressed church policy with the authority and assurance of a leading prelate. Readers of the London and Boston editions immediately guessed his authorship. Unlike his colonial foot soldiers, Secker adopted a mild, reasonable, and conciliatory tone. He conceded that the Church of England had persecuted the Puritans and observed that East Apthorp had used "a strong Expression or two" in his characterization of New England's founders. But he denied any design to convert all Protestant dissenters to the Anglican communion, maintaining that Episcopalians no more wanted "to *episcopize* New-England" than dissenters wanted "to *presbyterianize* England." He further denied that, if Episcopalians attained a legislative majority, they would impose a test act. Secker styled Mayhew's fear of the imposition of taxes for the support of bishops as even "more chimerical" than his fear of religious tests. The Bostonian's dire predictions about episcopacy were wholly unfounded.[39]

Secker addressed at length Mayhew's anxieties concerning an Anglican episcopate in New England. He said, with the ring of authority, that the Church of England only desired two or three American bishops for strictly pastoral and administrative purposes, and that such bishops would have no political power to "infringe or diminish any Privileges and Liberties enjoyed by any of the Laity, even of our own Communion. This is the real and the only Scheme that hath been planned for Bishops in *America*; and whoever hath heard of any other, hath been misinformed through Mistake or Design." Forgetting for a moment the Test and Corporation Acts, mandatory tithing, ecclesiastical courts, and the bishops' bench in the House of Lords, Secker maintained that prelacy had imposed no "bondage" in England and so would not oppress America. Had there ever been any intention of planting an Episcopal see in New England rather than such Episcopal colonies as Virginia and New York, such a bishop would exert his power cautiously, for fear of angering the Congregational and Presbyterian majority. "Therefore the Doctor would not need to be at all anxious for the Liberty of his dear Country," Secker assured Mayhew's readers. Speaking on behalf of all Episcopalians (including presumably Aplin, Browne, Apthorp, Caner, and Johnson), the archbishop concluded that churchmen desired only peaceful coexistence with their nonconforming brethren.[40]

On February 15, 1764, Israel Mauduit mailed Mayhew a copy of the archbishop's *Answer*. In his accompanying letter, Mauduit observed that Secker was the likely author, praised the pamphlet for its "moderation & Candour," and argued that, since the *Answer* conceded Mayhew's main points, "the Controversy has now answer'd its End." John Adams agreed that, despite the elegance of Secker's *Answer*, Mayhew seemed to have carried the day. Adams bemusedly wrote a friend in April that high-church Episcopalians, dazed by the good doctor's onslaught, "have Christen'd the Observations, the Devils Thunder Bolt." Thomas Hollis wrote Mayhew that month, informing him of the success of his *Defense* in London. The London *Monthly Review* gave it a positive review in January 1764, and public demand prompted a second edition of the London reprint after less than four months. Hollis added that he had been friends with Thomas Secker for twenty years, but the archbishop's determination to plant episcopacy in America persuaded Hollis, "pass me the boldness of the expression, to drop him wholly." In a second April letter, Hollis reported to Mayhew that the archbishop's *Answer* had not swayed many minds in London. He urged Mayhew, as he had the preceding December, to hammer Secker for going soft on Catholicism, whose rapid growth in England in the early 1760s gravely alarmed many English Protestant dissenters. Mauduit considered the Bishop Controversy—as it came to be known—at an end, but Hollis and Mayhew believed that Secker's *Answer* begged a reply.[41]

Mayhew published *Remarks on an Anonymous Tract* in Boston that June, on the heels of the *Answer's* publication in Boston. The eighty-page pamphlet complimented Secker for his "excellent sense," "happy talent at writing," absence of "the sordid, illiberal spirit of bigotry," for being, "in general, a fair reasoner," and for "doing justice to the merits of an opponent; a species of justice too seldom found in controversial writers." But Mayhew wrote that

Secker had not altered his opinion of the Episcopal Church and its ambitions for America. "Plausible colors may be put upon almost any thing, however false or wrong in itself, by men of great ingenuity, and *fine sense*," the minister riposted, but "*plain, common sense*, with a competent knowledge of *facts* and *circumstances*, . . . and much more, an equal capacity on the side of truth and right, will ever have the advantage in an argument." Historical experience made clear that bishops have "commonly been *the most useful members*, or *instruments*, that the crown or court had, in establishing tyranny over the bodies and souls of men."[42]

Mayhew granted that Secker's plan for a colonial bishop, outlined in his *Answer*, was "more plausible, and less exceptionable" than any other. However, he counted himself among those "misinformed" that an episcopate would be located in New England. "Since a mission was established at Cambridge, and a very sumptuous dwelling-house (for this country) erected there," remarked Mayhew, "that town [had] been talked of by episcopalians as well as others, as the proposed place of residence for a bishop; which I thought not improbable." Whatever might be the Church's real plan for a colonial episcopate, American Congregationalists and Presbyterians still had "great reason to deprecate the appointment of any *such bishops* here." Even if American bishops had strictly limited powers, as Secker promised, they would not be content for long with such diminished prestige and influence. "Ambition and avarice never want plausible pretexts, to accomplish their end," Mayhew reminded the primate. History demonstrated that those endowed with unaccountable power could be expected to seek still more power, and British history no farther back than Queen Anne's reign demonstrated that English bishops were hardly impervious to a lust for power, as in the case of Henry Sacheverell and Francis Atterbury.[43]

Secker also failed to persuade Mayhew that New England's Congregational and Presbyterian majority would be able to stop Episcopal ambitions. The archbishop dismissed as "chimerical" Mayhew's fear that Episcopalians would get a majority in the colonial legislatures, establish episcopacy in all colonies, introduce a test act to exclude nonconformists from the government, and impose taxes for the support of bishops. The doctor responded that he did not "imagine that these dangers were very near at hand in New-England," but "even remote evils may be reasonably apprehended, as well as those which are imminent; and are to be guarded against, as much as may be." "Bishops being once fixed in America," he predicted, "pretexts might easily be found, both for encreasing their number, and enlarging their powers." It was, after all, in the nature of power—both civil and religious—to expand to the detriment of liberty.[44]

Even if colonial prelacy did not grow oppressive in Mayhew's own time, he still feared for posterity. "People are not usually deprived of their liberties all at once, but gradually, by one encroachment after another, *as it is found they are disposed to bear them*," Mayhew sagely observed, "and things of the most fatal tendency are often introduced at first, under a comparatively plausible and harmless appearance." The best way to stop tyranny lay in "*opposing the first attempts.*" "*Obsta principiis*, was never thought an ill maxim by wise men," he taught, and "all prudent men act upon the same principle." As for a bishop, American nonconformists were "desirous to keep the apprehended evil at as great a distance as may be." Mayhew insisted that colonial opposition to an episcopate was due not to bigoted paranoia but to rational prudence.[45]

It was a central tenet of Real Whig political thought that the ambitions of designing men must be resisted from the outset before such plotters could grow into tyrants. Mayhew was repeating in his *Remarks* a warning he had sounded as far back as 1750, when he told the West Church congregation, "People have no security against being unmercifully *priest-ridden*, but by keeping all imperious BISHOPS and other CLERGYMEN who loved to 'lord it over God's heritage,' from getting their *foot* into the *stirrup* at all." He had long kept a wary eye upon the Episcopal clergy, lest they seek to regain the political influence they enjoyed before the Whig Party's ascendancy under Georges I and II. Mayhew generously granted to Secker that the political threat posed by high-church Episcopalians might lie in some indefinite future. But he had good reason to suspect that the old alliance of high-church clergy and Tory ministers was regaining power in England under George III. It was all the more critical for Americans to resist the encroachment of episcopacy in 1764, Mayhew cautioned, "if it be true, as many affirm, that *high-church, tory-principles* and maxims are lately revived in England; and favour'd greatly by some, whose influence may go far toward bringing them into as much reputation, as they have been in disgrace, since the death of Queen *Anne*."[46]

At least since Andrew Marvell denounced "the growth of popery and arbitrary government" in his 1677 pamphlet of the same name, Protestant dissenters believed that high-church religion and royalist politics rose and fell together—and that episcopacy was popery in a Protestant veil. Like many Presbyterians and Congregationalists on both sides of the Atlantic, Mayhew viewed the Church of England as a pale shadow of the hated Church of Rome. The doctor set off yelps among American Episcopalians when *Observations* offered a passing remark on the sinister resemblance between the episcopacy, hierarchy, and liturgy of the Anglican and Catholic Churches. He steered clear of the sensitive subject in his *Defense*. But Thomas Secker opened the door again in his *Answer*. The primate noted that the presence of bishops in New England should not be so offensive to Congregationalists, since Catholic bishops exercised their pastoral functions in England without offending Episcopalians. By way of preface to his response, Mayhew reaffirmed that he was "a warm friend to religious liberty in the largest sense," favoring tolerance of sectarian differences, "where the differences are *merely* of a *religious* nature, or such as do not affect the liberty, safety and natural rights of mankind." The Roman Catholic Church could not be tolerated, though, because of its radical hostility to constitutional government and individual rights, particularly liberty of conscience.[47]

Applying evidence provided by Thomas Hollis, Mayhew claimed that Catholicism flourished in London because magistrates no longer enforced the penal laws prohibiting public Catholic worship—a claim that the archbishop's own remark confirmed. Following France's defeat in Canada and the end of the Jacobite threat, the British state did increasingly indulge open worship by English and foreign Catholics.[48] Mayhew asked, "does not the prevalence of popery in England, afford matter for very serious reflexions?" He reminded the anonymous author of the *Answer*—who, he punned, "can be very *arch* when he pleases"—of the atrocities and betrayals Catholics committed against their Protestant brethren in the sixteenth and seventeenth centuries. These crimes still smoldered in the historical memory of New England Congregationalists. Mayhew angrily bewailed:

Are all their diabolical treacheries and cruelties buried in oblivion? Can they who believe the Pope's supremacy over all Kings, and consequently deny the independency of the British crown and empire, possibly be good loyal subjects to King GEORGE, or any other protestant King? Are there no laws now in force against papists? or is there no-body to execute them? Is the sword of the law rusted in the hands of the magistrates, as well as that of the Spirit, where it is said so *rarely* to come, in the mouths of the prelates?"[49]

For Mayhew, there was no contradiction in calling for the forcible suppression of Catholic worship and on the same page favorably citing Voltaire's *Treatise on Tolerance*. Only two years earlier, a French court had tortured to death an elderly Protestant in a sentence, Voltaire claimed in his *Treatise*, motivated by Catholic prejudice. Mayhew's anti-Catholicism was rooted as much in his commitment to the Enlightenment as to Protestantism, and he need not have looked all the way back to the seventeenth century for evidence of Catholic fanaticism and brutality.[50]

Having accused the Church of England of negligence in arresting the spread of Catholicism, Mayhew still reminded his readers of those times in Britain when "the pernicious practices of papists, and the increase of popery there, have been winked at." Collusion between the British state and the Catholic Church was obvious during the Stuart dynasty. There have also been "other times" when British ministers of state turned a blind eye to Catholic worship in return for support in Parliament from "the wealthier papists." Under such corrupted ministries, magistrates accordingly became lax in enforcing the penal laws. Meanwhile, English bishops "who aimed at riches or higher preferment, or both, observing the conduct of the ministry . . . , wholly connived also at the practices of papists, and the progress of popery." Thanks to such corruption of government ministers, members of Parliament, magistrates, and bishops, "cruel, blood-thirsty and rebel-hearted roman-catholics, had hardly any opposition made to them, or anything to fear in England, either from law or gospel." Mayhew was careful not to specify in what "times" such corruption of the British state had occurred.[51]

Deftly integrating the perspectives of New England Congregationalism and English Real Whiggism, Mayhew argued that the toleration of Catholicism by Britain's Church and state would lead to their corruption, which would in turn lead to religious and civil tyranny, as it had during the Stuart era. "By such-like means has the *Scarlet Whore*," Mayhew declaimed, "with whom the Kings and great men of the earth have committed *fornication*, at certain seasons got fairly mounted on her *horned beast*, and rode, with the cup of *abominations* in her hand, almost triumphant thro' England." Stepping back from this apocalyptic climax, the Boston pastor added unconvincingly, "Such has heretofore been the state of things in England. How it is at present, I pretend not particularly to know." Mayhew avoided a sedition charge by this hedge, but he maintained that "popery was fast gaining ground" in England in 1764. His implication was clear that Catholic corruption of Britain's Church, Parliament, ministry, and perhaps even king had already begun.[52]

Having launched that final, poisoned dart at the archbishop of Canterbury, Mayhew's *Remarks* concluded, "I take leave for the present, I hope forever, of this controversy, of which I am heartily weary." Modern historians have also found the Bishop Controversy not a little wearying to survey. "He is a brave scholar indeed," Clinton Rossiter wrote of its literature, "who can read over these mildewed pages with any feeling other than boredom aggravated by acute exasperation." In *Mitre and Sceptre*, his study of Protestant dissent as a source of the American Revolution, historian Carl Bridenbaugh had little to say about the specific arguments that Mayhew and his adversaries made during the First Bishop Controversy.[53]

The dispute was pregnant with significance for subsequent relations between Britain and the colonies. It shifted very quickly from a denominational squabble over the SPG's missionary activities to the troubling question of an American episcopate. This question in turn opened debate over the constitutional limits of colonial subjection to British authority. The First Bishop Controversy ended with Mayhew's thinly veiled allegation that Hanoverian Britain might soon join Bourbon France and Spain among the nations in thrall to the Papacy.

New England's Congregationalist and Presbyterian clergy premised their allegiance to Britain to a great degree on the protection their churches received from the Crown against persecution by Roman Catholics and high-church Episcopalians. Mayhew's claim that the Church of England and even Britain's civil government were increasingly friendly to Catholics and hostile to Protestant dissenters had explosive implications for New England's allegiance to the Crown. If Britain, admired by New Englanders as the scourge of popery, were to become its instrument, then Britain would become New England's enemy rather than defender. The First Bishop Controversy prompted Congregational and Presbyterian clergy to consider whether Britain—under

George III and such Tory advisors as the Earl of Bute—had finally succumbed to the temptations of Rome.

From the earliest settlement of Plymouth, Massachusetts-Bay, and Connecticut, New Englanders had abominated the Pope as the Antichrist described in the Book of Revelations. Yankee anti-Catholicism was not merely apocalyptic fanaticism or sectarian bigotry. Fearing the Roman Church as the world's foremost engine of persecution and abettor of royal absolutism, eighteenth-century Yankees interpreted the struggle between Protestantism and Catholicism as a conflict, in historian Pauline Maier's words, between "reason and authority, knowledge and ignorance, liberty and slavery." Historian Nathan O. Hatch argued that the menace of Catholic expansionism during the French and Indian War politicized the Congregational clergy, rendering them more sensitive in the 1760s to British threats to their civil and religious liberty. After the Stamp Act Crisis, Hatch posited, "New England ministers decided that the Pope of Rome no longer served as the primary embodiment of Antichrist and that Satan had redirected this evil power through another agency, that of oppressive and arbitrary civil governments." The furious response of Yankees to the Quebec Act of 1774, by which king-in-Parliament legalized the Catholic Church from the New England frontier to Minnesota, suggests otherwise. Against the act, the *Massachusetts Gazette* raised the battle cry "No Popery! No French Laws! No Protestant Popish King!" In his 1776 war sermon, Connecticut minister Samuel Sherwood similarly implied that the British state had become corrupted by Catholicism. Sherwood exhorted his congregation to rise up against, in Hatch's paraphrase, "the 'antichristian tyranny' which the British government represented; because the king's chief ministers has sipped the golden cup of fornication with 'the old mother of harlots.'" New England's clergymen feared and hated popery quite as much at the beginning of the Revolutionary War as they did at the end of the French and Indian War, and anti-Catholicism contributed to their alienation from Britain.[54]

These pastors did redirect the main thrust of their millenarian rhetoric from France to Britain but not because they thought the Pope was no longer the principal agent of evil in the world. Jonathan Mayhew persuaded them during the First Bishop Controversy that popery had begun to corrupt the British state itself and turn it toward despotic principles, as it previously had the French and Spanish states. In his campaign against the Church of England, Mayhew exposed a plan by the archbishop of Canterbury and his colonial allies to introduce an American episcopate, drew out a confession by high-church Episcopalians that they desired a monopoly over colonial government, compared the Church of England with the Church of Rome, and accused Britain's ministry, Parliament, and Church of complicity in the spread of Catholicism in England. Mayhew thereby gave the New England Congregational clergy—even normally apolitical evangelicals and politically conservative orthodox Calvinists—urgent cause to shift the focus of their dread of Antichrist from France to Britain. The doctor's Real Whig association of religious tyranny with civil tyranny, combined with his Congregationalist association of high-church Episcopalianism with Roman Catholicism (the "Protestant popery" critique), spurred Yankee divines to oppose British aggression after 1763 as ardently as they had opposed French aggression before 1763.[55]

Before the rise of the stamp-tax specter, Mayhew's three works on the First Bishop Controversy helped convince American and British nonconformists that American and British churchmen conspired to crush the colonies' civil and religious liberty. In April 1764, even George Whitefield, Episcopal missionary and English father of the Great Awakening, warned two New Hampshire pastors, "There is a deep laid plot against both your civil and religious liberties, and they will be lost." Rev. Francis Allison, Presbyterian minister and vice-provost of the College of Philadelphia, wrote Mayhew's admirer, the Rhode Island Congregationalist Rev. Ezra Stiles, that he feared Episcopalians were scheming to "induce the English Parliament to produce a test; or at least confine all offices in the army and Revenue to members of the Episcopal Church." In August 1764, Rev. William Gordon of New Hampshire wrote Dr. Joseph Bellamy of Connecticut about Presbyterians' widespread concern "that the government will send over some Bishops to settle in America," adding, "once Episcopacy has got a footing, there's no knowing where it will stop." Beginning in 1763 and 1764, fear of episcopacy and popery brought together New England's nonconformist clergymen—Congregationalist and Presbyterian, orthodox and heterodox, New Light and Old Light—as they had not been since the Great Awakening. By unifying them in defense of their churches, and mobilizing them against royal and parliamentary authority, the Bishop Controversy helped to transform New England's low-church Protestant clergy into the "black regiment," the ecclesiastical wing of the Whig opposition movement of the 1760s.[56]

Once ostracized by Boston's ministers for his rejection of Calvinism and Trinitarianism, Jonathan Mayhew found himself lionized by dissenters from the Anglican Church—Presbyterians and Congregationalists, Calvinists and rationalists, laymen and clergymen—from Philadelphia to Edinburgh. Carl Bridenbaugh observed that the pastor's audacious attacks upon the Church of England earned him "a transatlantic reputation as the champion of British Nonconformity, and it is doubtful if even Benjamin Franklin had as many readers." Mayhew's agitation of the public thwarted Thomas Secker's plan to press Parliament for an American episcopate in the early 1760s. The archbishop offered no public response to *Remarks on an Anonymous Tract*. In October 1764, East Apthorp locked the doors of Christ Church, shook the dust of Cambridge off his feet, and returned to England. Historian Robert Ingram has called the defeat of Secker's episcopate campaign by dissenters to be "their greatest victory during the eighteenth century in their ongoing battle with the orthodox," a "proxy war in which an ecclesiastical superpower was humiliated by a numerically smaller, highly motivated force."[57]

Mayhew's victory seemed complete, but he did not relent. At the beginning of the Stamp Act Crisis, the West Church pastor resumed his attack upon English Catholicism and its alleged Episcopalian abettors. Invited to give the annual Dudleian Lecture at Harvard College on May 8, 1765, he denounced Catholicism as an affront to man's senses and reason, maintained that "popery and liberty are incompatible," and renewed his accusation that the Church of England was criminally negligent in allowing Catholic priests to seduce weak-willed Protestants to "an impious, horrid system of tyranny over the bodies and souls of men." Mayhew died in 1766 and Secker in 1768, but the heated debate over episcopacy and its associations with Catholicism resumed shortly after the Stamp Act Crisis. The Second Bishop Controversy raged for the better part of a decade, with Thomas Bradbury Chandler taking up Secker's cause and Charles Chauncy carrying on in his friend Mayhew's place.[58]

Advocates of an episcopate faced resistance not only from Congregationalists and Presbyterians but also from low-church Episcopalians in the mid-Atlantic and southern colonies. In the absence of bishops, Episcopal laymen administered their own churches through a vestry system that resembled Presbyterian church government. Most colonial Episcopalians were not eager to submit this control to a royal appointee as unelected and unaccountable as a stamp-tax collector. Just as anti-Catholicism had helped meld the English, Welsh, and Scots into one British nation in the early eighteenth century, so shared hostility toward prelates and popes—along with revenue-men and redcoats—turned the colonists away from Britain and unified them as Americans. As John Adams put it in 1815, "the apprehensions of Episcopacy contributed fifty years ago, as much as any other cause, to arouse the attention, not only of the inquiring mind, but of the common people, and urge them to close thinking on the constitutional authority of parliament over the colonies."[59]

While the Bishop Controversy helped unite nonconformists and low-churchmen against British authority, it also often served to separate Patriot sheep from Loyalist goats with the approach of war. In her study *Revolutionary Anglicanism*, historian Nancy L. Rhoden noted that these debates did more than make the colonists identify the Episcopal Church of England with an increasingly despotic British state. She contended:

The episcopacy controversy also created the fault line along which clerical opinion would divide during the Revolutionary War. One can notice clearly a link between pro-episcopal opinion and later loyalism, as well as between anti-episcopal opinion and patriotism. Although decisions of patriotism or loyalism rested upon many considerations, views on episcopacy served as a successful predictor in many notable cases. The most prominent episcopal spokesmen in each colony, namely Thomas Bradbury Chandler, Henry Caner, Jonathan Boucher, and John Camm, became loyalist exiles. Their episcopal opinions formed part of a larger, more encompassing political philosophy which favored deference to hierarchical authority.[60]

In Revolutionary Massachusetts, certainly, the ideological "fault line" between Congregationalists and Episcopalians divided not only the clergy but the laity as well.[61]

While the battle over writs of assistance in the early 1760s polarized Massachusetts into two hostile political factions—Otis's friends of liberty and Hutchinson's friends of government—the Bishop Controversy at the same time helped to polarize the province into two hostile political ideologies: Whiggism and Toryism. A handful of royal appointees within the Episcopal clergy and the royal government stood against New England's Whig majority in maintaining that political and religious authority flowed from the Crown (or king-in-Parliament) downward rather than from the people upward. It is fitting that Yankees should have divided into Whigs and Tories while debating essentially the same issues that were at stake when those two ideologies originated—the period from 1673–1683, when England was rocked successively by the Test Act Controversy, the Popish Plot, and the Exclusion Crisis. Then, as during the Bishop Controversy, fears of Catholic corruption and a despotic alliance of high-churchmen and royalists alienated Protestant dissenters and low-church Episcopalians from the Crown.[62]

And in the 1760s, as in the 1670s, questions about religious liberty and church government prompted debates about the limits of civil liberty and state power. During the First Bishop Controversy, Mayhew attacked the Church of England as a threat to colonial self-government. His Episcopalian adversaries responded by asserting the authority of England's Crown, Parliament, and Church over America's congregations and legislatures. By defining the religious conflict between Congregationalists and Episcopalians in terms of Whig revolution principles and Tory obedience principles—in terms of liberty versus tyranny and order versus licentiousness—Mayhew and his antagonists drew the philosophical battle lines of the American Revolution before constitutional debates over taxation had begun in earnest. By the time Parliament passed statutes striking directly at the colonies' civil liberty, Mayhew and his allies in the Congregational and Presbyterian clergy had already mobilized their congregations for the fierce defense of their rights. With passage of the Stamp Act in 1765, Parliament stuck its nose into a hornet's nest too recently stirred by Thomas Secker's prelatical crook.

6

The Whig Dilemma

Members of the British imperial establishment, from the archbishop of Canterbury to the royal governor of Massachusetts, viewed Dr. Jonathan Mayhew as a radical who abused press and pulpit to shake the pillars of church and state to their foundations. Mayhew viewed himself as a conservative who understood Whig revolution principles as foundational to the British Empire. He had concluded his passionate defense of resistance and regicide, the 1750 *Discourse Concerning Unlimited Submission*, with the reminder: "Let us all learn to be *free*, and to be *loyal*." He had told his readers that, since American colonists enjoyed liberty under Hanoverian rule, it "becomes us, therefore, to be contented and dutiful subjects" and "to *lead a quiet and peaceable life*." In a 1758 sermon on the French and Indian War, Mayhew claimed that "it would be highly criminal" for persons "who have the happiness of living under such a free, mild government as the British, and a King, with whom the laws are so sacred as they have ever been with his present majesty, either to raise or countenance any kind of rebellion, or sedition in the state."[1]

After denouncing rebellion and sedition, the Boston divine immediately added that, because "the privileges we enjoy under the British government" are "so precious and invaluable, we are bound in reason and duty, if there should ever be occasion, to stand up in the defence of them," even against corrupt elements within the British government itself. He observed that Americans "cannot be true hearty friends to the free English government, to the principles of the revolution, to the present Royal Family, or to the protestant religion, without detesting tyranny; and opposing in our several places, and to the utmost of our power, if ever there should be occasion given for it, all arbitrary, illegal proceedings, whether in church or state, whether of great men or little ones." Imagining the Hanoverian British state as still based upon "the principles of the revolution," Mayhew considered loyalty and freedom, the subjection to law and the right of resistance, as logically compatible and mutually reinforcing.[2]

In this respect, Mayhew's political thought and political activism were true to the British Real Whig tradition. In her study *From Resistance to Revolution*, historian Pauline Maier described that tradition as "an ideology of resistance and restraint." Understanding liberty as the individual's "absolute freedom in all actions" concerning himself alone, Maier explained, it could be violated both by the tyranny of the state or the anarchy of the mob, and it required the protection of the rule of law. Sometimes tyranny could only be restrained by extralegal force, hence the natural right of resistance. Such British Whig philosophers as John Locke and Benjamin Hoadly maintained, however, that the people could resort to arms in defense of their liberty only as a last resort, when all peaceful options had been exhausted. Even when justified, armed resistance might be avoided from prudential considerations. "An account had to be taken of the chances of success," Maier noted, "and some balance struck between the evils possibly arising from violence and those inherent in continued submission." One could style their struggle to strike this balance "the Whig dilemma." When does the defense of liberty justify extralegal resistance, and how can one resist tyranny without unleashing anarchy?[3]

Mayhew grounded his commitment to Whig revolution principles in his British Enlightenment conception of humans as capable of rationality, moral agency, informed consent, and hence political self-government. He considered the people as endowed by God with the natural capacity to think for themselves and therefore judge their governors, identify abuses of power, and determine for themselves when resistance to government was both morally justified and prudentially warranted. For him, the right of resistance followed from the right of private judgment. Throughout his career, the West Church pastor unabashedly preached Real Whig politics and educated the public on British violations of colonial rights in the 1760s. By characterizing the activities of the Church of England as part of a conspiracy against New England's civil and religious liberty, Mayhew successfully raised a clamor among New Englanders sufficient to thwart Archbishop Secker's colonial episcopate without need for violence or disorder, mobilizing public opinion rather than public force.

This clamor was also sufficient, however, to put Yankees in a state of extreme agitation that did not dissipate after East Apthorp closed his Episcopal mission in Cambridge. The ill-timed actions of the British state confirmed New Englanders' worst fears of a British plot to enslave them. When Parliament passed the Stamp Act of 1765 on the heels of the Bishop Controversy and the Sugar Act, Bostonians' heightened anxiety exploded into rage. Having urged the people to rise in protest against tyranny, Mayhew and New England's Whig opposition leaders found it difficult to restrain them from resorting to anarchy. "The experience of most popular leaders and the lesson they derived from the uprisings of 1765," Maier observed, "were personified in the plight of Boston's radical minister Jonathan Mayhew." During the Stamp Act Crisis of 1765–1766, the oppressiveness of the stamp tax and the fury of the New England public against it prompted Mayhew to wrestle with the dilemma that had long haunted Whigs on both sides of the Atlantic: how to save liberty without destroying it in the process.[4]

For Mayhew, the Church of England's plan to impose bishops and the British Parliament's plan to impose taxes were not necessarily coordinated conspiracies. But they sprang from the same principles, and these attacks upon religious and civil liberty were mutually reinforcing, amounting to a siege against America's free institutions. Passage of the Sugar Act on April 5, 1764, made all the more cogent his warnings that Parliament would tax the colonies to support royally appointed bishops. Against Secker's claim that fear of such taxation was fanciful, Mayhew wrote in his *Remarks on an Anonymous Tract*:

Nay, if bishops were speedily to be sent to America, it seems not wholly improbable, from what we hear of the *unusual* tenor of some late parliamentary acts and bills, for raising money on the poor colonies *without their consent*, that provision might be made for the support of these bishops, if not of all the church clergy also, in the *same way*.[5]

Even before Parliament's passage of the sugar and stamp taxes, Secker's plan for an American episcopate had prompted nonconformists and Episcopalians to debate the constitutional limits of Britain's jurisdiction over the colonies. John Adams wrote in 1815 that "the apprehensions of Episcopacy contributed fifty years ago, as much as any other cause, to arouse the attention, not only of the inquiring mind, but of the common people, and urge them to close thinking on the constitutional authority of parliament over the colonies." If the Stamp Act Crisis was, as historian Edmund S. Morgan put it, the "prologue to Revolution," then the First Bishop Controversy was the prologue to the Stamp Act Crisis.[6]

Mayhew's principled defense of civil and ecclesiastical liberty won him powerful friends, including "dissenters" outside of New England, such as William Allen, the Pennsylvania Chief Justice and leader of Pennsylvania's Presbyterian party. Allen corresponded with Mayhew as an ally against the plots of high-church Episcopal clergymen throughout the northern colonies. Writing Mayhew in October 15, 1764, the chief justice warned:

Bishop's-weed is a very noxious one, and when it once gets into a country there is no getting clear of it. The Archbishop of Canterbury, and many of the Society [for the Propagation of the Gospel] are fond of transplanting it into the Colony. But, from what I should observe, the Bishops, nor their office have not many friends among the Nobility, and Gentry: if ever they are sent among us it will be with Political views to make us more tame, and submissive to the Yoke intended to be laid on us. I am sorry to say it, there is, at present, an evileye over America, and that odious Stamp-act is intended for a precedent for much greater impositions. The power of our own Legislatures is to be annihilated; for if the Parliament lay internal taxes on us, they are in a great measure rendered useless.[7]

If Parliament could nullify the independence of colonial lower houses with taxes, then it could nullify the independence of colonial meetinghouses with bishops. Civil liberty and religious liberty would rise or fall together, Allen and Mayhew believed, and both must be upheld in principle against the first appearance of tyranny.

Like Mayhew, Allen viewed bishops and taxes as two prongs of the trident that Britannia turned menacingly toward her colonies. The Pennsylvania chief justice also shared Mayhew's commitment to the Real Whig principle of *obsta principiis*, but the question remained of how to oppose tyranny without unleashing anarchy. Allen told the Boston divine that the best response of the colonies to the proposed Stamp Act would be to cease trading with English merchants, who under duress would then intercede with Parliament on the colonies' behalf. "The internal taxation is what we should oppose with Sobriety, and Manliness, and consider it a negative that will bring us and our Posterity, should it take place, into Slavery," he gravely cautioned the minister. While Parliament's attack on colonial liberty had to be opposed with manly resolve, Allen and Mayhew agreed that such nonviolent, sober, rational tactics as commercial nonimportation would preserve the appropriate balance between liberty and order.[8]

When George III came to the throne, the young prince was firmly under the sway of John Stuart, the third Earl of Bute, who impressed upon him the importance of royal prerogative within the British constitutional system. In the 1760s, British court politics took a distinctly Tory direction for the first time since the death of the last Stuart monarch, Queen Anne. Under pressure from Whigs in Britain's Parliament and press, Bute formally resigned as lord treasurer in April 1763. The same month, William Pitt, darling of the Real Whigs and Bute's relentless nemesis, resigned as prime minister in protest against the king's policies. Bute secured the position of lord treasurer and de facto prime minister for George Grenville, one of his political protégés, who began implementing the earl's program of colonial taxation and rigorous enforcement of colonial commercial regulations. It appeared to Real Whigs on both sides of the Atlantic that the new king intended to desert traditional Hanoverian support for Whig revolution principles, the dissenting interest, and colonial rights.

In a May 1763 letter to Mayhew, Thomas Hollis attributed this disturbing trend to Bute's secret influence over the king. That November, Mayhew wrote his English friend that the available evidence tended to "confirm the Apprehensions which I have all along had concerning the P[rin]ce; and make me almost tremble for the Consequences. May God unite the Hearts of all wise and good men;—all who love liberty and Great-Britain, and hate French ambition and S[cotc]h Politicks." He added grimly, "The Contests in England seem to me to have arisen almost as high already, as they can possibly rise, without terminating in what I so much dread the thoughts of, that I shall not even mention it." Mayhew wrote Hollis in 1764, "The account which you give me, as well as others, of the political state of Affairs in England, is extremely afflictive to me, and fills me with very gloomy apprehensions, though I think there is nothing in my natural temper, inclining to melancholy, or a dejection of spirits." The warnings Mayhew had issued ten years earlier about the menace of British corruption and high-church Toryism to American virtue and liberty seemed to be proving prescient.[9]

Nonconforming Whigs like Hollis and Mayhew had long heaped praise on the House of Hanover for preserving the gains of the Glorious Revolution: the Bill of Rights, the Toleration Act, and the Protestant Succession. The abrupt change in imperial policy initiated by Bute suggested ominously that George III had embraced the Tory obedience principles that Hollis and Mayhew attributed to his Scottish Stuart advisor. Mayhew wrote in his *Remarks on an Anonymous Tract* that he feared it was true, "as many affirm, that *high-church, tory-principles* and maxims are lately revived in England; and favour'd greatly by some, whose influence may go far towards bringing them into as much reputation, as they have been in disgrace, since the death of Queen *Anne*." By the time Parliament voted overwhelmingly in favor of the Stamp Act on March 22, 1765, he and Hollis worried that Britain had started down a path that could only end in tyranny, civil war, and revolution comparable to the horrors of the 1640s.[10]

Over the preceding fifteen years, Mayhew's dogged advancement of Whig revolution principles in New England's political culture had helped make Massachusetts fertile ground for both elite and popular protest against this new imposition of British authority on the American colonies. Mayhew's recent agitation of the Episcopal threat, in particular, served to mobilize New England's Congregational clergy against the hateful stamp tax scheduled to take effect on November 1, 1765. On May 29, 1765, Rev. Andrew Eliot gave the annual election sermon to the Massachusetts General Court. Although a Whig in principle, Eliot was a mild and moderate person by temperament, lacking his friend Mayhew's ardor of spirit. His sermon was, in historian Bernard Bailyn's characterization, "platitudinous throughout," with one glaring exception, "an unexpected, and altogether unintegrated, paragraph" in which Eliot's language suddenly ran hot.[11] The minister of Boston's New North Church told the assembled leaders that

> where men . . . pervert their power to tyrannical purposes; submission, if it can be avoided, is so far from being a duty, that it is a crime. It is an offense against the state of which we are members, and whose happiness we ought to prefer to our chief joy. It is an offense against mankind, whose rights we meanly betray. It is an offense against God, who is good to all, and who has appointed government for the welfare and happiness, and not the destruction of his creatures.[12]

Bailyn did not address this strange burst of Whig resistance theory in a sermon otherwise conventional in style and conciliatory in tone.

Listening to Eliot's election sermon, Governor Bernard, so deeply offended by the sentiments Mayhew expressed in his *Discourse Concerning Unlimited Submission*, might well have noted the similarity between Eliot's rhetorical flourish and a similar passage in Mayhew's older work. Where Eliot's 1765 election sermon stated that submission to tyranny "is a crime . . . an offense against the state. . . . an offense against mankind. . . . an offense against God," Mayhew wrote in his 1750 *Discourse* that submission to tyranny is "as great *treason* as ever man uttered; it is treason,—not against one *single* man, but the state—against the whole body politic;—'tis treason against mankind:—'tis treason against common sense—'tis treason against GOD." Mayhew's influence on Eliot is unmistakable. The West Church pastor's political activism, particularly against the high-church Episcopal clergy, helped radicalize New England Congregational pastors like Eliot who were not ordinarily inclined to preach politics, let alone revolution principles.[13]

These revolutionary sentiments and a corresponding outrage at the Stamp Act were not confined to Mayhew, Eliot, and a handful of elite clergymen, however. Nor were they confined entirely to New England. On August 8, 1765, Mayhew wrote Hollis:

The Colonies are universally and greatly alarmed at the Measures lately taken respecting them. These Measures appear to me extremely hard and injurious. If long persisted in, they will at best greatly cramp, and retard the population of, the Colonies, to the very essential detriment of the Mother country. And what may, in time, be the consequence of raising a general and great disaffection in the people of this large Continent, no one can certainly foresee. But you and I, Sir, are at least clear in this point, that no people are under a *religious obligation* to be slaves, if they are able to set themselves at liberty.[14]

For years, the West Church pastor had toiled to convince New Englanders that they had no religious duty of nonresistance to tyrants, and he soon would have proof that the people learned this lesson all too well. Mayhew did not have to wonder for long how the general public would respond to the Stamp Act. "When I last wrote," Mayhew informed Hollis eleven days later, "I did not think the spirit of opposition to the Stamp-Act would break out so soon, in any open Acts of Violence, as it has done."[15]

On August 14, Bostonians woke to find provincial secretary Andrew Oliver—who had been sent a royal commission as distributor of tax stamps in the city—hanging in effigy from an elm tree in downtown Boston. Also hanging from the tree was a boot with its sole colored a "vile" shade of green: a visual pun on Bute and Grenville. A leering devil peeked out of the boot, representing the power of Antichrist that was ultimately responsible for the ministerial innovations. "Some thousands of people went that day to see it," Mayhew wrote, "and it seemed to give general satisfaction to the people." At sundown, the crowd tore down the new stamp office, sawed off the head of the Oliver effigy, and then burned the wood and the effigies in front of Oliver's house, "amidst loud acclamations." Later that night, some members of the crowd attacked and damaged Oliver's private residence. Their intimidation worked; Oliver vowed to reject his commission as a stamp-tax collector. The following evening, the mob marched to the home of Thomas Hutchinson, the lieutenant governor and chief justice of Massachusetts, who was widely and falsely thought guilty of encouraging passage of the Stamp Act. Upon arrival of the mob, Hutchinson concealed himself, "and they departed without doing any Mischief." The common people of Boston displayed in action their devotion to Whig revolution principles, their repugnance for Tory obedience principles, and their opinion of the Stamp Act.[16]

Mayhew concluded from the violent protests of the preceding days that any attempt to enforce the Stamp Act would provoke armed resistance in the colonies. He told Hollis in the letter of August 19 that American hatred of the Stamp Act was so intense and so universal that "I am satisfied it will never be carried into execution, unless it is done at the point of the Sword, by a large army, or rather by a number of considerable ones, at least one in each Colony; there being about sixty thousand fighting men in this Province only: And it is given out by many, that they will spend their last blood in this cause." Mayhew added that he was only stating the facts of the case, not his evaluation of them, but he wrote that Britain would be foolish to wage war to enforce "this odious tax." Such a war between Britain and the colonies would result in either America's destruction or America's independence, both of which would be bad for Britain. "God forbid there should be an intire Breach between them," he told Hollis, "which might prove very fatal to both!"[17]

Mayhew feared a fratricidal war between Britain and America, but he also feared the subjugation of New England by a corrupt British government. He resolved to make his own contribution to the Whig opposition by preaching both self-defense and self-restraint. On the afternoon of August 25, the pastor gave a sermon to the congregation of the West End meetinghouse on the nature and value of civil liberty. While Mayhew's original notes do not remain, a few days later he wrote a memorandum of his sermon on Galatians 5:12–13. In one of the few systematic explications of the meaning of liberty by an American colonist, Mayhew enumerated the various ways in which eighteenth-century British subjects used the word: "philosophical liberty, or freedom of choice and action"; "gracious liberty," the God-given ability to resist sin; "religious liberty, or that natural right which every man has to worship God as he pleases"; and Christian liberty, freedom from the obligations of Jewish law, the one Paul addressed in his letter to the Galatians. Another species was natural liberty, which "every man has, in what is commonly called a state of nature, or antecedent to the consideration of his being a member of civil society; consisting in a right to act as he pleases, in opposition to being bound by any human laws; always, provided that he violates no laws of God, nature, or right reason; which no man is at liberty to do."[18]

The subject that commanded Mayhew's interest that day, however, was civil liberty, liberty as it exists in a "civil Society, or a body politic." The attainment of civil liberty, he told his assembled brethren, requires that individuals "give up some part of their natural liberty, or the right which they have in a state of nature, to act as they please, each individual for himself." He said of civil liberty:

It supposeth the restraint of laws, some persons to govern, and some to be governed. For people [in the memorandum, he struck out "men" and added "people"] do not enjoy civil liberty, where each individual does what is right in his own eyes, without any regard to others. This is a State of anarchy & confusion; as distant from a state of civil liberty, as slavery itself, in which it often terminates, one extreme leading to another, seemingly the most opposite thereto.[19]

Liberty can be made compatible with subjection to civil law, the pastor explained, when the laws "are made by common consent & choice; that all have some hand in framing them, at least by their representatives, chosen to act for them, if not in their own persons." If people are "governed contrary to, or independently of, their own will & consent," then they are "in a state of slavery." Lest he be accused of hyperbole in comparing the stamp tax to enslavement, he explained what he meant by slavery in principle. "For the essence of slavery consists in being subjected to the arbitrary pleasure of others," Mayhew posited, "whether many, few, or but one, it matters not." For him, representation was an attribute essential to a free government. "The essence of civil liberty does not consist in, or depend upon, the number of persons, by whom a nation is governed," he expounded, "but in their being governed by such persons & laws, as they approve of."[20]

Both monarchy and democracy, Mayhew contended, are constitutional forms compatible with civil liberty, so long as the people remain sovereign and the government remains accountable to their will. A people can still be free under monarchy, "provided it is by their own choice, and they delegate the powers of government to him, still reserving to themselves a right to judge, whether he discharges his trust well or ill, to discard him, and appoint another in his stead." And a people can still be enslaved under democracy, if those who exercise power in the people's name do so "only for their own interest, pleasure or profit, contrary to the will of the governed." The people are "real slaves" if they have laws imposed on them by governors whom they have not approved. It does not matter if their "masters" are kindly. The people are still enslaved if the question of "whether they shall be ruled justly & mercifully, or not, depends on the mere pleasure of a master, or many masters." In light of Mayhew's Real Whig political principles, the essential difference between civil liberty and slavery was the difference between government with or without the consent of the governed.[21]

The only New England clergyman to take an explicit and public stand against the stamp tax, Mayhew boldly applied his political principles to the current political crisis. He observed that "a mother-country" could remain free while "her colonies may be kept in a state of real slavery to her." Mayhew made clear enough to his listeners that he had in mind Britain's imposition of the Stamp Act on the American colonists. He told them:

For if they are to possess no property, nor to enjoy the fruits of their own labor, but by the mere precarious pleasure of the mother, or of a distant legislature, in which they neither are, nor can be represented; this is really slavery, not civil liberty. Only slaves are bound to labor for the pleasure & profit of others; and to subsist merely on what their masters are pleased to allow them, tho' they may possibly have kind masters, who treat them with tenderness & humanity, still they are as really in a state of slavery, as those who have hard & cruel masters."[22]

He added, in a footnote, that this proposition was "agreeable to the reasonings of the most approved English writers on liberty, before as well as since the Revolution; tho' contrary to Hobbs, Filmer, and suchlike betrayers of the liberties & rights of their country, into the hands of arbitrary princes." Taxation without consent is slavery, he declaimed, regardless of whether the tax be large or small.[23]

Having distinguished civil liberty from slavery, Mayhew then distinguished it from anarchy. In his sermon of August 25, he reminded the congregation that, while Paul told the Galatians that they had been "called unto liberty," he also reminded them, "Only use not liberty for an occasion to the flesh." As examples of abusers of liberty, he cited those who "disregard the wholesome laws of Society, made for the preservation of the order and common good thereof," "who causelessly & maliciously speak evil of their rulers; endeavouring to make them appear odious or contemptible, or to weaken their influence, and proper authority, in their several stations," and "who cause factions, or insurrections against the government, under which they live; & who rebel against, or resist their lawful rulers, in the due discharge of their offices." Mayhew equated civil liberty with self-government, but political self-government required moral self-government—the regulation and direction of the passions by reason and virtue.[24]

Popular lawlessness nullified civil liberty, but so did laws contrary to popular consent. Having made clear that he was no advocate of mob rule, Mayhew then turned to the touchy subject of resistance to oppressive laws like the Stamp Act. When "a nation is something actually abused by their rulers to a great degree," he observed, the question naturally arises, "whether passive obedience and non-resistance were the duty of such a people; or whether opposing such rulers, and the execution of unrighteous & oppressive laws, could properly be accounted using liberty for an occasion to the flesh?" Mayhew maintained in this sermon, as he had in his political sermons over the preceding fifteen years, that the people have the right to resist tyranny by force—and the right to judge when the acts of their rulers warrant such resistance. Whatever else he told his congregation about resistance and obedience on August 25, he did not record in the memorandum.[25]

The day after Mayhew's sermon on liberty, the Boston mob provided a dramatic example of using liberty as an occasion to the flesh. Mayhew's young admirer from Braintree, the Whiggish law student Josiah Quincy, Jr., recorded this pivotal incident in his diary the following day. In the evening of August 26, Bostonians mobbed the private homes of two officers of the customs commission and friends of the governor: William Story (one of Mayhew's antagonists in the "Indian Affair") and Benjamin Hallowell. The two mobs united into one giant mob and marched on Thomas Hutchinson's house. The lieutenant governor resolved not to flee again but told his children to leave. His eldest daughter refused to go without him, and Hutchinson relented. The "rage-intoxicated rabble," as Quincy put it, swept into the house and destroyed or stole everything of value inside. They inflicted enormous structural damage on the building, tearing the cupola off the roof. The mob made a point of ransacking Hutchinson's papers, perhaps to destroy records relating to ongoing prosecutions of Boston shippers for violations of the Navigation Acts. Quincy was particularly outraged that they destroyed "some of the most valuable records of the country, and other ancient papers," which Hutchinson had collected for future volumes of his history of Massachusetts. "This is a loss greatly to be deplored," the law student lamented, "as it is absolutely irretrievable."[26]

The anarchic attack on Hutchinson's house stunned and horrified most Bostonians, including Jonathan Mayhew. Despite the lieutenant governor's close collaboration with Governor Bernard, Mayhew always had a high opinion of his mind and character, enjoyed a good working relationship with him on the Harvard Board of Overseers, and kept a portrait of Hutchinson at home. In a private letter to Hollis, the pastor praised Hutchinson—with some reservations—as "very full in the principles of liberty, civil and religious." On August 27, Mayhew wrote Hutchinson to offer him "condolence, on account of the almost unparall'd outrages committed on your house the last evening." The minister insisted vehemently, "God is my witness, that from the bottom of my heart, I detest these proceedings." He understood, though, that some of his "numerous and causeless enemies" claimed that he approved the proceedings and "had indeed encouraged them in a Sermon which I preached the last Lord's day on Gal. 5. 12, 13." Defending himself against the smear, Mayhew wrote:

This I absolutely deny. I did indeed express myself strongly in favor of civil & religious liberty, [as I hope I shall ever continue to do;] and spoke of the late Stamp Act as a great grievance, likely to prove detrimental in a high degree, both to the Colonies, and to the Mother Country; which, I believe, is the Sense of almost every person of understanding in the Plantations; And, particularly, I have heard your Honor speak to the same Purpose. But then, as my text led me to do, I cautioned my Hearers very particularly against the abuses of liberty; and intimated my hopes, that no persons among ourselves had encouraged the bringing of such a burden on their country, notwithstanding it had been strongly suspected. Let me add, that when in private company I have often heard your Honor spoken of as one, who was supposed to have been an encourager of the Act aforesaid, I have as often taken the Liberty to say, I had heard you express yourself in a manner that strongly implied the contrary; which I did with a view to remove those prejudices which I perceived some persons had against you in that aspect. And, in truth, I had rather lose my hand than be an encourager of such outrages as were committed last night.[27]

Standing on his reputation for always telling the truth, even to the point of indiscretion, he begged Hutchinson to believe him and disregard the accusations made against him. The lieutenant governor was not persuaded, perhaps prejudiced against Mayhew by the unpleasantness of the Indian Affair.[28]

Mayhew's friend Andrew Eliot, an eyewitness to the attack on Hutchinson's house, denied the Tory charge. The day after the first anniversary of the infamous riot, Eliot wrote Thomas Hollis that Mayhew had preached "a sermon on liberty" on August 25, but he "said not one word of the attack" on Andrew Oliver on August 14. Although some "malevolent persons" accused Mayhew of inciting the August 26 riot, "the plan was laid before, and it is questioned whether [even] one of the rioters had ever heard of the Doctor's sermon." Eliot confided to Hollis that Mayhew told him privately, "Of the 14th of August, I choose to say nothing," but "the proceedings of the 26th I abhor, from my very soul."[29]

Just as the myth that Hutchinson favored the Stamp Act persisted in some circles, so the myth that Mayhew incited the Hutchinson attack persisted in other circles. The wealthy merchant Richard Clarke, a full member of the

West Church, blamed Mayhew for the mob action and withdrew his family from the congregation. The pastor wrote Clarke a long letter pleading his case. With uncharacteristic humility, he confessed:

> I readily acknowledge, what I was not so well aware of before, that it was a very unfortunate time to preach a sermon, the chief aim of which was to show the importance of Liberty, when people were before so generally apprehensive of the danger of losing it. They certainly needed rather to be moderated and pacified, to the contrary: And I would freely give all that I have in the world, rather than have preached that sermon; tho' I am well assured, it was very generally liked and commended by the hearers at the time of it.[30]

Though "composed in a high strain of liberty," he was certain that "no person could, without abusing & perverting it, take encouragement from it to go to mobbing, or to commit some abominable outrages as were lately committed, in defiance of the laws of God and man. I did, in the most formal, express manner, discountenance everything of that kind." Mayhew reminded Clarke that he concluded his sermon with the exhortation for the people not to "use any method, for the defense of our rights & privileges, besides those which are honest & honourable." Considering all of the caveats he offered in the sermon about the abuse of liberty, Mayhew told Clarke, "it is humbly conceived the author ought in common justice to be acquitted, as no encourager of mobs and riots."[31]

On September 1, he gave a sermon to the West Church denouncing the August 26 attack in such strong language that some friends of liberty considered Mayhew a traitor to the cause. "I still love liberty as much as ever," Mayhew wrote Richard Clarke, "but have apprehensions of the greatest inconveniences likely to follow on a forceable, violent opposition to an act of parliament; which I consider, in some sort, as proclaiming war against Great Britain." Despite the pastor's long and heartfelt letter, Clarke did not reconcile with him or return to the West Church. Mayhew's old enemies perpetuated the accusation of incitement. On September 5, Rev. Henry Caner, rector of King's Chapel, reported to the archbishop of Canterbury that "Dr. Mayhew has distinguished himself in the pulpit upon this Occasion (it is said) in One of the most seditious Sermons ever delivered, advising the people to stand up for their rights to the last drop of their Blood." In a letter of October 5, Hutchinson claimed that Mayhew had intended his sermon of August 25 to incite the mob against Governor Francis Bernard. Sixteen years later, Hutchinson's brother-in-law, the Tory historian Peter Oliver, accused Mayhew of preaching on August 25 "so seditious a Sermon, that some of his Auditors, who were of the Mob, declared, whilst the Doctor was delivering it they could scarce contain themselves from going out of the Assembly & beginning their Work." It was a smear that the friends of government never substantiated and Mayhew never escaped.[32]

Boston's August tumults touched off similar protests and riots throughout the colonies. In July, George III dismissed George Grenville over a dispute unrelated to the Stamp Act. The king's choice of the Marquis of Rockingham, a moderate Whig, as prime minister gave many Bostonians hope for repeal. Mayhew, however, believed that Parliament would not withdraw the Stamp Act until convinced of its destructive effects. On September 26, he anxiously wrote Thomas Hollis:

You can hardly conceive how the minds of people in the colonies are inflamed by the late Parliamentary regulations, particularly the Stamp-Act. The violent Measures which have been taken already in most of them, to make the Stamp-Officers resign their posts, and many other things, confirm me in the opinion which I intimated to you in the last, That this Act will never be carried into execution, without the effusion of much blood: For it is the general voice of the people, that they had rather die by the sword, than submit to such slavery as they conceive they shall be under, by submitting to such a kind of taxation.[33]

In attempt to take opposition to the Stamp Act out of the hands of the mob, nine provincial legislatures sent delegates, gentlemen of property and education, to an intercolonial congress like that held at the beginning of the French and Indian War. On October 1, 1765, the day the Stamp Act Congress convened in New York City, Mayhew conveyed to Hollis his fear that the crisis would end in open armed revolt. He wrote:

For my own part, I have both privately and publicly delivered my opinion of the inexpediency and great danger of any *forcible*, *riotous* and *illegal* proceedings, in opposition to parliamentary authority, even though the Colonies should be oppressed. *We are not able to contend in this way with Great Britain.* But far the greater part of the People in the Colonies seem at present resolved to *run all hazzards* rather than submit: For they say nothing worse can happen to us than such slavery.[34]

Despite all the looming signs of civil war, Mayhew continued to hope that the Stamp Act could be repealed through nonviolent measures: cogent argumentation offered by American and British Whigs as well as economic boycott organized by American merchants, the colonial legislatures, and the Congress.

One of the American Whigs combating the Stamp Act with pen rather than sword was the young Bostonian lawyer, John Adams. In the fall of 1765, he published his first political tract in four installments in the *Boston Gazette*. Throughout, it bore the marks of Mayhew's influence upon his thinking, with references to his *Discourse Concerning Unlimited Submission*, his *Observations*, and the Dudleian lecture on Catholicism that Mayhew gave at Harvard in May 1765. In the last installment of his four-part series, published on October 21, Adams praised—with Mayhewesque audacity—the old English spirit of resistance to tyranny, "the same great spirit, which once gave Caesar so warm a reception; which denounced hostilities against John 'till Magna Charta was signed; which severed the head of Charles the first from his body, and drove James the second from his kingdom." Also like Mayhew, Adams observed that the spirit of liberty must be governed and directed by reason. "This spirit however without knowledge," he added, "would be little better than a brutal rage. Let us tenderly and kindly cherish, therefore the means of knowledge. Let us dare to read, to think, speak and write." For Adams as for Mayhew, the individual right of private judgment—cherished by New England Congregationalists and British Protestant dissenters—meant that the people were free to think on political subjects and sit in judgment of their own rulers.[35]

Applying the lessons of the Bishop Controversy to the Stamp Act Crisis, Adams repeated Mayhew's warning of a British plot to subvert America's civil and religious liberty. The Yankee lawyer grimly wrote:

The prospect, now before us, in America, ought . . . to engage the attention of every man of learning to matters of power and of right, that we may be neither led nor driven blindfolded to irretrievable destruction. Nothing less than this seems to have been meditated for us, by somebody or other in Great-Britain. There seems to be a direct and formal design on foot, to enslave all America. This however must be done by degrees. The first step that is intended seems to be an entire subversion of the whole system of our Fathers, by an introduction of the cannon and feudal law, into America.... The designs and labours of a certain society, to introduce the former of them into America, have been well exposed to the public by a writer of great abilities, and the further attempts to the same purpose that may be made by that society, or by the ministry or parliament, I leave to the conjectures of the thoughtful.[36]

Mayhew could take credit for teaching young Whigs like Adams to resist tyranny from the beginning, including the religious tyranny threatened by the Church of England. He could also take the blame, however, for agitating the public during the Bishop Controversy into such a frantic state that they were prepared to resort to violence against persons and property as the first response to tyranny rather than the last. The pastor worried that the fear of conspiracy and dread of tyranny he had helped excite in the New England mind with his political sermons and pamphlets might prove too powerful for informed reason to restrain from destructive consequences.

Mayhew and Hollis did their utmost to attain peaceful repeal of the Stamp Act and thereby avert a bloody civil war against the world's mightiest empire, a war the American colonists could not possibly have won in 1765 (and only narrowly won in 1783). A man of extraordinary political influence, Hollis asked the Marquis of Rockingham for an audience, which the prime minister granted the following day, October 23. Hollis showed him Mayhew's letter of August 19—predicting that the Stamp Act could not be enforced without great bloodshed—and cited it as evidence that Parliament should repeal the act. "His Lordship treated me with great civility, read the letter attentively, but did by no means seem to feel the importance of it," Hollis recorded in his diary, "nor to apprehend the very imminent danger there is at this time of losing our northern colonies." He wrote Mayhew on November 18 "extremely concerned, afflicted at the present sad, melancholy state of affairs betwixt England and her Colonies." "All my *little* Energies have been and shall be *exerted* on this occasion," Hollis reassured him, "for how can they be more nobly engaged, than in good offices betwixt the Mother Country and her Colonies?" Toward that end, Hollis arranged and paid for the English reprint of John Adams's pamphlet. The four installments appeared in the *London Chronicle* on November 23, November 28, December 3, and December 26, under Hollis's title *A Dissertation on the Feudal and the Canon Law*. His efforts with the government having stalled, Hollis used the press in hopes of rallying British public opinion against the Stamp Act.[37]

The failure of the Rockingham ministry to advance the cause of repeal, and the determination of New Englanders to resist the tax by force, left Mayhew despondent about the future. "I am daily more and more confirmed in the opinion, that the said Act will never be received without much bloodshed," he wrote Hollis on January 7, 1766. "Great Britain has doubtless power to enforce it; but not without the destruction of the Colonies, or what is scarce better." He feared for the fate of "the whole British empire," which was being led to ruination by Rockingham and "a pensioned, bribed H[ouse] of C[ommo]ns and H[ouse] of L[ords]." Seven days later, William Pitt, a former prime minister widely admired for his devotion to Real Whig principles and successful wartime strategy against the French, returned to the British House of Commons and rose to speak. He baldly stated his opinion that "this kingdom has no right to lay a tax upon the colonies," because the colonial assemblies "have ever been in possession of this, their constitutional right, of giving and granting their own money. They would have been slaves if they had not enjoyed it." A fierce debate ensued between Pitt and Grenville.[38]

Greatly aided by the economic pressure placed on British merchants and manufacturers by colonial nonimportation, Pitt had turned the House of Commons in favor of repeal by February 22. Archbishop Secker urged the bishops' bench in the House of Lords to vote for repeal, hopeful of resuming his crusade for an American episcopate once the colonies' antistamping fever had broken. A majority of nobles and bishops in the House of Lords passed the repeal bill on March 11; on March 18, King George III approved it, to the huzzahs of the London multitudes. In a happy resolution of the Whig dilemma, America used successfully political and economic pressure rather than force to avert tyranny, holding fast to its liberty without renouncing order and resorting to bloodshed.[39]

America's British friends exulted in this stunning reversal of fortune. Many attributed repeal to the eloquence of William Pitt. On March 18, a jubilant Hollis wrote in his diary: "Englishmen, Scottishmen, Irishmen, Colonists, Brethren, rejoice in the wisdom, fortitude, of *one* man, which have saved you from civil war and your enemies!" Another English propagator of Whig revolution principles, Rev. Michaijah Towgood, wrote Mayhew on April 6, congratulating him on repeal, which he attributed to the Americans' unflagging spirit of resistance to tyranny. He hypothesized that "the Reluctance you have shown to have the *Episcopal* Bit put into your Mouth, may have hasten'd your being saddled with that disagreeable Tax." The British government plot to reduce the colonists to obedience with bishops and taxes having been thwarted, Towgood imagined great things for the future of America. "I think, we see a flourishing & great Empire rising up on your Continent," he ecstatically wrote, "where civil & religious Liberty will be better understood & more fully enjoyed than [where] it hath been on this Side [of the Atlantic].—*You must increase, but we must decrease*."[40]

Ahead of letters to Mayhew from Towgood and Hollis, news of repeal reached Boston by one of John Hancock's ships in the earliest hours of May 17. Having narrowly averted war with the most powerful nation in Europe, deliriously joyful Bostonians ignited the sky with fireworks and bloodied the streets with rum. Six days later, in a sermon called *The Snare Broken*, Mayhew gave thanks to God, king, and Pitt for the deliverance of America from catastrophe. Having shared their gloomy apprehension of the consequences of the Stamp Act, the pastor told his congregation, "I now partake no less in your common joy, on account of the REPEAL of that act; whereby these colonies are emancipated from a slavish, inglorious bondage; are re-instated in the enjoyment of their ancient rights and privileges, and a foundation is laid for lasting harmony between Great Britain and them, to their mutual advantage." As pastor of the West Church and a celebrated spokesman for the cause of American liberty, Mayhew used this opportunity to present New Englanders' understanding of their rights and reflect on the Stamp Act's danger to those rights.[41]

He began by outlining his basic premises, the Whig revolution principles that most New Englanders now considered self-evident. Speaking for the people, he took it "for granted" that, as "free-born" men, "we have a natural right to *our own*, till we have freely consented to part with it, either in person, or by those whom we have appointed to represent and to act for us." He averred, "this natural right is declared, affirmed and secured to us, as we are British subjects, by Magna Charta; all acts contrary to which, are said to be *ipso facto* null and void: And, that this natural, constitutional right has been further confirmed to most of the plantations by particular subsequent royal charters." He saw British and colonial law as confirming and securing the natural rights of man and maintained the unity of the colonists' natural, British, and charter rights. Mayhew asserted the rights of the people not to be taxed without consent or tried without juries as "of the utmost importance, being essential to liberty." The colonies were correct to petition Parliament for repeal of the Stamp Act, which invaded both of these rights, "tending directly to reduce us to a state of slavery." This reiteration of his premises in *The Snare Broken* was one of the most succinct statements of the Real Whig political philosophy that Mayhew, more than any other colonial clergyman, had established as the popular consensus in New England over the preceding nineteen years.[42]

Although Mayhew believed the colonists fully justified in opposing the Stamp Act, he was—like the British Whig philosophers before him—less clear and confident about the proper means of resisting an unjust law. In *The Snare Broken*, the pastor opposed "any methods of opposition to that measure, on the part of the colonies, besides those of humble petitioning." In a final attempt to clear himself of the charge of inciting the attack on Hutchinson's house on August 26 of the previous year, Mayhew said: "I take for granted, that we are all perfectly agreed in condemning the riotous and felonious proceedings of certain *men of Belial*, as they have been justly called, who had the effrontery to cloke their rapacious violences with the pretext of zeal for liberty." He offered the mob no credit for advancing repeal by intimidating stamp distributors like Andrew Oliver. Mayhew attributed repeal to the nonimportation of British goods by American merchants, the eloquence of William Pitt, and the rational interestedness of king and Parliament. He insisted that corrupt Tory ministers—perhaps in the pay of France and the Stuart Pretender—had duped George III and the Parliament into passing the bill, and he hoped they would be duly punished. Because reason and nonviolent measures prevailed against corruption and duplicity, Mayhew and the people of New England were spared the terrible choice of either submitting to "slavery" or resisting Britain by force of arms.[43]

While Mayhew never made it clear whether the Stamp Act would have warranted armed resistance, he made it abundantly clear that "our late apprehensions, and universal consternation, on account of ourselves and posterity, were far, very far indeed, from being groundless." The colonists' fear of tyranny was not exaggerated or paranoiac. Stamp tax revenue, he insisted, would have made Crown-appointed officers independent of pay by colonial legislatures, thereby rendering them unaccountable to the people's will. The tax could also have been used to fund a standing peacetime army for awing the colonists "into an implicit obedience to ministerial measures" and to "maintain a standing army of bishops."[44] While the pastor did not think that all of these concerns had equal weight, he insisted that the colonists were correct to characterize parliamentary taxation as enslavement. Mayhew maintained:

For *They*, as we generally suppose, are really slaves to all intents and purposes, who are obliged to labor and toil only for the benefit of others; or, which comes to the same thing, the fruit of whose labour and industry may be *lawfully* taken from them without their consent, and they justly punished if they refuse to surrender it on demand, or apply it other purposes than those, which their masters, of their mere grace and pleasure, see fit to allow.[45]

Reaffirming the arguments of his notorious sermon of August 25, 1765, he said that it makes no difference to a people whether they are taxed "by a *single* person, under the title of an absolute Monarch" or "by a far-distant legislature consisting of *many* persons, in which they are not represented." Liberty means living by one's own private judgment, under laws to which one has consented, and slavery means living by the arbitrary judgment of an unaccountable master, even if one's master is "confessedly the most humane and generous in the world."[46]

New England having broken free of its snare and escaped enslavement, Mayhew assumed the pastoral role of peacemaker, urging all to forgive not only Britain for its mistake but also one another for the strife excited by partisan differences. He spoke from the bitter personal experience of his anti–Stamp Act sermon on August 25 and his anti-riot sermon on September 1 in alluding to how, at the height of the Stamp Act Crisis, "it was hardly safe for any man to speak his thoughts on the times, unless he could patiently bear to lie under the imputation of being a coward, an incendiary, rebel, or enemy to his country; or to have some other odium cast upon him." At the height of the crisis, the courts were closed and the government at war with itself, producing a "state of general disorder, approaching so near to anarchy," that some wicked men "took an opportunity to gratify their private resentments, and to get money in an earlier and more expeditious way than that of labor;

committing abominable excesses and outrages on the persons or property of others." A friend to liberty and not anarchy, to individual rights and not mob rule, Mayhew lamented this abandonment of "religion, virtue and good order." Just as Massachusetts "had the honor to lead in a spirited, tho' decent and respectful application for the redress of our late grievances," so the people "should now be ambitious to have the honor of leading in a prudent, temperate, wise behavior, in consequence of the success." He urged Bostonians to make peace with one another and to return to the ordinary course of business.[47]

For such statements, scholar Alan Heimert characterized Mayhew in *Religion and the American Mind* as an elite champion of "hierarchy and subordination" who considered himself superior to the people, hated the Sons of Liberty more than the Stamp Act, and was "phlegmatic and indifferent" toward British tyranny.[48] Mayhew's denunciation of the Hutchinson mobbing and his pleas for reconciliation earned him similar accusations in his own time. Against the specious smear of being a crypto-Tory, he said:

Let none suspect that, because I thus urge the duty of cultivating a close harmony with our mother-country, and a dutiful submission to the King and Parliament, our chief grievances being redressed, I mean to disswade people from having a just concern for their own rights, or legal, constitutional privileges. History, one may presume to say, affords no example of any nation, country or people long free, who did not take some care of themselves; and endeavour to guard and secure their own liberties. Power is of a grasping, encroaching nature. . . . Power aims at extending itself, and operating according to mere will, where-ever it meets with no balance, check, controul or opposition of any kind. For which reason it will always be necessary, as was said before, for those who would preserve and perpetuate their liberties, to guard them with a wakeful attention; and in all righteous, just and prudent ways, to oppose the first encroachments on them. "Obsta principiis." After a while it will be too late.[49]

Despite the chaos that opposition to the Stamp Act Crisis had unleashed, Mayhew never deserted the heartfelt commitment to individual liberty, popular self-government, and the Whig revolution principles he had displayed in his political sermons for nineteen years.

In a personal aside, the forty-five-year-old minister reflected upon the passion for liberty that ran like a golden thread throughout his life. "I would not, I cannot now, and tho' past middle age, relinquish the fair object of my youthful affections, LIBERTY," he sighed, "whose charms, instead of decaying with time in my eyes, have daily captivated me more and more."[50] Repeal of the Stamp Act brought the goddess Liberty back to American soil, inspiring Mayhew to offer a classical apostrophe to his life's greatest love. He wrote:

> Once more then, Hail! celestial Maid, the daughter of God, and, excepting his Son, the first-born of heaven; Welcome to these shores again; welcome to every expanding heart! Long mayest thou reside amongst us, the delight of the wise, good and brave; the protectress of innocence from wrongs and oppression, the patroness of learning, arts, eloquence, virtue, rational loyalty, religion! And if any miserable people on the continent or isles of Europe . . . be driven, in their extremity, to seek a safe retreat from slavery in some far-distant climate; let them find, O let them find one in America under thy brooding, sacred wings; where our oppressed fathers once found it, and we now enjoy it, by the favor of Him, whose service is the most glorious freedom![51]

In Mayhew's British Enlightenment worldview, liberty was to be cherished because it makes rationality, virtue, religion, science, wealth, happiness, and every other value possible. For him, to lose liberty was to lose everything for which life was worth living.

He loved America—and New England, in particular—as an asylum for freedom-loving people everywhere. For all of his pleas for peace and reconciliation, Mayhew left his congregation and readers with a reaffirmation of the duty to remain vigilant against abuses of power by their government. He expressed his hope to Americans that "they will never lose a just sense of liberty, or what they may reasonably expect from the mother-country." Mayhew added:

> And if ever there should be occasion, as I sincerely hope and pray there may not, their late experience and success will teach them how to act, in order to obtain the redress of grievances; I mean, by joint, manly and spirited, but yet respectful and loyal petitioning. Setting aside some excesses and outrages, which all sober men join in condemning, I believe history affords few examples of a more general, generous and just sense of liberty in any country, than has appeared in America within the year past.[52]

He wished that Americans would never have to contemplate the option of armed resistance to royal authority. The pastor remarked:

My immediate aim in what I now say, being only to recommend industry, good order and harmony, I will not meddle with the thorny question, whether, or how far, it may be justifiable for private men, at certain extraordinary conjunctures, to take the administration of government in some respects into their own hands. Self-preservation being a great and primary law of nature, and to be considered as antecedent to all civil laws and institutions, which are subordinate and subservient to the other; the right of so doing, in some circumstances, cannot well be denied. But certainly, there is no plausible pretence for such a conduct among us now.[53]

Real Whig political philosophy was, as historian Pauline Maier put it, an "ideology of resistance and restraint." At what point the threat of tyranny warrants violent resistance, and how to resist it without unleashing anarchy: this was the Whig dilemma. Mayhew did not solve it. Thanks to the peaceful repeal of the Stamp Act, he never had to.[54]

While lying in his bed at sunrise on June 8, 1766, Mayhew had an idea. He was thinking about the ecclesiastical council in Rutland, Massachusetts, for which he would depart the following morning. Congregational ministers had an old practice of coordinating their responses to common religious problems, like the one waiting for him in Rutland, by correspondence. It then occurred to Mayhew that the American colonists could coordinate responses to common political problems by creating a similar system of correspondence. New England's *communion of churches* suggested to him the advantage of "a *communion of colonies.*"[55]

That day, he wrote a letter to his old college friend, James Otis, Jr., leader of the Whig opposition party in the Massachusetts House of Representatives. Mayhew proposed to Otis that the House send "circular congratulatory letters" to the lower houses of the other colonial legislatures in the wake of the repeal of the Stamp Act. The purpose of such correspondence would be "to cement & perpetuate union among ourselves, by all practicable & laudable methods." The Stamp Act Congress of the preceding autumn had laid the foundation for such a political union of the American colonies; Mayhew encouraged Otis to build upon that foundation without delay. "Cultivating a good understanding and hearty friendship between these Colonies, and their several Houses of Assembly," he wrote, "appear to me to be so necessary a part of prudence & good policy, all things considered, that no favorable opportunity for that Purpose ought to be omitted." Mayhew had supported a colonial union twelve years before, during the darkest days of the French and Indian War, when it was under consideration by the Albany Congress. The Stamp Act Crisis returned Mayhew's thoughts to that vision with a new urgency.[56]

After repeal of the Stamp Act, most colonists, even in radicalized New England, rejoiced that their liberty was once again safe under the British constitution and Hanoverian rule. The West Church reverend, however, recognized that power was always a menace to liberty unless kept under constitutional limits, and he recommended a coordinated defense against future British invasions of American rights. On the use of correspondence as the framework for union, Mayhew wrote:

> Pursuing this track, and never losing sight of it, may be of the utmost importance to the colonies on some future occasions; perhaps the only means of perpetuating their liberties; for what may be hereafter we cannot tell, how favourable soever present appearances may be. It is not safe for the colonies to sleep[,] since they will probably always have some *watchful* enemies in Britain; & if they should be such children as to do so, I hope there are at least some persons too much of men, & friends to them, to rock the cradle, or sing lullabies to them.[57]

Mayhew looked to Otis as one person who was too much of a man to let the people sink into complacency.

Five days earlier, in his address to the Massachusetts General Court, Governor Bernard proposed revoking the right of the House of Representatives to nominate candidates to the Massachusetts Provincial Council and instead stocking it with royal appointees. On behalf of the House, Samuel Adams and James Otis reproached the governor for his high-handed treatment of the people's representatives. Outraged at Bernard for "so open & flagrant an attack upon our charter rights & priviledges," Mayhew told Otis that his "spirited" response to the governor was appropriate, "unless we could be content to have an absolute & uncontroulable instead of a limited, Constitutional G[overno]r." In the spirit of *obsta principiis*, he applauded Otis's "firmness, in adhering to our rights, in opposition to all encroachments."[58]

Mayhew hastened to write Otis about his idea before departing for Rutland on June 9, for fear that the indignant governor might prorogue or dissolve the House before the pastor's return. Otis apparently took no action on the suggestion at the time. In November 1772, Samuel Adams proposed that the Boston Town Meeting create a committee of correspondence to coordinate the defense of charter rights with the other towns of Massachusetts. In time, a system of committees of correspondence developed also among the lower houses of several colonies, unifying them in a common defense of American liberty, as the West Church minister had suggested. It is unknown whether Otis ever discussed Mayhew's proposal with Adams. Otis's sister, Mercy Otis Warren, made a point of reprinting the pastor's letter in her *History of the American Revolution*, and she noted that the idea for committees of correspondence "had been contemplated by several gentlemen, a year or two before it took place; among others, by the learned and excellent doctor Jonathan Mayhew of Boston."[59]

Having always preached that eternal vigilance is the price of liberty, Mayhew conceived committees of correspondence as a system, operated by responsible gentleman-politicians within the existing constitutional order, for detecting and arresting tyranny at its first appearance, thereby averting the need for mob violence and armed resistance. It was his response to the Whig dilemma, his last, best effort to save Americans from having to wrestle again with the frightful prospect of civil war. Whether or not the pastor may be rightly credited with originating the idea that Samuel Adams later implemented to so great effect, Mayhew's letter to Otis belies the criticism of modern scholar Alan Heimert, who questioned the depth and sincerity of Mayhew's attachment to popular self-government after the Hutchinson Riot. The Boston divine's love of liberty, and his anxiety for its defense against British tyranny, was unflagging, even in the final weeks of his life. "To a good man, all time is holy enough, and none too holy, to do good, or to think upon it." That was the first sentence of Mayhew's letter to Otis, the last letter he would ever write. This good man could not have known then just how little time he had remaining.[60]

Conclusion

Having written his letter to James Otis on June 8, 1766, Jonathan Mayhew proceeded to Rutland, New Hampshire, for an ecclesiastical council arbitrating the disputed dismissal of the town's Congregational minister, Thomas Frink. Mayhew recorded the proceedings. The ministers completed their work on June 18, and Mayhew made the sixty-mile trip back home to Boston. Exhausted by the work and the journey, he experienced a severe headache over the days following his return but received no medical attention. On June 24, the pastor suffered a stroke that paralyzed the right half of his body. Six days later, Thomas Hollis received a letter from his American friend, shipped out from Boston on May 30. Mayhew wrote the note in haste to accompany copies of his freshly printed sermon on repeal of the Stamp Act, *The Snare Broken*. He dedicated the work to William Pitt, "who was so strenuous an Assertor, and able Vindicator of the oppressed Liberties of America." Mayhew asked Hollis to deliver a copy of the sermon to the former British prime minister, which he faithfully did. The West Church pastor ended his letter: "It is long since I heard from you." Hollis would not hear from him again.[1]

In the days following his stroke, Mayhew slipped into a coma. According to tradition, Dr. Samuel Cooper, a moderate Calvinist, visited his old friend on his deathbed and asked if Mayhew wished to recant any of his heterodox opinions before meeting his Maker. "My integrity I hold fast," the dying man replied, "and will not let it go." This account of Mayhew's last words is likely apocryphal, considering Cooper's charitable nature and Andrew Eliot's later characterization of the stricken pastor. Dr. Eliot informed Hollis, "I saw him often in his sickness, but he never appeared to have the clear exercise of reason. The distemper attacked him with such violence, that I could not wish for his life, of which some entertained hopes. He would have been only the *shadow* of Dr. Mayhew."[2]

On Wednesday, July 9, death padded in on soft paws to bay at the foot of his bed. "This morning at five of Clock," Boston merchant John Rowe recorded in his diary, "the Rev. Dr. Mayhew died much lamented by Great Numbers of people." Two days later, the pastor's flock assembled in the West Church, where Dr. Charles Chauncy gave a prayer for the dead, the first ever given in one of New England's Congregational meetinghouses. Although the temperature that Friday afternoon rose to ninety degrees, Bostonians thronged to pay their last respects. Marching in pairs, 114 gentlemen of Mayhew's congregation led the train. Following behind Mayhew's coffin were six ministers: Nathaniel Appleton, Ebenezer Gay, Charles Chauncy, Andrew Eliot, Ebenezer Pemberton, and Samuel Cooper. Next came the ladies of the congregation, and then the other clergy and gentry of the town, following in fifty-seven carriages and sixteen coaches and chariots.[3]

Up to that moment, it was the longest funeral procession in Boston's history and a solemn occasion by all accounts. John Winthrop IV, the Hollis Professor of Mathematics and Natural Philosophy at Harvard College, observed that his former student's funeral was attended "by all ranks of people of every denomination," "a striking instance of that universal esteem he justly merited, and that charity he was remarkable for when alive, being in all respects worthy so great and benevolent a character." The melancholy nature of the moment seized strangers as well as friends. "Being a Spectator of the solemn Funeral of the late worthy and reverend Dr. JONATHAN MAYHEW," an anonymous teenager wrote the *Massachusetts Gazette*, he "was so sensibly touched with the Loss of this great Friend to civil and religious Liberty" that he lamented in verse: "MAYHEW is gone! ah weep! Nov Anglia, weep! / Thy Friend, thy Champion, and thy dear Delight / Now lives no more!" Coming three months before his forty-sixth birthday, the pastor's death was sudden and unexpected, dealing a great shock to a town that had endured so many shocks over the preceding year. Mayhew's final resting place went unmarked. His remains were most likely deposited at the burying ground near the old city granary, the Congregational cemetery nearest his church. If so, then Mayhew was joined in the years to come by many of his friends, such as James Otis, Paul Revere, Edmund Quincy, Josiah Quincy, Samuel Quincy, and Robert Treat Paine.[4]

The eulogies for Mayhew were not without criticism, but a recurring theme was New England's grateful admiration for his stubborn defense of liberty. On July 13, Charles Chauncy manned the West Church's vacant pulpit to preach a funeral discourse that Sabbath day. He praised Mayhew as "eminently a friend to liberty both civil and religious," who asserted "the liberty of thinking for himself," opposed "the attempts of those who would make slaves either of men's souls or bodies," cherished New England for its God-given freedom, and "vigorously laid himself out in opposing any designs that might have been formed to subvert it." In his *Massachusetts Gazette* obituary of Mayhew, Professor Winthrop hailed the late clergyman for "his declared enmity to every priestly usurpation of authority over the consciences of men," "his strength of mind, integrity of soul, and unconquerable resolution," his "endearing character [as] a steady and able advocate for religious and civil liberty," his service to "this continent [as] a resolute and strong defender of its religious independency" and to "mankind [as] a bold and nervous assertor of their rights." Dr. Benjamin Church—a physician, poet, and Whig now best remembered for his treason to the Revolution—heaped laurels on "god-like *Mayhew*" in an anonymous elegy. "His earliest Joy was *Liberty*, for this, / His Soul to Labours, Watchings, Prayers he gave," the poet declaimed, "Freedom was all his Ardor, all his Bliss, / His Heart turn'd Rebel at that Tho't, a Slave." After receiving news of his dear friend's demise, Thomas Hollis submitted to the London newspapers this epitaph: "Readers, pursue this plan, the good of North-America, and of Mankind; live, like him, to great ends; nor dread, from the excess of it, his exit." He commissioned an engraved print of Mayhew's image that saluted him as "an Assertor of the Civil and Religious Liberties of His Country and Mankind, who, Overplied by Public Energies, Died of a Nervous Fever."[5]

Hollis died in 1774, and John Adams emerged as the keeper of Mayhew's flame. Like Hollis, Adams believed that the minister's unrelenting exertions in fighting tyranny, as well as the abuse he received from the Tory press, contributed to his premature death. "That Art and Power which has destroyed a Thatcher, a Mayhew, an Otis," he wrote in his diary in February 1772, "may destroy the Health and the Lives of these Gentlemen, but can never subdue their Principles or their Spirit." In 1774, when he considered writing a history of the constitutional crisis between Britain and the colonies, Adams listed twenty-three persons whom he would need to describe, naming Mayhew the eighteenth of these historic figures, after Samuel Adams and before John Hancock.[6] On the eve of the battles of Lexington and Concord, Adams memorialized the Boston pastor during his famous newspaper debate with Massachusetts Tory Daniel Leonard. Adams wrote:

Dr. Mayhew was a Whig of the first magnitude, a clergyman equalled by very few of any denomination in piety, virtue, genius, or learning, whose works will maintain his character as long as New-England shall be free, integrity esteemed, or wit, spirit, humour, reason, and knowledge admired. How was he treated from the press? Did not the Reverend Tories, who were pleased to write against him, the Missionaries of Defamation, as well as Bigotry and passive obedience, in their pamphlets and newspapers, bespatter him all over with their filth? With equal falsehood and malice charge him with every thing evil?[7]

Adams heard Mayhew speak from the pulpit on many occasions and had been influenced by Mayhew's sermons and pamphlets since his adolescence. But it was only a year before the minister's death, at the Dudleian Lecture in May 1765, that Adams first made his acquaintance, "which was likely to become a lasting and intimate Friendship." By securing Mayhew's place in history, Adams proved himself the doctor's shortest known but most devoted friend.[8]

While the present book was inspired by John Adams's two-century-old view of the Revolution and Mayhew's importance to it, its conclusions are the result of archival research in the documentary record, and its claims have been informed by academic debates of historians and political theorists over the last century. This study contends that Mayhew's political thought and activism should be understood primarily in light of his rationalism. The principle that all humans must think for themselves and be free to act on their judgment was fundamental for Mayhew. Commitment to his own independent thinking, reinforced by his Harvard education, set him at odds with religious and political authority and attracted him to intellectual traditions—heterodox Protestantism, classical moral philosophy, natural rights philosophy, Real Whig political thought—that appeared to affirm the epistemological primacy of reason, the moral primacy of happiness, and the political primacy of individual rights. Mayhew's rationalist views on basic philosophic and theological issues drew him to radically individualistic conclusions regarding the nature and purpose of government.

Mayhew embraced the British Whig "revolution principles" of individual natural rights, the sovereignty of the people, government by consent, limited and delegated powers, the conditionality of allegiance, and the right of resistance, on which Locke, Hoadly, and the Real Whigs believed Britain's Revolution Settlement had been grounded. Consequently, the pastor could consider himself a conservative defender of the British Constitution and the Hanoverian monarchy while invoking revolutionary ideas expounded by English commonwealthmen like Sidney and Milton. These revolution principles, in turn, inspired Mayhew to promote doggedly the incomparable value of individual liberty, informing the New England public of the nature of their rights and the proper limits of political power. Mayhew infused young Yankee gentlemen like Adams, Robert Treat Paine, Paul Revere, and the Quincy brothers with the very principles on which they would act during the Imperial Crisis and the Revolutionary War. So far from blinding him with irrational fears, Real Whig ideology enabled the Boston divine to discern the long-term consequences of British policies, recognizing threats to liberty in the bud. Preaching opposition to tyranny at its first beginnings, he warned the people of New England of machinations against their civil and religious liberty formed within Parliament, the Massachusetts royal government, and the Church of England on both sides of the Atlantic. In turn, the pastor's involvement in practical politics prompted him to wrestle with the great question bedeviling colonial Whigs: whether Britain could be trusted with America's liberty and how a subject could oppose an abusive government without unleashing still greater abuses.

Father of Liberty has sought to understand Mayhew's political thought and activism in the context of the events of his own personal experiences and intellectual development, as well as the political events and cultural developments of the Hanoverian British Empire and eighteenth-century New England, from the rise of the Enlightenment and the First Great Awakening to the French and Indian War and the Imperial Crisis. Drawing upon the insights of such scholars as Bailyn, Maier, Zuckert, and Clark, it has also offered analysis of Mayhew's politics by reference to the religious and political ideas of his Anglo-American Atlantic world, particularly New England's heterodox Congregationalism and Britain's Protestant dissent, the "natural religion" of British Enlightenment rationalism, and Real Whig political ideology.

Although Mayhew considered himself a conservative defender of Britain's Revolution Settlement and champion of New England's free institutions, this study has emphasized his radicalism in theology and politics. Another scholar examining the same materials might instead emphasize the continuities of Mayhew's political and religious thought with those of his Calvinist ancestors and his colleagues in the Congregational clergy. With the 250th anniversary of Mayhew's death having passed and the 300th anniversary of his death at hand, perhaps *Father of Liberty* will encourage or provoke further scholarly investigation of his political thought and activism, as well as new research into his theology, moral philosophy, biography, and family life. Although noted frequently in the historical scholarship of the last sixty years, Mayhew has not yet received the academic attention warranted by the extent of his contributions to early American thought and culture. Moreover he has all but entirely disappeared from the collective memory of the general public over the last century. In time, the American people—indeed, all men and women who cherish their own right to think and live for themselves—would do well to recover the principles, character, and example of Jonathan Mayhew. It is upon the spirit of such men that our freedom depends.

NOTES

PREFACE

1. John Adams, *The Works of John Adams*, vol. 10, ed. Charles Francis Adams (Boston: Little and Brown, 1856), 287–288.

INTRODUCTION

1. *Boston Gazette, and The Country Journal* (September 2 and 3, 1765); *Boston Gazette, and The Country Journal* (September 3, 1765); Josiah Quincy, Jr., *Reports of Cases Argued and Adjudged in the Superior Court of Judicature of the Province of Massachusetts Bay between 1761 and 1772* (Boston: Little and Brown 1865), 168–173; Bernard Bailyn, "Religion and Revolution: Three Biographical Studies," *Perspectives in American History*, vol. 4 (1970): 116–117; Bailyn, *The Ordeal of Thomas Hutchinson* (Cambridge, Mass.: Harvard University Press, 1973), 35–38; for Hutchinson's private reasons for blaming Mayhew for incitement of the riot, see the fourth chapter of this work.
2. Jonathan Mayhew Papers, Bortmann Collection, Boston University, Folder No. 91; Mayhew has been popularly credited with coining "no taxation without representation" or "taxation without representation is tyranny," but this passage from the August 25 sermon is the closest Mayhew came to saying it; for an example of this error, see Matthew Stewart, *Nature's God: The Heretical Origins of the American Republic* (New York: W. W. Norton, 2014), 60.
3. For the argument that Mayhew's sermon did not incite the Hutchinson Riot, and for an alternative explanation of the riot's origins, see J. Patrick Mullins, "The Sermon That Didn't Start the Revolution: Jonathan Mayhew's Role in the Boston Stamp Act Riots," in *Community without Consent: New Perspectives on the Stamp Act*, ed. Zachary McLeod Hutchins (Hanover, N.H.: Dartmouth College Press, 2016), 3–35; Jonathan Mayhew, "Letter of Rev. Jonathan Mayhew to Richard Clarke, 1765," *The New England Historical and Genealogical Register* (Boston: New England Historic Genealogical Society, 1892): 15–19; Charles W. Akers, *Called unto Liberty: A Life of Jonathan Mayhew, 1720–1766* (Cambridge, Mass.: Harvard University Press, 1964), 205, 210.
4. Lester J. Cappon, ed., *The Adams-Jefferson Letters: The Complete Correspondence between Thomas Jefferson and Abigail and John Adams* (Chapel Hill: University of North Carolina Press, 1999), 527; John Adams, *The Works of John Adams*, vol. 10, ed. Charles Francis Adams (Boston: Little and Brown, 1856), 187–188, 191, 271–272, 301; Robert Treat Paine quoted in John Wingate Thornton, *The Pulpit of the American Revolution, or The Political Sermons of the Period of 1776* (Boston: Gould and Lincoln, 1860), 43
5. Carl Bridenbaugh, *Mitre and Sceptre: Transatlantic Faiths, Ideas, Personalities, and Politics, 1689–1775* (New York: Oxford University Press, 1962), 242.

6. Adams, *Works*, vol. 10, 287–288; John Adams, *Diary and Autobiography of John Adams*, vol. 3, ed. L. H. Butterfield (Cambridge, Mass.: Harvard University Press, 1961), 286.
7. Jonathan Mayhew, *Remarks on an Anonymous Tract, Entitled an Answer to Dr. Mayhew's Observations on the Charter and Conduct of the Society for the Propagation of the Gospel in Foreign Parts, Being a Second Defence of the Said Observations* (Boston: Richard and Samuel Draper, Edes and Gill, and Thomas and John Fleet, 1764), 63.
8. Thomas Jefferson, *Thomas Jefferson: Writings*, ed. Merrill D. Peterson (New York: Library of America, 1984), 1500–1501.
9. Douglas Adair and John A. Schutz, eds., *Peter Oliver's Origin and Progress of the American Revolution: A Tory View* (San Marino, CA: Huntington Library, 1961), 43–44.
10. Alden Bradford, *Memoir of the Life and Writings of Rev. Jonathan Mayhew, D.D.* (Boston: Little, 1838); Cyrus Bartol, *The West Church and Its Ministers: The Fiftieth Anniversary of the Ordination of Charles Lowell, D.D.* (Boston: Crosby, Nicholas, 1856), 81–132; Theodore Parker quoted in John Weiss, *Life and Correspondence of Theodore Parker*, 2 vols. (New York: D. Appleton and Company, 1864), 1: 82; I must thank Professor Paul Teed for bringing Theodore Parker's opinion of Jonathan Mayhew to my attention; Thornton, *Pulpit of the American Revolution*, 40–104; Frank Moore, ed., *The Patriot Preachers of the American Revolution, with Biographical Sketches* (New York: Charles T. Evans, 1862), 7–48; Samuel A. Eliot, *Heralds of a Liberal Faith, Volume One: The Prophets* (Boston: American Unitarian Association, 1910), 34–48, esp. 40–41.
11. Alice M. Baldwin, *The New England Clergy and the American Revolution* (Durham, N.C.: Duke University Press, 1928), xi–xiii, 44–45, 90–92, 168–172; for other, more delimited contributions to the Whig argument for the intellectual influence of the clergy on the Revolution, see Arthur Lee Cross, *The Anglican Episcopate and the American Colonies* (London: Longmans, Green, 1902); see also C. H. Van Tyne, "Influence of the Clergy, and of Religious and Sectarian Forces, on the American Revolution," *American Historical Review* (October 1913): 44–64.
12. For notable representatives of the Progressive interpretation of the American Revolutionary era, consider Carl L. Becker, *The History of Political Parties in the Province of New York, 1760–1776* (Madison: University of Wisconsin Press, 1908); Charles A. Beard, *An Economic Interpretation of the Constitution of the United States* (New York: Macmillan, 1913); Arthur Meier Schlesinger, *The Colonial Merchants and the American Revolution, 1763–1776* (New York: Columbia University Press, 1917); and J. Franklin Jameson, *The American Revolution Considered as a Social Movement* (Princeton, N.J.: Princeton University Press, 1926); for examples of the Progressive "propaganda" analysis of Revolutionary political writing, see John C. Miller, *Sam Adams: Pioneer in Propaganda* (Boston: Little, Brown, 1936);

see also Philip Davidson, *Propaganda and the American Revolution, 1763–1783* (Chapel Hill: University of North Carolina Press, 1941).
13. Clinton Rossiter, *Seedtime of the Republic: The Origins of the American Tradition of Political Liberty* (New York: Harcourt, Brace, 1953), 1–11, 19–35, 37–43, 149, 228, 234, 243–246; for another neo-Whig work taking note of Mayhew's contribution to American political culture, see Max Savelle, *Seeds of Liberty: The Genesis of the American Mind* (New York: A. A. Knopf, 1948), 309–311; for a variation upon Baldwin's argument that liberal political ideas were communicated from the seventeenth century to the Revolution by a chain of Whig intellectuals, see Caroline Robbins, *The 18th Century Commonwealthman* (Indianapolis: Liberty Fund, 2004 [1959]); for the classic neo-Whig statement of the thesis that colonial Americans were naturally inclined to John Locke's natural rights philosophy by their New World circumstances, see Louis B. Hartz, *The Liberal Tradition in America: An Interpretation of American Political Thought since the Revolution* (San Diego, Calif.: Harcourt, Brace, 1991 [1952]), 3–13, 19, 52–53, 58–62.
14. Akers, *Called unto Liberty*, 2.
15. Bridenbaugh, *Mitre and Sceptre*, xi–xiv, 20, 56–59, 99–103, 174–177, 193, 211–220, 225–229, 246–259, 323, 335–338, 355; Trevor Colbourn, *The Lamp of Experience: Whig History and the Intellectual Origins of the American Revolution* (Indianapolis: Liberty Fund, 1998 [1965]), 4–5, 72–79, 81–82, 227, 229–232, 333–336.
16. Bernard Bailyn, ed., *Pamphlets of the American Revolution, 1750–1776, Volume I, 1750–1765* (Cambridge, Mass.: Harvard University Press, 1965), iv–x, 204, 209–211; Bailyn, *The Ideological Origins of the American Revolution* (Cambridge, Mass.: Harvard University Press, 1992 [1967]); for his analysis of Mayhew's role in the Boston Stamp Act riots, see Bailyn, "Religion and Revolution," 111–139; J. G. A. Pocock, *The Machiavellian Moment: Florentine Political Thought and the Atlantic Republican Tradition* (Princeton, N.J.: Princeton University Press, 1975), esp. Chapter 15; Gordon S. Wood, "Rhetoric and Reality in the American Revolution," *William and Mary Quarterly* (January 1966): 4–32; Gordon S. Wood, *The Creation of the American Republic, 1776–1787* (Chapel Hill: University of North Carolina Press, 1969); for a republican-revisionist study in which Mayhew figures prominently, see Pauline Maier, *From Resistance to Revolution: Colonial Radicals and the Development of American Opposition to Britain, 1765–1776* (New York: Random House, 1972), 9–13, 28, 32, 60, 146, 229, 235, 271.
17. Alan Heimert, *Religion and the American Mind: From the Great Awakening to the Revolution*. (Cambridge, Mass.: Harvard University Press, 1966), esp. 239–293; Edmund S. Morgan, "Review of Alan Heimert's *Religion and the American Mind*," *William and Mary Quarterly* (July 1967): 454–459.
18. Nathan O. Hatch, *The Sacred Cause of Liberty: Republican Thought and the Millennium in Revolutionary New England* (New Haven, Conn.: Yale University Press, 1977), 17, 38, 46, 82–83; Patricia U. Bonomi, *Under the Cope of Heaven: Reli-*

gion, Society and Politics in Colonial America (New York: Oxford University Press, 1986), 186, 188, 196–209, 216; Harry S. Stout, *The New England Soul: Preaching and Religious Culture in Colonial New England* (New York: Oxford University Press, 1986), 240–244, 282–285.

19. J. C. D. Clark, *The Language of Liberty, 1660–1832: Political Discourse and Social Dynamics in the Anglo-American World* (Cambridge: Cambridge University Press, 1994), 14–16, 30–31, 36–40, 43–45, 158–169, 296–316, 364–370; see also Clark, *English Society, 1660–1832: Ideology, Social Structure, and Political Practice during the Ancien Regime* (Cambridge: Cambridge University Press, 2000 [1985]), esp. Chapters 4 and 5; James E. Bradley, *Religion, Revolution, and English Radicalism: Nonconformity in Eighteenth-Century Politics and Society* (Cambridge: Cambridge University Press, 1990); Bradley, "The Religious Origins of Radical Politics in England, Scotland, and Ireland, 1662–1800," in *Religion and Politics in Enlightenment Europe*, ed. James E. Bradley and Dale K. Van Kley (Notre Dame, Ind.: University of Notre Dame Press, 2001), 188–190, 192–194, 234–235; for a thoughtful elaboration upon Clark's proposition that political radicalism follows from anti-Trinitarianism, see A. M. C. Waterman, "The Nexus between Theology and Political Doctrine in Church and Dissent," in *Enlightenment and Religion: Rational Dissent in Eighteenth-Century Britain*, ed. Knud Haakonssen (Cambridge: Cambridge University Press, 1996), 193–218.

20. For the origination of the interpretive concept "Rational Dissent," see Anthony Lincoln, *Some Political and Social Ideas of English Dissent* (Cambridge: Cambridge University Press, 1938), 30; for an introduction to the scholarship on Rational Dissent, see Haakonssen, *Enlightenment and Religion*; for a classic formulation of the Enlightenment as paradigmatically materialist, skeptical, anticlerical, and French, see Peter Gay, *The Enlightenment: The Rise of Modern Paganism* (New York: Alfred A. Knopf, 1966); for the argument that the Reformation's failure to resolve doctrinal disputes by reference to Scripture gave rise to rationalism, see Brad S. Gregory, "The Reformation Origins of the Enlightenment's God," in *God in the Enlightenment*, ed. William J. Bulman and Robert G. Ingram (Oxford: Oxford University Press, 2016), 201–214; John Corrigan, *The Prism of Piety: Catholick Congregational Clergy at the Beginning of the Enlightenment* (Oxford: Oxford University Press, 1991); for his interpretation of Mayhew and his friend Charles Chauncy in terms of Rational Dissent, see Corrigan, *The Hidden Balance: Religion and the Social Theories of Charles Chauncy and Jonathan Mayhew* (Cambridge: Cambridge University Press, 1987); for Mayhew as an example of the "New England Arminians" who represented the "moderate Enlightenment" in opposition to orthodox Calvinism and the First Great Awakening, see Henry F. May, *The Enlightenment in America* (Oxford: Oxford University Press, 1976), 56–58, 87.

21. For the contention that "sacrifice of individual interests to the greater good of the whole formed the essence of republicanism and comprehended for Americans

the idealistic goal of the Revolution," see Wood, *Creation of the American Republic*, 53–65; for a more recent presentation of the principles of the Revolution (and even Mayhew personally) as communitarian, see Barry Alan Shain, *The Myth of American Individualism: The Protestant Origins of American Political Thought* (Princeton, N.J.: Princeton University Press, 1994), esp. 168, 282, 290; Steven M. Dworetz, *The Unvarnished Doctrine: Locke, Liberalism, and the American Revolution* (Durham, N.C.: Duke University Press, 1990), 7–10, 30–36, 56, 60–61, 135–138, 150–151, 160–163, 173–183; Michael P. Zuckert, *The Natural Rights Republic: Studies in the Foundation of the American Political Tradition* (Notre Dame, Ind.: University of Notre Dame Press, 1996), 2–12, 95, 153–159, 171–172, 195–201; Thomas G. West, in "The Transformation of Protestant Theology as a Condition of the American Revolution," *Protestantism and the American Founding*, ed. Thomas S. Engeman and Michael P. Zuckert (Notre Dame, Ind.: Notre Dame University Press, 2004), 187–223; for a magisterial study demonstrating the prominence of the natural rights political philosophy in the early modern Anglophone world, see Lee Ward, *The Politics of Liberty in England and Revolutionary America* (Cambridge: Cambridge University Press, 2004); for a much-needed study of American political thought before the Revolution, demonstrating how distinctive New World conditions contributed to the popularity of natural rights philosophy with the colonists, see Craig Yirush, *Settlers, Liberty, and Empire: The Roots of Early American Political Theory, 1675–1775* (Cambridge: Cambridge University Press, 2011).

22. Gilles Kepel, *The Revenge of God: The Resurgence of Islam, Christianity, and Judaism in the Modern World*, trans. Alan Braley (University Park: Pennsylvania State University Press, 1994); for "Christian republicanism," a synthesis of Real Whig political thought with Protestantism, of which Mayhew's *Discourse Concerning Unlimited Submission* was an early representative, see Mark Noll, *America's God: From Jonathan Edwards to Abraham Lincoln* (Oxford: Oxford University Press, 2002), esp. 79–81, 138–140; for "biblical republicanism," a synthesis of classical republicanism with biblical typology, see Eran Shalev, *American Zion: The Old Testament as a Political Text from the Revolution to the Civil War* (New Haven, Conn.: Yale University Press, 2013), esp. Chapter 1; James P. Byrd, *Sacred Scripture, Sacred War: The Bible and the American Revolution* (Oxford: Oxford University Press, 2013), 1–9, 29–30, 116–129.

23. Robert A. Ferguson, *The American Enlightenment, 1750–1820* (Cambridge, Mass.: Harvard University Press, 1997), 1, 7–8, 22, 35, 42–46, 49, 55–56, 62–63, 72–73; for his fuller development of the relationship between religion and politics, in which Mayhew also figures, see Ferguson, "The Dialectic of Liberty: Law and Religion in Anglo-American Culture," *Modern Intellectual History*, vol. 1, no. 1 (2004): 27–54; Gregg L. Frazer, *The Religious Beliefs of America's Founders: Reason, Revelation, and Revolution* (Lawrence: University Press of Kansas, 2012), 6–22, 59–68, 78–81, 105–106; for John Adams's "Enlightenment rationalism," reconciled with

Protestantism by way of Mayhew's influence, see C. Bradley Thompson, *John Adams and the Spirit of Liberty* (Lawrence: University Press of Kansas, 1998), esp. Chapter 1; for the interrelation of "Biblical religion or faith and Enlightenment reason or philosophy" in American Revolutionary thought and the persistent use of biblical rhetoric by Enlightenment thinkers, see Dustin Gish and Daniel Klinghard, "The Mutual Influence of Biblical Religion and Enlightenment Reason at the American Founding," in *Resistance to Tyrants, Obedience to God: Reason, Religion, and Republicanism at the American Founding*, ed. Dustin Gish and Daniel Klinghard (Lanham, Md.: Lexington Books, 2013), Chapter 1; for the thesis that modern Western secularism was an unintended by-product of the Protestant Reformation, see Brad S. Gregory, *The Unintended Reformation: How a Religious Reformation Secularized Society* (Cambridge, Mass.: Harvard University Press, 2012).

24. James B. Bell, A *War of Religion: Dissenters, Anglicans, and the American Revolution* (Houndmills, U.K.: Palgrave McMillan, 2008), x–xiv, 67–80, 84–92, 211–221; Jonathan Clark, "The American Revolution: A War of Religion?" *History Today*, vol. 39, no. 12 (December 1989): 10–16; Clark, *Language of Liberty*.

25. T. H. Breen, *American Insurgents, American Patriots: The Revolution of the People* (New York: Hill and Wang, 2010), 241–261; Joseph S. Tiedemann, "Presbyterianism and the American Revolution in the Middle Colonies," *Church History*, vol. 74, no. 2 (June 2005): 306–344; Nancy L. Rhoden, *Revolutionary Anglicanism: The Colonial Church of England Clergy during the American Revolution* (New York: New York University Press, 1999); for an earlier study in a similar interpretive vein analyzing anti-Catholicism as an intellectual and political cause of the Revolution, see Francis D. Cogliano, *No King, No Popery: Anti-Catholicism in Revolutionary New England* (Westport, Conn.: Greenwood Press, 1995); for a modest step toward a religious account of the Revolution's southern origins (e.g., a brief overview of the Parson's Cause and other political challenges facing the Anglican Church in Virginia in the 1760s and 1770s), see James B. Bell, *Empire, Religion and Revolution in Early Virginia, 1607–1786* (Houndmills, U.K.: Palgrave Macmillan, 2013), Chapter 10.

26. Jonathan Mayhew, *The Snare Broken, a Thanksgiving-Discourse, Preached at the Desire of the West Church, in Boston, N.E., Friday May 23, 1766, Occasioned by the Repeal of the Stamp-Act* (Boston: Richard and Samuel Draper, Edes and Gill, 1766), 35.

27. Ibid., 35.

CHAPTER 1. THE RIGHT OF PRIVATE JUDGMENT

1. Robert Treat Paine, Jr., *The Works in Verse and Prose, of the Late Robert Treat Paine, Junior, Esquire, with Notes, to Which Are Prefixed, Sketches of His Life, Character and Writings* (Boston: J. Belcher, 1812), 74.

2. Robert Treat Paine, *Diaries, 1746–1756* (Reel 10 of 19), Robert Treat Paine Papers (1659–1862), Massachusetts Historical Society.
3. Charles W. Akers, *Called unto Liberty: A Life of Jonathan Mayhew, 1720–1766* (Cambridge, Mass.: Harvard University Press, 1964), 9–10; "Memoirs of Prince's Subscribers," *New England Historical and Genealogical Register* (July 1859): 248.
4. Richard W. Cogley, *John Eliot's Mission to the Indians before King Philip's War* (Cambridge, Mass.: Harvard University Press, 1999); Perry Miller, *Errand into the Wilderness* (Cambridge, Mass.: Harvard University Press, 1956); and Janice Knight, *Orthodoxies in Massachusetts: Rereading American Puritanism* (Cambridge, Mass.: Harvard University Press, 1994).
5. Experience Mayhew, *A Discourse Shewing That God Dealeth with Men as with Reasonable Creatures* (Boston: Green, 1720), 6–7, 16.
6. Ibid., 14–15, 22–26; Miller, *Errand into the Wilderness*, 72, 96–97.
7. Akers, *Called unto Liberty*, 14–16, 20–22; Jonathan Mayhew, *Remarks on an Anonymous Tract, Entitled an Answer to Dr. Mayhew's Observations on the Charter and Conduct of the Society for the Propagation of the Gospel in Foreign Parts, Being a Second Defence of the Said Observations* (Boston: Richard and Samuel Draper, Edes and Gill, and Thomas and John Fleet, 1764), 81.
8. Harry S. Stout, *The New England Soul: Preaching and Religious Culture in Colonial New England* (New York: Oxford University Press, 1986), 130–131; Clifford K. Shipton, *Sibley's Harvard Graduates, Volume 5: 1701–1712* (Boston: Massachusetts Historical Society, 1937), 271; see John Corrigan, *The Prism of Piety: Catholick Congregational Clergy at the Beginning of the Enlightenment* (Oxford: Oxford University Press, 1991).
9. Ned C. Landsman, *From Colonials to Provincials: American Thought and Culture, 1680–1760* (Ithaca, N.Y.: Cornell University Press, 1997), 66–70; Robert J. Wilson III, *The Benevolent Deity: Ebenezer Gay and the Rise of Rational Religion in New England, 1696–1787* (Philadelphia: University of Pennsylvania Press, 1984), 12–13, 16, 19–21, 65; Benjamin Rand, "Philosophical Instruction in Harvard University from 1636 to 1900," *The Harvard Graduates' Magazine* (September 1928): 36.
10. Jonathan Mayhew Papers, Bortman Collection, Boston University, Folder Nos. 8 and 13; Patricia U. Bonomi, *Under the Cope of Heaven: Religion, Society, and Politics in Colonial America* (New York: Oxford University Press, 1986), 149; Conrad Wright, *Beginnings of Unitarianism in America* (Boston: Beacon Press, 1955), 40, 64.
11. Mayhew Papers, Folder Nos. 12, 14, and 15.
12. Ibid., Folder No. 13; for an example of his return to worldliness by December 1743, see ibid., Folder No. 16.
13. Akers, *Called unto Liberty*, 32; Mayhew Papers, Folder Nos. 9 and 10.
14. Mayhew Papers, Folder No. 10; John Spurr, "Rational Religion in Restoration England," *Journal of the History of Ideas*, vol. 49, no. 4 (October–December 1988): 563–585.

15. [Richard Steele], *The Ladies' Library*, vol. 3 (London: Jacob Tonson, 1732), 2–3.
16. Isaac Watts, *Logick: or, The Right Use of Reason in the Enquiry after Truth, with a Variety of Rules to Guard against Error, in the Affairs of Religion and Human Life, as Well as in the Sciences* (London: T. Longman, T. Shewell, and J. Brackstone, 1745), 1–4; Steele, *Ladies' Library*, vol. 1, vii, 1, and vol. 2, 38–41; Mayhew Papers, Folder No. 10, extract 1.
17. Steele, *Ladies' Library*, vol. 3, 83–98; note that Mayhew's extract from page 97 corresponds to pages 94–95 in this edition; Mayhew Papers, Folder No. 10, extracts 19 and 20.
18. Mayhew Papers, Folder No. 10.
19. *American Magazine* (July 1744), 483; Clifford K. Shipton, *Sibley's Harvard Graduates, Volume 11: 1741–1745* (Boston: Massachusetts Historical Society, 1960), 441–443; Francis G. Walett, ed., *The Diary of Ebenezer Parkman, 1703–1782, Part One: 1719–1755* (Worcester, Mass.: American Antiquarian Society, 1974), 157; Akers, *Called unto Liberty*, 58–59; Wilson, *Benevolent Deity*, 129.
20. Mayhew Papers, Folder No. 21; Akers, *Called unto Liberty*, 41–43; Wilson, *Benevolent Deity*, 124–126, 136, 138.
21. Akers, *Called unto Liberty*, 44–47, 53; John Corrigan, *The Hidden Balance: Religion and the Social Theories of Charles Chauncy and Jonathan Mayhew* (Cambridge: Cambridge University Press, 1987), 116, 120–121; Landsman, *From Colonials to Provincials*, 21–22; John Gascoigne, *Cambridge in the Age of the Enlightenment: Science, Religion, and Politics from the Restoration to the French Revolution* (Cambridge: Cambridge University Press, 1987), 9n, 143.
22. *Boston Evening-Post* (March 9, 1747); Mayhew Papers, Folder No. 133; Shipton, *Sibley's Harvard Graduates, Volume 11: 1741–1745*, 12–14; Akers, *Called unto Liberty*, 47–50; Wilson, *Benevolent Deity*, 139; Wright, *Beginnings of Unitarianism*, 65–66; Colman to Foxcroft, May 1747, H. H. Edes Papers, Massachusetts Historical Society; Colman to Anonymous, June 1747, Benjamin Colman Papers, Massachusetts Historical Society.
23. Akers, *Called unto Liberty*, 66–68.
24. Jonathan Mayhew, *Seven Sermons upon the Following Subjects* (Boston: Rogers and Fowle, 1749), 3–7; Samuel Clarke, *The Works of Samuel Clarke* (New York: Garland Publishing, 1978), 312; John Locke, *An Essay Concerning Human Understanding*, ed. Peter H. Nidditch (Oxford: Clarendon Press, 1975), 49.
25. Mayhew, *Seven Sermons*, 11–17; Clarke, *Works*, 143–155, 312; Locke, *Essay*, 49, 229, 258; Joseph Butler, *Sermons* (Oxford: Clarendon Press, 1896), 34–35; for the importance of happiness within Mayhew's theology, see E. Brooks Holifeld, *Theology in America: Christian Thought from the Age of the Puritans to the Civil War* (New Haven, Conn.: Yale University Press, 2003), 131–134.
26. Mayhew, *Seven Sermons*, 99–101; Daniel Walker Howe, *The Unitarian Conscience: Harvard Moral Philosophy, 1805–1861* (Middletown, Conn.: Wesleyan University Press, 1988), 49; Arthur Herman, *How the Scots Invented the Modern World* (New

York: Three Rivers Press, 2001), 76–78; Frederick C. Beiser, *Sovereignty of Reason: The Defense of Rationality in the Early English Enlightenment* (Princeton, N.J.: Princeton University Press, 1996), 30–31, 41.
27. Mayhew, *Seven Sermons*, 30–39.
28. Ibid., 39–40; Watts, *Logick*, 1; Steele, *Ladies' Library*, vol. 3, 82–83.
29. Mayhew, *Seven Sermons*, 43–45; Locke, *Essay*, 237, 263–264; Watts, *Logick*, 231–233, 240–241.
30. Mayhew, *Seven Sermons*, 51–52; Locke, *Essay*, 101.
31. Mayhew, *Seven Sermons*, 46–47.
32. Ibid., 11.
33. Ibid., 59–60; compare with Elisha Williams, "Essential Rights and Liberties of Protestants," in *Political Sermons of the American Founding Era, 1730–1805*, ed. Ellis Sandoz (Indianapolis: Liberty Fund, 1991), 61–65.
34. Mayhew, *Seven Sermons*, 60–62.
35. Ibid., 63–65.
36. Ibid., 65–66.
37. Clarke, *Works*, 659–662.
38. Mayhew, *Seven Sermons*, 73, 75–76.
39. Ibid., 91, 88.
40. Ibid., 148–153; for Mayhew's discussion of sin and justification in heretical Pelagian terms, see his March 1749 sermon manuscript, Mayhew Transcripts, Huntington Library.
41. Mayhew, *Seven Sermons*, 86–89.
42. Jonathan Mayhew, *A Discourse Concerning Unlimited Submission and Non-Resistance to the Higher Powers* (Boston: Daniel Fowle, 1750), 36n.
43. Akers, *Called unto Liberty*, 67; Mayhew, *Seven Sermons*, i–ii, 77–78, 111n, 87; Mayhew Papers, Folder Nos. 24, 25, 26, 28, 29, 31, and 135; Wright, *Beginnings of Unitarianism*, 79; for Benjamin Avery and the Dissenting Deputies, see Carl Bridenbaugh, *Mitre and Sceptre: Transatlantic Faiths, Ideas, Personalities, and Politics 1689–1775* (New York: Oxford University Press, 1962), 40–44; see also Bernard Lord Manning, *The Protestant Dissenting Deputies*, ed. Ormond Greenwood (Cambridge: Cambridge University Press, 1952), 2, 29–30.
44. Jonathan Mayhew, *Sermons upon the Following Subjects* (Boston: Richard Draper, 1755), iii, 254, 267–269, 269n, 417–418n; Akers, *Called unto Liberty*, 117–122; Letter from Josiah Cotton to John Cushing (July 28, 1750), William Cushing Papers, Massachusetts Historical Society; for Mayhew's most complete statement of his anti-Trinitarianism, see "Brief Notes on the Creed of St. Athanasius," Mayhew Papers, Folder No. 124; Mayhew's position (denial of the Trinity but not the divinity of Christ) is best described as Arian, but for his mistaken characterization as a Socinian (one who denies the divinity of Christ), see Matthew Stewart, *Nature's God: The Heretical Origins of the American Republic* (New York: W. W. Norton, 2014), 60–61.

45. Akers, *Called unto Liberty*, 67, 169; Corrigan, *Hidden Balance*, 116, 120–121; Lester J. Cappon, ed., *The Adams-Jefferson Letters* (Chapel Hill: University of North Carolina Press, 1959), 527; Letter from Gideon Richardson to Robert Treat Paine (April 24, 1750) and Diaries (1746–1756), Robert Treat Paine Papers, Massachusetts Historical Society; for membership of Cranch and Edmund Quincy, see "Records of the West Church, Boston," *New England Historical and Genealogical Register* (July 1939): 259–260.
46. John Adams, *The Works of John Adams*, vol. 1, ed. Charles Francis Adams (Boston: Little and Brown, 1856), 41, 14–15, 30–36; for Richard Cranch, see "Researches among Funeral Sermons," *New England Historical and Genealogical Register* (July 1853): 250.
47. John Adams, *Diary and Autobiography*, vol. 1, ed. Lyman H. Butterfield (Cambridge, Mass.: Harvard University Press, 1961), 219–220.
48. For the thesis that theology (specifically Christology) turned Protestant dissenters into radical Whigs and mobilized them for resistance, see J. C. D. Clark, *The Language of Liberty, 1660–1832: Political Discourse and Social Dynamics in the Anglo-American World* (Cambridge: Cambridge University Press, 1994), 330–339.

CHAPTER 2. THE RIGHT OF RESISTANCE

1. John Adams, *The Works of John Adams*, vol. 10, ed. Charles Francis Adams (Boston: Little and Brown, 1856), 282–283, 271–272.
2. Ibid., 284, 287–288; Bernard Bailyn, ed., *Pamphlets of the American Revolution 1750–1776, Volume I, 1750–1765* (Cambridge, Mass.: Harvard University Press, 1965), 210–211.
3. Adams, *Works*, vol. 10, 359; Bailyn, *Pamphlets of the American Revolution*, 210–211.
4. Francis Bremer, "In Defense of Regicide: John Cotton on the Execution of Charles I," *William and Mary Quarterly* (January 1980): 103–124.
5. K. H. D. Haley, *The First Earl of Shaftesbury* (Oxford: Clarendon Press, 1968), 160–164, 171, 180; Richard L. Greaves, *Deliver Us from Evil: The Radical Underground in Britain, 1660–1663* (Oxford: Oxford University Press, 1986), 21–48, 131–133; Mark Kishlansky, *A Monarchy Transformed: Britain, 1603–1714* (London: Penguin Books, 1996), 213–239.
6. Greaves, *Deliver Us from Evil*; Kishlansky, *A Monarchy Transformed*, 213–239.
7. W. M. Spellman, *The Latitudinarians and the Church of England, 1660–1700* (Athens: University of Georgia Press, 1992); Frederick C. Beiser, *Sovereignty of Reason: The Defense of Rationality in the Early English Enlightenment* (Princeton, N.J.: Princeton University Press, 1996).
8. Haley, *First Earl of Shaftesbury*, 707–724; Jonathan Scott, *Algernon Sidney and the Restoration Crisis, 1677–1683* (Cambridge: Cambridge University Press, 1991), 272, 287–291, 336–341; Richard L. Greaves, *Secrets of the Kingdom: British Radicals from the Popish Plot to the Revolution of 1688–1689* (Stanford, Calif.: Stanford University Press, 1992), 99–128, 153–160, 175–188, 192–196, 204–216, 230–235, 241; Kishlan-

sky, *A Monarchy Transformed*, 263–286; J. R. Jones, *Country and Court: England, 1658–1714* (Cambridge, Mass.: Harvard University Press, 1978), 234–255; Lee Ward, *The Politics of Liberty in England and Revolutionary America* (Cambridge: Cambridge University Press, 2004), 274–283; for the Revolution Settlement, see William A. Speck, *Reluctant Revolutionaries: Englishmen and the Revolution of 1688* (Oxford: Oxford University Press, 1989), 139–187; for the best explanation of Tory and Whig ideology in the 1690s, see H. T. Dickinson, *Liberty and Property: Political Ideology in Eighteenth-Century Britain* (London: Methuen, 1979 [1977]), 13–90; see also J. P. Kenyon, *Revolution Principles: The Politics of Party, 1689–1720* (Cambridge: Cambridge University Press, 1977), 5–60.

9. Kishlansky, *A Monarchy Transformed*, 287–313; Scott, *Algernon Sidney and the Restoration Crisis*, 107; Greaves, *Secrets of the Kingdom*, 336–344; Ward, *Politics of Liberty*, 283–284; Kenyon, *Revolution Principles*, 60–101.

10. William Gibson, *Enlightenment Prelate: Benjamin Hoadly, 1676–1761* (Cambridge: James Clarke, 2004); Andrew Starkie, *The Church of England and the Bangorian Controversy, 1716–1721* (London: Boydell, 2007); John Shute Barrington, *The Rights of Protestant Dissenters* (London: n.p., 1704); Knud Haakonssen, ed., *Enlightenment and Religion: Rational Dissent in Eighteenth-Century Britain* (Cambridge: Cambridge University Press, 1996); Alan P. F. Sell, *John Locke and the Eighteenth-Century Divines* (Cardiff: University of Wales Press, 1997); John Gascoigne, *Cambridge in the Age of Enlightenment: Science, Religion, and Politics from the Restoration to the French Revolution* (Cambridge: Cambridge University Press, 1989); Bernard Lord Manning, *The Protestant Dissenting Deputies*, ed. Ormond Greenwood (Cambridge: Cambridge University Press, 1952); for analysis of the lobbying efforts of the Dissenting Deputies, see James E. Bradley, *Religion, Revolution, and English Radicalism: Nonconformity in Eighteenth-Century Politics and Society* (Cambridge: Cambridge University Press, 1990), 52–61.

11. Jones, *Country and Court*; Frank O' Gorman, *The Long Eighteenth Century: British Political and Social History, 1688–1832* (London: Arnold, 1997), 65–75; Ward, *Politics of Liberty*, 286–287; Kenyon, *Revolution Principles*, 102–145.

12. Jones, *Country and Court*, 334–337; Ward, *Politics of Liberty*, 288–304; Kenyon, *Revolution Principles*, 146–208; for a sampling of Trenchard and Gordon's reassertion of Whig revolution principles, see David L. Jacobson, ed., *The English Libertarian Heritage: From the Writings of John Trenchard and Thomas Gordon in The Independent Whig and Cato's Letters* (San Francisco: Fox and Wilkes, 1994 [1965]), xxxiii–xlvii, 30, 63, 67–72, 85–137; for New England dissenters' attachment to Britain as defender of the "Protestant interest," see Thomas S. Kidd, *The Protestant Interest: New England after Puritanism* (New Haven, Conn.: Yale University Press, 2004).

13. Andrew Trebeck, *A Sermon Preach'd before the Honourable House of Commons, at St. Margaret's Westminster, on Friday, January 30, 1746-7* (London: L. Gulliver and W. Owne, [1747]), 6, 11, 17; Richard Osbaldeston, *A Sermon Preached before*

the House of Lords, in the Abbey-Church of Westminster, on Saturday, January 30th, 1747: Being the Day Appointed to Be Observed as the Day of the Martyrdom of King Charles I (London: John Oliver, 1748), 17, 9, 11, 15; Thomas Pickering, *A Sermon Preach'd before the Right Honourable, the Lord Mayor, the Aldermen and Citizens of London, in the Cathedral Church of St. Paul, on Tuesday, January the 30th, 1749–50* (London: John Clarke, 1750), 1–9.

14. Pickering, *A Sermon Preach'd before the Lord Mayor*, 12–15.
15. Henry Wilder Foote, ed., *Annals of Kings Chapel: From the Puritan Age of New England to the Present Day*, vol. 2 (Boston: Little and Brown, 1896), 23–26, 33–34, 37, 114; Letter of Charles Brockwell to the Bishop of London (April 13, 1750), the Fulham Papers, 1700–1800, Lambeth Palace Library.
16. Jonathan Mayhew, *A Discourse Concerning Unlimited Submission and Non-Resistance to the Higher Powers* (Boston: Daniel Fowle, 1750), 37; Jonathan Mayhew Papers, Bortmann Collection, Boston University, Folder No. 10; for the transmission of political ideas from the Commonwealthmen through the English radical Whigs to the American Patriots, see Caroline Robbins, *The Eighteenth-Century Commonwealthman* (Indianapolis: Liberty Fund, 2004 [1959]); in a major contribution to Mayhew scholarship, historian Chris Beneke has persuasively interpreted Mayhew's *Discourse* in multiple political contexts of the late 1740s, from the Jacobite Rising of 1745 and royal veto of the Currency Act to the Knowles anti-impressment riot and contemporary debate over a colonial episcopate; for his insightful analysis, see Chris Beneke, "The Critical Turn: Jonathan Mayhew, the British Empire, and the Idea of Resistance in Mid-Eighteenth-Century Boston," *Massachusetts Historical Review*, vol. 10 (2008): 23–56.
17. Charles W. Akers, *Called unto Liberty: A Life of Jonathan Mayhew, 1720–1766* (Cambridge, Mass.: Harvard University Press, 1964), 90; Bailyn, *Pamphlets of the American Revolution*, 205–209, 697n.
18. Mayhew, *Unlimited Submission*, vi; Jonathan Mayhew, *The Snare Broken, a Thanksgiving-Discourse, Preached at the Desire of the West Church, in Boston, N.E., Friday May 23, 1766, Occasioned by the Repeal of the Stamp-Act* (Boston: Richard and Samuel Draper, Edes and Gill, 1766), 34.
19. Mayhew, *Unlimited Submission*, v–vi; for excerpts from *The Independent Whig*, see Jacobson, *English Libertarian Heritage*, 3–36; for the Real Whig anticlericalist critique of the Church of England as an engine of civil tyranny, particularly as articulated by John Trenchard and Thomas Gordon, see J. A. I. Champion, *The Pillars of Priestcraft Shaken: The Church of England and Its Enemies, 1660–1730* (Cambridge: Cambridge University Press, 1992), 173–179.
20. Mayhew, *Unlimited Submission*, 7; Dickinson, *Liberty and Property*, 15.
21. Mayhew, *Unlimited Submission*, 15–16.
22. Ibid., 6–13, 14n, 10–11n, 12n, 14–18, 24, 26–28, 35n; see Benjamin Hoadly, "The Measures of Submission to the Civil Magistrate Considered," *The Works of Benjamin Hoadly*, ed. John Hoadly (London: W. Bowyer and J. Nichols, 1773), esp.

18–25, 38–39; compare with John Milton, "The Tenure of Kings and Magistrates," *Political Writings*, ed. Martin Dzelzainis (Cambridge: Cambridge University Press, 1991), 15.
23. Mayhew, *Unlimited Submission*, 25, 29–30; Bailyn, *Pamphlets of the American Revolution*, 206.
24. For popular sovereignty, delegated political authority as a trust, and the people capable of judging when that trust has been violated, see Milton, *Political Writings*, 9–13; see also John Locke, *Two Treatises of Government*, ed. Peter Laslett (Cambridge: Cambridge University Press, 1992 [1960]), 414–416, 426–428; see also "Cato's Letters, No. 38," in Jacobson, *English Libertarian Heritage*, 94.
25. Mayhew, *Unlimited Submission*, 36n.
26. Ibid., 37.
27. Ibid.
28. Ibid., 38–41; Bailyn, *Pamphlets of the American Revolution*, 206.
29. Mayhew, *Unlimited Submission*, 40–41, 41–42n.
30. Ibid., 42.
31. Ibid., 40, 42–44.
32. Ibid., 45–48; compare with "The Independent Whig, No. 24," in Jacobson, *English Libertarian Heritage*, 25–30; John Locke, *Political Essays*, ed. Mark Goldie (Cambridge: Cambridge University Press, 1997), 365.
33. Mayhew, *Unlimited Submission*, 47–48; Adams, *Works*, vol. 10, 288.
34. *Boston Evening-Post*, February 19 and 26, 1750; Akers, *Called unto Liberty*, 90; Bailyn, *Pamphlets of the American Revolution*, 697; Letter of Charles Brockwell to the Bishop of London (April 13, 1750), Fulham Papers.
35. Letter of James MacSparran to the Bishop of London (March 15, 1749), Fulham Papers; for more letters on the *Discourse* controversy, see *Boston Evening-Post*, March 5, 12, and 19, 1750, April 2, 17, and 23, 1750, May 21, 1750, June 18, 1750, and July 9, 1750; *Boston Gazette, or Weekly Journal*, March 13 and 20, 1750, April 3, 1750, May 8 and 29, 1750, and April 24, 1753.
36. Mayhew Papers, Folder Nos. 28, 31, and 113; Bailyn, *Pamphlets of the American Revolution*, 697–698.
37. Mayhew Papers, Folder No. 31; Alan Heimert, *Religion and the American Mind: From the Great Awakening to the Revolution* (Cambridge, Mass.: Harvard University Press, 1966), 293.
38. Mayhew, *Unlimited Submission*, iv.
39. Richard Baron, ed., *The Pillars of Priestcraft and Orthodoxy Shaken, Vol. II* (London: R. Griffiths, 1752), 258–335; for another example of *The Independent Whig*'s influence on colonial political culture, see William Livingston, *The Independent Reflector: Or, Weekly Essays on Sundry Important Subjects More Particularly Adapted to the Province of New-York*, ed. Milton M. Klein (Cambridge, Mass.: Harvard University Press, 1963).
40. Lester J. Cappon, *The Adams-Jefferson Letters: The Complete Correspondence be-

tween Thomas Jefferson and Abigail and John Adams, vol. 2 (Chapel Hill: University of North Carolina Press, 1999), 527.

41. Bremer, "In Defense of Regicide," 103–124; for the waxing and waning of the eighteenth-century historical reputation of Cromwell and the regicides, see Alfred F. Young, *Liberty Tree: Ordinary People and the American Revolution* (New York: New York University Press, 2006), 144–179; see also Brendan McConville, *The King's Three Faces: The Rise and Fall of Royal America, 1688–1776* (Chapel Hill: University of North Carolina Press, 2008), 95–100.

42. Adams, *Works*, vol. 10, 282–283; for examples of the popularization of radical Whig ideas by New England's Congregationalist clergy, see Ellis Sandoz, ed., *Political Sermons of the Founding Era, 1730–1805*, vol. 1 (Indianapolis: Liberty Fund, 1999); Trevor Colbourn, *The Lamp of Experience: Whig History and the Intellectual Origins of the American Revolution* (Indianapolis: Liberty Fund, 1998 [1965]), 71–99; J. C. D. Clark, *The Language of Liberty, 1660–1832: Political Discourse and Social Dynamics in the Anglo-American World* (Cambridge: Cambridge University Press, 1994), 330–339; C. H. Van Tyne, "Influence of the Clergy, and of Religious and Sectarian Forces, on the American Revolution," *American Historical Review* (October 1913): 44–64; Alice M. Baldwin, *The New England Clergy and the American Revolution* (Durham, N.C.: Duke University Press, 1928); Nathan O. Hatch, *The Sacred Cause of Liberty: Republican Thought and the Millennium in Revolutionary New England* (New Haven, Conn.: Yale University Press, 1977); James F. Cooper, Jr., *Tenacious of Their Liberties: The Congregationalists in Colonial Massachusetts* (New York: Oxford University Press, 1999); Steven M. Dworetz, *The Unvarnished Doctrine: Locke, Liberalism and the American Revolution* (Durham, N.C.: Duke University Press, 1994); Michael P. Zuckert, *The Natural Rights Republic: Studies in the Foundation of the American Political Tradition* (Notre Dame, Ind.: University of Notre Dame Press, 1996); Thomas G. West, "The Transformation of Protestant Theology as a Condition of the American Revolution," in *Protestantism and the American Founding*, ed. Thomas S. Engerman and Michael P. Zuckert (Notre Dame, Ind.: University of Notre Dame Press, 2004): 187–224.

43. Adams, *Works*, vol. 10, 301; Bailyn, *Pamphlets of the American Revolution*, 204, 210–211.

CHAPTER 3. VIRTUE AND LIBERTY

1. Sermon manuscript (undated), Mayhew Family Papers, Houghton Library, Harvard University; Jonathan Mayhew, *Seven Sermons upon the Following Subjects* (Boston: Rogers and Fowle, 1749), 11, 37, 46–47, 86–87.

2. Jonathan Mayhew, *A Discourse Concerning Unlimited Submission and Non-Resistance to the Higher Powers* (Boston: Daniel Fowle, 1750), 36n.

3. Jonathan Mayhew Papers, Bortmann Collection, Boston University, Folder Nos. 24 and 25.

4. Ibid., Folder Nos. 28, 29, and 30.

5. Ibid., Folder No. 31.
6. Ibid., Folder Nos. 29, 30, 31, and 32.
7. Ibid., Folder Nos. 30, 38.
8. For Mayhew's radical Whig view of the British constitution, see Mayhew, *Unlimited Submission*, 41n.
9. Jonathan Mayhew, *Christian Sobriety: Being Eight Sermons on Titus II:6, Preached with a Special View to the Benefit of the Young Men Usually Attending the Public Worship at the West Church in Boston* (Boston: Richard and Samuel Draper, Edes and Gill, and Thomas and John Fleet, 1763), 2–38.
10. Jonathan Mayhew, *A Sermon Preached at Boston in New-England, May 26, 1751, Occasioned by the Much-Lamented Death of His Royal Highness Frederick, Prince of Wales* (Boston: Richard Draper and Daniel Gookin, 1751), 9–11; Mayhew, *Unlimited Submission*, 35–36n; for the importance of the concept of government as a "trust" in Mayhew's *Discourse*, see Clinton Rossiter, *Seedtime of the Republic: Origin of the American Tradition of Political Liberty* (New York: Harcourt, Brace, 1953), 236–243; David L. Jacobson, ed., *The English Libertarian Heritage: From the Writings of John Trenchard and Thomas Gordon in The Independent Whig and Cato's Letters* (San Francisco: Fox and Wilkes, 1994 [1965]), 94.
11. Mayhew, *Death of Frederick*, 13–15; Jacobson, *English Libertarian Heritage*, 85.
12. Mayhew, *Death of Frederick*, 16–22.
13. Ibid., 24–29, 34; for key examples of the theme of the corrupting influence of power in *Cato's Letters*, see Jacobson, *English Libertarian Heritage*, 61–68, 80–93.
14. For the tradition of the Massachusetts election sermon, see A. W. Plumstead, ed., *The Wall and the Garden: Selected Massachusetts Election Sermons, 1670–1775* (Minneapolis: University of Minnesota Press, 1968), 6–37.
15. Mayhew Papers, Folder Nos. 25, 28, and 31; for Shirley's legal and political career, see George Arthur Wood, *William Shirley, Governor of Massachusetts, 1741–1756: A History*, 2 vols. (New York: Columbia University Press, 1920).
16. Mayhew Papers, Folder No. 36; Plumstead, *Wall and Garden*, 285.
17. Jonathan Mayhew, *A Sermon Preach'd in the Audience of His Excellency, William Shirley, Esq.; Captain General, Governour and Commander in Chief, the Honourable His Majesty's Council, and the Honourable House of Representatives of the Province of the Massachusetts-Bay, in New-England, May 29, 1754. Being the Anniversary for the Election of His Majesty's Council for the Province* (Boston: Samuel Kneeland, 1754), 3–6; Plumstead, *Wall and Garden*, 291n.
18. Mayhew, *William Shirley*, 7.
19. Ibid., 8–9; John Locke, *Two Treatises of Government*, ed. Peter Laslett (Cambridge: Cambridge University Press, 1992 [1960]), 271, 323–324, 326, 328–333, 344, 353.
20. Mayhew, *William Shirley*, 10–11.
21. Ibid., 12–14.
22. Ibid., 19.
23. Ibid., 19–20.

24. Ibid., 21–23.
25. Ibid., 23; for the thesis that the Puritan founders of the Massachusetts-Bay colony and their English patrons were indeed committed to civil and religious liberty, including the colony's sovereign independence from Britain, see Michael P. Winship, "Godly Republicanism and the Origins of the Massachusetts Polity," *William and Mary Quarterly* (July 2006): 427–462.
26. Mayhew, *William Shirley*, 23–24.
27. Ibid., 28–32, 33n, 48n.
28. Ibid., 33–34, 36–37.
29. Ibid., 37–38.
30. Ibid., 37, 39–41, 43, 45–47; Plumstead, *Wall and Garden*, 313n.
31. Mayhew, *William Shirley*, 40, 45, 49–50.
32. Ibid., 34–35, 37.
33. Plumstead, *Wall and Garden*, 309n; for Mayhew's personal copy of the Albany Plan of Union, see Mayhew Papers, Folder No. 125; for a positive English review of the London edition of Mayhew's election sermon, see *The Monthly Review, or, Literary Journal*, vol. 11 (London: R. Griffiths, 1754), 479–480.
34. Fred Anderson, *Crucible of War: The Seven Years' War and the Fate of Empire in British North America, 1754–1766* (New York: Random House, 2000), 77–85; William W. Fowler, Jr., *Empires at War: The French and Indian War and the Struggle for North America, 1754–1763* (New York: Walker, 2005), 69–73.
35. Jonathan Mayhew, *A Discourse on Rev. XV, 3rd and 4th, Occasioned by the Earthquakes in November 1755* (Boston: Edes and Gill, 1755), 61–63.
36. Ibid., 66.
37. Mayhew Papers, Folder Nos. 39, 50, and 51.
38. Jonathan Mayhew, *Two Discourses Delivered November 23rd, 1758, Being the Day Appointed by Authority to Be Observed as a Day of Public Thanksgiving: Relating, More Especially, to the Success of His Majesty's Arms, and Those of the King of Prussia, the Last Year* (Boston: Richard Draper, Edes and Gill, and Green and Russell, 1758), 8–11.
39. Jonathan Mayhew, *Two Discourses Delivered October 25th, 1759, Being the Day Appointed by Authority to Be Observed as a Day of Public Thanksgiving, for the Success of His Majesty's Arms, More Particularly in the Reduction of Quebec, the Capital of Canada, with an Appendix* (Boston: Richard Draper, Edes and Gill, and Thomas and John Fleet, 1759), 27, 36.
40. Ibid., 28, 32.
41. Ibid., 29–32.
42. Ibid., 41–50, 54, 57.
43. Ibid., 50–51, 60.
44. Ibid., 61.
45. John Adams, *Works of John Adams*, vol. 1, ed. Charles Francis Adams (Boston: Little and Brown, 1856), 23–24.

46. Mayhew, *Reduction of Quebec*, 63–66; sermon manuscript (undated), Mayhew Family Papers, Houghton Library, Harvard University.
47. Mayhew, *Two Discourses Delivered October 9th, 1760. Being the Day Appointed to Be Observed as a Day of Public Thanksgiving for the Success of His Majesty's Arms, More Especially in the Intire Reduction of Canada* (Boston: Edes and Gill, 1760), 53–54; Nathan O. Hatch, *The Sacred Cause of Liberty: Republican Thought and the Millennium in Revolutionary New England* (New Haven, Conn.: Yale University Press, 1977), 3, 12, 40–43.
48. Mayhew, *Reduction of Canada*, 54–60, 64–65.
49. Jonathan Mayhew, *A Discourse Occasioned by the Death of King George II and the Happy Accession of His Majesty King George III to the Imperial Throne of Great-Britain, Delivered January 4th, 1761* (Boston: Edes and Gill, 1761), 16–17, 23–26, 28–30.
50. Ibid., 30–34.
51. Ibid., 33–35, 37–39, 41.
52. Mayhew Papers, Folder No. 58; see also John Reynolds's 1759 letter in Mayhew Papers, Folder No. 53.

CHAPTER 4. POWER AND CORRUPTION

1. Jonathan Mayhew Papers, Bortmann Collection, Boston University, Folder No. 91; Jack P. Greene, ed., *Colonies to Nation, 1763–1789: A Documentary History of the American Revolution* (New York: Norton, 1967), 61–62; Andrew Eliot, "Letters from Andrew Eliot to Thomas Hollis," *Collections of the Massachusetts Historical Society*, 4th ser., vol. 4 (Boston: Massachusetts Historical Society, 1858), 407; Bernhard Knollenberg, ed., "Thomas Hollis and Jonathan Mayhew: Their Correspondence, 1759–1766," *Proceedings of the Massachusetts Historical Society*, vol. 69 (1947–1950): 162–163; Edmund S. Morgan, "Thomas Hutchinson and the Stamp Act," *New England Quarterly* 21 (1948): 471; Clifford K. Shipton, *Sibley's Harvard Graduates, Volume 11, 1741–1745* (Boston: Massachusetts Historical Society, 1960), 465; Thomas Hutchinson, *The History of the Colony and Province of Massachusetts-Bay*, vol. 3, ed. Lawrence Shaw Mayo (Cambridge, Mass.: Harvard University Press, 1936), 89.
2. Knollenberg, "Thomas Hollis and Jonathan Mayhew," 128–129; Colin Nicolson, *The "Infamas Govener": Francis Bernard and the Origins of the American Revolution* (Boston: Northeastern University Press, 2000), 77.
3. Douglass Adair and John A. Schutz, eds., *Peter Oliver's Origin and Progress of the American Rebellion: A Tory View* (San Marino, CA: Huntington Library, 1963), 29, 41–45.
4. Nicolson, "*Infamas Govener*," 20–32, 36, 40–49; Edward Channing and Archibald Cary Coolidge, eds., *The Barrington-Bernard Correspondence and Illustrative Matter, 1760–1770* (Cambridge, Mass.: Harvard University Press, 1912), vii–ix, xvi–xix; Hiller B. Zobel, *The Boston Massacre* (New York: W. W. Norton, 1970),

6; M. H. Smith, *The Writs of Assistance Case* (Berkeley: University of California Press, 1978), 199.
5. John R. Galvin, *Three Men of Boston: Leadership and Conflict at the Start of the American Revolution* (Washington, D.C.: Brassey's, 1976), 24–25; Nicolson, "*Infamas Govener*," 64–66; Oliver M. Dickerson, *The Navigation Acts and the American Revolution* (Philadelphia: University of Pennsylvania Press, 1951), 254.
6. Charles W. Akers, *Called unto Liberty: A Life of Jonathan Mayhew, 1720–1766* (Cambridge, Mass.: Harvard University Press, 1964), 10, 151; Mayhew Papers, Folder No. 36; Jonathan Mayhew, *A Discourse Occasioned by the Death of the Honourable Stephen Sewall, Esq.; Chief-Justice of the Superiour Court of Judicature, Court of Assize, and General-Goal-Delivery; as Also a Member of His Majesty's Council for the Province of the Massachusetts-Bay in New-England: Who Departed This Life on Wednesday-Night, September 10, 1760, Delivered the Lord's-Day after His Decease* (Boston: Richard Draper, Edes and Gill, and Thomas and John Fleet, 1760), 24, 32–39, 45, 56–60.
7. Mayhew, *Discourse Occasioned by the Death of Stephen Sewall*, 60, 37–38; John J. Waters and John A. Schutz, "Patterns of Massachusetts Colonial Politics: The Writs of Assistance and the Rivalry between the Otis and Hutchinson Families," *William and Mary Quarterly* (October 1967): 558; Galvin, *Three Men of Boston*, 22.
8. Waters and Schutz, "Patterns of Massachusetts Colonial Politics," 559–561; Galvin, *Three Men of Boston*, 16–21; Smith, *Writs of Assistance Case*, 207–211.
9. Galvin, *Three Men of Boston*, 25–26; Smith, *Writs of Assistance Case*, 434n; see Josiah Quincy, Jr., *Reports of Cases Argued and Adjudged in the Superior Court of Judicature of the Province of Massachusetts Bay, between 1761 and 1772*, ed. Samuel M. Quincy (Boston: Little and Brown, 1865), 541–552.
10. Galvin, *Three Men of Boston*, 27–30, 39–40; A. J. Langguth, *Patriots: The Men Who Started the American Revolution* (New York: Simon and Schuster, 1989), 20–24; *Journals of the House of Representatives of Massachusetts* (Boston, 1919–1989), vol. 38, pt. 1: 11–17.
11. Channing and Coolidge, *Barrington-Bernard Correspondence*, 42–45; Richard L. Bushman, *King and People in Provincial Massachusetts* (Chapel Hill: University of North Carolina Press, 1985), 55.
12. Mayhew Papers, Folder No. 61.
13. Akers, *Called unto Liberty*, 106–110; Mayhew Papers, Folder No. 115; Thomas Hollis, *Letters from Thomas Hollis of Lincoln's Inn to Andrew Eliot*, ed. William H. Bond (Cambridge, Mass.: Houghton Library, 1988), 90; for the 1771 assessment of the wealth of the full members of the West Church congregation, see John Corrigan, *The Hidden Balance: Religion and the Social Theories of Charles Chauncy and Jonathan Mayhew* (Cambridge: Cambridge University Press, 1987), 120–121.
14. Mayhew Papers, Folder No. 61.
15. Charles H. Lippy, *Seasonable Revolutionary: The Mind of Charles Chauncy* (Chicago, 1981), 109; Mayhew Papers, Folder No. 61.

16. *Journals of the House*, vol. 38, pt. 1: 5–6.
17. Mayhew Papers, Folder No. 61.
18. Walter Muir Whitehill and Lawrence W. Kennedy, *Boston: A Topographical History* (Cambridge, Mass.: Harvard University Press, 2000 [1959]), 18; Mayhew Papers, Folder No. 61.
19. Mayhew Papers, Folder No. 61; Akers, *Called unto Liberty*, 153–155.
20. Mayhew Papers, Folder No. 61.
21. Ibid.
22. Ibid.
23. Ibid.; Mayhew Papers, Folder No. 62.
24. Mayhew Papers, Folder No. 61.
25. Ibid.
26. Ibid.; the Mayhew-Bernard quarrel closely fits the pattern of "political gossip" described in Joanne B. Freeman, *Affairs of Honor: National Politics in the New Republic* (New Haven, Conn.: Yale University Press, 2001).
27. Mayhew Papers, Folder No. 61; David L. Jacobson, ed., *The English Libertarian Heritage: From the Writings of John Trenchard and Thomas Gordon in The Independent Whig and Cato's Letters* (San Francisco: Fox and Wilkes, 1994 [1965]), 38–44.
28. Mayhew Papers, Folder No. 61.
29. Ibid.
30. Akers, *Called unto Liberty*, 78–79.
31. Freeman, *Affairs of Honor*, xvi; Bushman, *King and People*, 23–36, 55–63, 78–85; Mayhew Papers, Folder Nos. 61 and 62.
32. Mayhew Papers, Folder No. 62.
33. Mayhew Papers, Folder No. 61.
34. Ibid.
35. Ibid.
36. Ibid.
37. Lee Ward, *The Politics of Liberty in England and Revolutionary America* (Cambridge: Cambridge University Press, 2004), esp. 274–288; H. T. Dickinson, *Liberty and Property: Political Ideology in Eighteenth-Century Britain* (London: Methuen, 1979 [1977]), 33–42, 70–79; see also J. P. Kenyon, *Revolution Principles: The Politics of Party 1689–1720* (Cambridge: Cambridge University Press, 1977).
38. Nicolson, "*Infamas Govener*," 37–39; Jonathan Mayhew, *A Discourse Occasioned by the Death of King George II and the Happy Accession of His Majesty King George III to the Imperial Throne of Great-Britain, Delivered January 4th, 1761* (Boston: Edes and Gill, 1761), 16–17, 23–26.
39. Mayhew Papers, Folder No. 61.
40. Jonathan Mayhew, *A Sermon Preached at Boston in New-England, May 26, 1751, Occasioned by the Much-Lamented Death of His Royal Highness Frederick, Prince of Wales* (Boston: Richard Draper and Daniel Gookin, 1751), 9–15.

41. Mayhew Papers, Folder No. 61.
42. Ibid.
43. Ibid.
44. Ibid.
45. Ibid.
46. Knollenberg, "Thomas Hollis and Jonathan Mayhew," 128–129.
47. Akers, *Called unto Liberty*, 160–164; "Jasper Mauduit: Agent in London for the Province of Massachusetts-Bay, 1762–1765," *Collections of the Massachusetts Historical Society*, vol. 74 (Boston: Massachusetts Historical Society, 1918), xxix, 68–73, 70–71n; Clifford K. Shipton, *Sibley's Harvard Graduates, Volume 8, 1726–1730* (Boston: Massachusetts Historical Society, 1951), 315–317.
48. "Jasper Mauduit," 74: xx–xxiv, 29–38.
49. Carl Bridenbaugh, *Mitre and Sceptre: Transatlantic Faiths, Ideas, Personalities, and Politics, 1689–1776* (New York: Oxford University Press, 1962), 210; Nicolson, "Infamas Govener," 76; Knollenberg, "Thomas Hollis and Jonathan Mayhew," 129–131; Mayhew Papers, Folder No. 67; Andrew Eliot to Jasper Mauduit, June 1, 1763, the Jasper Mauduit Papers (1760–1767), Massachusetts Historical Society, Boston.
50. Mayhew Papers, Folder No. 61; Akers, *Called unto Liberty*, 160–161; for a discussion of the Indian Affair as an affair of honor, see J. Patrick Mullins, "'A Kind of War, Tho' Hitherto an Un-Bloody One': Jonathan Mayhew, Francis Bernard, and the Indian Affair," *Massachusetts Historical Review*, vol. 11 (2009): 27–56.

CHAPTER 5. SCEPTRE AND SURPLICE

1. David L. Jacobson, ed., *The English Libertarian Heritage: From the Writings of John Trenchard and Thomas Gordon in The Independent Whig and Cato's Letters* (San Francisco: Fox and Wilkes, 1994 [1965]), 30.
2. Jonathan Mayhew, *A Discourse Concerning Unlimited Submission and Non-Resistance to the Higher Powers* (Boston: Daniel Fowle, 1750), vi, 45–48.
3. Donald F. M. Gerardi, "Samuel Johnson and the Yale 'Apostasy' of 1722," *Historical Magazine of the Protestant Episcopal Church* (June 1978): 153–175; Don R. Gerlach and George DeMille, "Samuel Johnson and the Founding of King's College, 1751–1755," *Historical Magazine of the Protestant Episcopal Church* (September 1975): 335–352; for the most important example of Presbyterian criticism of the Episcopal clergy's growing power in New York in the mid-1750s, see William Livingston, *The Independent Reflector: or, Weekly Essays on Sundry Important Subjects More Particularly Adapted to the Province of New-York*, ed. Milton M. Klein (Cambridge, Mass.: Harvard University Press, 1963).
4. Carl Bridenbaugh, *Mitre and Sceptre: Transatlantic Faiths, Ideas, Personalities, and Politics, 1689–1776* (New York: Oxford University Press, 1962), 98–99, 99n; Nancy L. Rhoden, *Revolutionary Anglicanism: The Colonial Church of England Clergy during the American Revolution* (New York: New York University Press,

1999), 55; for the classic study of the long struggle by Episcopalians to introduce a bishop to America, on political as well as religious motives, see Arthur Lyon Cross, *The Anglican Episcopate and the American Colonies* (London: Longmans, Green, 1902).
5. Stephen Taylor, "Whigs, Bishops, and America: The Politics of Church Reform in Mid-Eighteenth-Century England," *Historical Journal* (June 1993): 331–356; for the definitive study of Thomas Secker's theological views and the reformist motivation behind his campaign for colonial episcopacy, see Robert G. Ingram, *Religion, Reform and Modernity: Thomas Secker and the Church of England* (London: Boydell, 2007), esp. 76–77, 108, and Chapter 7.
6. Bridenbaugh, *Mitre and Sceptre*, 215–217.
7. Ibid., 110–111.
8. Ibid., 215, 211.
9. *Boston Gazette, and The Country Journal*, January 12, 1761.
10. Jonathan Mayhew Papers, Bortmann Collection, Boston University, Folder Nos. 54 and 55.
11. Bridenbaugh, *Mitre and Sceptre*, 210; Colin Nicolson, *The "Infamas Govener": Francis Bernard and the Origins of the American Revolution* (Boston: Northeastern University Press, 2000), 76; Bernhard Knollenberg, ed., "Thomas Hollis and Jonathan Mayhew: Their Correspondence, 1759–1766," *Proceedings of the Massachusetts Historical Society*, vol. 69 (1947–1950): 129–131.
12. Bridenbaugh, *Mitre and Sceptre*, 210; Ingram, *Religion, Reform and Modernity*, 231–234; Mayhew Papers, Folder No. 67; Andrew Eliot to Jasper Mauduit, June 1, 1763, the Jasper Mauduit Papers (1760–1767), Massachusetts Historical Society, Boston.
13. Knollenberg, "Thomas Hollis and Jonathan Mayhew," 131; Bridenbaugh, *Mitre and Sceptre*, 220.
14. Bridenbaugh, *Mitre and Sceptre*, 212–213, 219–220.
15. East Apthorp, *Considerations on the Institution and Conduct of the Society for the Propagation of the Gospel in Foreign Parts* (Boston: Green and Russell, Thomas and John Fleet, 1763), 23, 7.
16. Ibid., 10–17; Mayhew Papers, Folder No. 68.
17. Jonathan Mayhew, *Observations on the Charter and Conduct of the Society for the Propagation of the Gospel in Foreign Parts: Designed to Shew Their Non-Conformity to Each Other* (Boston: Richard and Samuel Draper, Edes and Gill, and Thomas and John Fleet, 1763), 6–7.
18. Ibid., 39–46.
19. Ibid., 53–57, 107.
20. Ibid., 155.
21. Ibid., 156.
22. Ibid., 157, 175.
23. Knollenberg, "Thomas Hollis and Jonathan Mayhew," 138; Harrison Gray to Jas-

per Mauduit, Boston, May 3, 1763, Mauduit Papers; Mayhew Papers, Folder No. 70.

24. [John Aplin], *Verses on Doctor Mayhew's Book of Observations on the Charter and Conduct of the Society for the Propagation of the Gospel in Foreign Parts: With Notes, Critical and Explanatory* (Providence, R.I.: William Goddard, 1763), 3–18; [Arthur Browne], *Remarks on Dr. Mayhew's Incidental Reflections, Relative to the Church of England, as Contained in His Observations on the Charter and Conduct of the Society, &c.* (Portsmouth, N.H.: Fowle, 1763), 3–4, 18–19, 24.

25. Aplin, *Verses on Dr. Mayhew's Book*, 18; Browne, *Remarks on Dr. Mayhew's Incidental Reflections*, 26–28.

26. Mayhew Papers, Folder No. 72.

27. [Henry Caner], *A Candid Examination of Dr. Mayhew's Observations on the Charter and Conduct of the Society for the Propagation of the Gospel in Foreign Parts, to Which Is Added, a Letter to a Friend, Containing a Short Vindication of the Said Society against the Mistakes and Misrepresentations of the Doctor in His Observations on the Conduct of That Society, by One of Its Members [Samuel Johnson]* (Boston: Thomas and John Fleet, Green and Russell, Edes and Gill, 1763), 77–78, 88.

28. Caner, *Candid Examination*, 27–29, 34–39, 47–55, 75–77, 86.

29. Jonathan Mayhew, *A Defence of the Observations on the Charter and Conduct of the Society for the Propagation of the Gospel in Foreign Parts, against an Anonymous Pamphlet Falsely Intitled, A Candid Examination of Dr. Mayhew's Observations, &c., and Also against the Letter to a Friend Annexed Thereto, Said to Contain a Short Vindication of Said Society, by One of Its Members* (Boston: Richard and Samuel Draper, Edes and Gill, and Thomas and John Fleet, 1763), 39–41.

30. Ibid., 41–43, 48–49, 54–55, 63, 79.

31. Ibid., 62, 50–51, 57.

32. Ibid., 57–58.

33. For discussion of the system of multiple establishments in provincial Massachusetts, and how the principle of religious liberty began to challenge that system in the years preceding the Revolution, see Chris Beneke, *Beyond Toleration: The Religious Origins of American Pluralism* (Oxford: Oxford University Press, 2006), 137–145.

34. Mayhew, *Defence of the Observations*, 50–51, 57, 58n, 60–62.

35. Leonard W. Levy, *The Establishment Clause: Religion and the First Amendment* (New York: Macmillan, 1986), 19–20; Mary Sarah Bilder, *The Transatlantic Constitution: Colonial Legal Culture and the Empire* (Cambridge, Mass.: Harvard University Press, 2004), 146–147, 159–160, 162, 165; John D. Cushing, "Notes on Disestablishment in Massachusetts, 1780–1833," *William and Mary Quarterly* (April 1969): 169–172;

36. Mayhew, *Defence of the Observations*, 54–55.

37. Ibid., 90–92.

38. Knollenberg, "Thomas Hollis and Jonathan Mayhew," 142–143.

39. [Thomas Secker], *An Answer to Dr. Mayhew's Observations on the Charter and Conduct of the Society for the Propagation of the Gospel in Foreign Parts* (Boston: Reprinted by Richard and Samuel Draper, Edes and Gill, and Thomas and John Fleet, 1764 [London, 1764]), 5–7, 9, 29, 47, 54.
40. Ibid., 51–57.
41. Mayhew Papers, Folder No. 74; Lyman Butterfield, ed., *Adams Family Papers*, vol. 1 (Cambridge, Mass.: Harvard University Press, 1963), 20; Knollenberg, "Thomas Hollis and Jonathan Mayhew," 143–148; Thomas Hollis, *The Memoirs of Thomas Hollis*, ed. Francis Blackburne (London: [publisher not identified], 1780), 96, 227–228, 490.
42. Jonathan Mayhew, *Remarks on an Anonymous Tract, Entitled an Answer to Dr. Mayhew's Observations on the Charter and Conduct of the Society for the Propagation of the Gospel in Foreign Parts, Being a Second Defence of the Said Observations* (Boston: Richard and Samuel Draper, Edes and Gill, and Thomas and John Fleet, 1764), 3–4, 83, 12; for American Patriots' use of the Whig interpretation of history, see H. Trevor Colbourn, *The Lamp of Experience: Whig History and the Intellectual Origins of the American Revolution* (Indianapolis: Liberty Fund, 1998 [1965]).
43. Mayhew, *Remarks*, 57–61.
44. Ibid., 59–67; for the contention (against the Bridenbaugh thesis) that the Church of England posed no political danger to New England Protestant dissenters, and that Mayhew feared only Anglican conversion of Congregationalists, see William M. Hogue, "The Religious Conspiracy Theory of the American Revolution: Anglican Motive," *Church History*, vol. 45, no. 3 (September 1976): esp. 287–292; on the contrary, the pastor maintained in his pamphlets that Anglican dominance posed an objective political threat to the liberties of the Congregationalists, even if not all of his Anglican disputants held explicit political objectives in their push for a colonial episcopate (and some clearly did).
45. Mayhew, *Remarks*, 62–63.
46. Mayhew, *Discourse Concerning Unlimited Submission*, vi; Mayhew, *Remarks*, 63.
47. Mayhew, *Remarks*, 70–71.
48. For the decline of English elite anti-Catholicism and the reasons for the British government's softening of its enforcement of the penal laws, see Colin Haydon, *Anti-Catholicism in Eighteenth-Century England, c. 1714–80* (Manchester: Manchester University Press, 1983), 165–172, 180–182.
49. Mayhew, *Remarks*, 73.
50. Voltaire, *Treatise on Tolerance and Other Writings*, ed. Simon Harvey (Cambridge: Cambridge University Press, 2000); official leniency towards Catholics was particularly galling to English Protestant dissenters who continued to be disenfranchised under statutory law, and this aggravation was shared by theologically orthodox and heterodox dissenters alike, according to Haydon, *Anti-Catholicism*, 182–186.
51. Mayhew, *Remarks*, 74–75.

52. Ibid., 75; for the reasons for fear of English Catholicism within Thomas Hollis's circle, and the thesis that the Church of England and Crown government were being corrupted by Catholicism, see Haydon, *Anti-Catholicism*, 184–191.
53. Mayhew, *Remarks*, 85; Clinton Rossiter, "The Life and Mind of Jonathan Mayhew," *William and Mary Quarterly* (October 1950): 538; Bridenbaugh, *Mitre and Sceptre*, 218–229; Richard James Hooker, "The Mayhew Controversy," *Church History*, vol. 5, no. 3 (September 1936): 239–255; happily there has been recent scholarship addressing the Bishop Controversy, with notable studies including Ingram, *Religion, Reform and Modernity*, Chapter 7; Peter M. Doll, *Revolution, Religion, and National Identity: Imperial Anglicanism in British North America, 1745–1795* (Madison, N.J.: Fairleigh Dickinson University Press, 2000); James B. Bell, *A War of Religion: Dissenters, Anglicans, and the American Revolution* (Houndsmills, U.K.: Palgrave Macmillan, 2008), esp. Chapters 6 and 7; James B. Bell, *The Imperial Origins of the King's Church in Early America, 1607–1783* (Houndmills, U.K.: Palgrave McMillan, 2004), esp. Chapter 11; and Kenneth R. Elliott, *Anglican Church Policy, Eighteenth Century Conflict, and the American Episcopate* (New York: Peter Lang, 2011).
54. Pauline Maier, "The Pope at Harvard: The Dudleian Lectures, Anti-Catholicism, and the Politics of Protestantism," *Proceedings of the Massachusetts Historical Society*, vol. 97 (1985): 23–24; Nathan O. Hatch, *The Sacred Cause of Liberty: Republican Thought and the Millennium in Revolutionary New England* (New Haven, Conn.: Yale University Press, 1977), 17, 87, 21; Francis D. Cogliano, *No King, No Popery: Anti-Catholicism in Revolutionary New England* (Westport, Conn.: Greenwood Press, 1995), 46–52.
55. Ruth H. Bloch, *Visionary Republic: Millennial Themes in American Thought, 1756–1800* (Cambridge: Cambridge University Press, 1985), 57–58; Cogliano, *No King, No Popery*, 43–45, 49–51, 55.
56. Bridenbaugh, *Mitre and Sceptre*, 244–245.
57. Ibid., 242, 246–254; Ingram, *Religion, Reform and Modernity*, 239–240.
58. Jonathan Mayhew, *Popish Idolatry: A Discourse Delivered in the Chapel of Harvard-College in Cambridge, New-England, May 8, 1765, at the Lecture Founded by the Honorable Paul Dudley, Esquire* (Boston: Richard and Samuel Draper, Edes and Gill, and Thomas and John Fleet, 1765), esp. 48–50; Maier, "The Pope at Harvard," 23–24.
59. Frederick V. Mills, Sr., "The Internal Anglican Controversy over an American Episcopate, 1763–1775," *Historical Magazine of the Protestant Episcopal Church* (September 1975): 257–276; John Adams, *The Works of John Adams*, vol. 10, ed. Charles Francis Adams (Boston: Little and Brown, 1856), 185; for the thesis that anti-Catholicism was the keystone of British national identity, see Linda Colley, *Britons: Forging the Nation, 1707–1837* (New Haven, Conn.: Yale University Press, 1992), 18–25.
60. Rhoden, *Revolutionary Anglicanism*, 63; for the centrality of denominational loy-

alties in the Revolution, see also J. C. D. Clark, *The Language of Liberty, 1660–1832: Political Discourse and Social Dynamics in the Anglo-American World* (Cambridge: Cambridge University Press, 1994).

61. For the tendency of high-church Anglicans in the colonies to support royal government during the Imperial Crisis and Revolutionary War, see Carla Gardina Pestana, *Protestant Empire: Religion and the Making of the British Atlantic World* (Philadelphia: University of Pennsylvania Press, 2009), 220–225; see also Doll, *Revolution, Religion, and National Identity*, 188; for the Church of England itself as a cause of the Revolution, see Bell, *A War of Religion*, 211–221; for membership in the Presbyterian denomination as a compelling (though not determinative) factor in political affiliation during the Revolution, see Joseph S. Tiedemann, "Presbyterianism and the American Revolution in the Middle Colonies," *Church History*, vol. 74, no. 2 (June 2005): 306–344.

62. For the origins of the Court-Country and Whig-Tory distinctions in Restoration Britain, see William A. Speck, *Reluctant Revolutionaries: Englishmen and the Revolution of 1688* (Oxford: Oxford University Press, 1989), 25–41; for the fear among low-church Whigs, during the Test Act Controversy of 1673–1675, of an alliance of high-church clergy and royalist ministers against the people's civil and religious liberty, see John Locke, *Political Essays*, ed. Mark Goldie (Cambridge: Cambridge University Press, 1997), 360–365.

CHAPTER 6. THE WHIG DILEMMA

1. Jonathan Mayhew, *Two Discourses Delivered November 23rd, 1758, Being the Day Appointed by Authority to Be Observed as a Day of Public Thanksgiving: Relating, More Especially, to the Success of His Majesty's Arms, and Those of the King of Prussia, the Last Year* (Boston: Richard Draper, Edes and Gill, and Green and Russell, 1758), 48.
2. Ibid., 48–49.
3. Pauline Maier, *From Resistance to Revolution: Colonial Radicals and the Development of American Opposition to Britain, 1765–1776* (New York: Random House, 1972), 27–29, 38; for more recent scholarship seeking to reconcile Mayhew's radicalism with his conservatism, and emphasizing his conservatism more than the present work, see John Oakes, "Conservative Revolutionaries: A Study of the Religious and Political Thought of John Wise, Jonathan Mayhew, Andrew Eliot, and Charles Chauncy," Ph.D. dissertation, Simon Fraser University, 2008, esp. 111–162; for a similar analysis, with focus on the Hutchinson Riot, see Howard L. Lubert, "Jonathan Mayhew: Conservative Revolutionary," *Journal of Political History*, vol. 32 (Winter 2011): 589–616.
4. Maier, *From Resistance to Revolution*, 48, 60.
5. Jonathan Mayhew, *Remarks on an Anonymous Tract, Entitled An Answer to Dr. Mayhew's Observations on the Charter and Conduct of the Society for the Propagation of the Gospel in Foreign Parts, Being a Second Defence of the Said Observations*

(Boston: Richard and Samuel Draper, Edes and Gill, and Thomas and John Fleet, 1764), 67.
6. John Adams, *The Works of John Adams*, vol. 10, ed. Charles Francis Adams (Boston: Little and Brown, 1856), 185.
7. Jonathan Mayhew Papers, Bortmann Collection, Boston University, Folder No. 83.
8. Ibid.
9. Bernhard Knollenberg, ed., "Thomas Hollis and Jonathan Mayhew: Their Correspondence, 1759–1766," *Proceedings of the Massachusetts Historical Society*, vol. 69 (1947–1950): 139–141, 148–150, 159, 165–166.
10. Mayhew, *Remarks on an Anonymous Tract*, 63; for the classic argument that Toryism resurged early in the reign of George III, see G. H. Guttridge, *English Whiggism and the American Revolution* (Berkeley: University of California Press, 1963); for a rebuttal of Guttridge's thesis, see Ian R. Christie, "Was There a 'New Toryism' in the Earlier Part of George III's Reign?" *Journal of British Studies*, vol. 5, no. 1 (1965): 60–75; for the British revival of neo-Toryism by the Anglican clergy during the reign of George III, see James E. Bradley, "The Anglican Pulpit, the Social Order and the Resurgence of Toryism during the American Revolution," *Albion*, vol. 21 (1989): 361–388; for high-church Anglican anxieties about British Protestant dissent in the late eighteenth century, see G. M. Ditchfield, "'The Right of Private Judgement, with the Care of the Public Safety': The Church of England's Perceptions of Protestant Dissent in the Later Eighteenth Century," *Enlightenment and Dissent*, vol. 28 (2012): 1–23.
11. Bernard Bailyn, *Faces of Revolution: Personalities and Themes in the Struggle for American Independence* (New York: Random House, 1992), 12–13.
12. Andrew Eliot, *A Sermon Preached before His Excellency Francis Bernard, Esq.; Governor, the Honorable His Majesty's Council, and the Honorable House of Representatives, of the Province of the Massachusetts-Bay in New-England, May 29th, 1765. Being the Anniversary for the Election of His Majesty's Council for the Province* (Boston: Green and Russell, 1765), 47–48.
13. Jonathan Mayhew, *A Discourse Concerning Unlimited Submission and Non-Resistance to the Higher Powers* (Boston: D. Fowle, 1750), 36n.
14. Knollenberg, "Thomas Hollis and Jonathan Mayhew," 173.
15. Ibid., 175.
16. Ibid.
17. Ibid.
18. Mayhew Papers, Folder No. 91.
19. Ibid.
20. Ibid.
21. Ibid.
22. Ibid.
23. Ibid.
24. Ibid.

25. Ibid.
26. Jack P. Greene, ed., *Colonies to Nation, 1763–1789: A Documentary History of the American Revolution* (New York: Norton, 1967), 61–62.
27. Mayhew Papers, Folder No. 91.
28. Knollenberg, "Thomas Hollis and Jonathan Mayhew," 162–163; Mayhew Papers, Folder No. 91; Thomas Hutchinson, *The History of the Colony and Province of Massachusetts-Bay*, vol. 3, ed. Lawrence Shaw Mayo (Cambridge, Mass.: Harvard University Press, 1936), 89.
29. Andrew Eliot, "Letters from Andrew Eliot to Thomas Hollis," *Collections of the Massachusetts Historical Society*, 4th ser., vol. 4 (Boston: Massachusetts Historical Society, 1858), 407; Edmund S. Morgan, "Thomas Hutchinson and the Stamp Act," *New England Quarterly* (December 1948): 471.
30. Jonathan Mayhew, "Letter of Rev. Jonathan Mayhew to Richard Clarke, 1765," *New England Historical and Genealogical Register* (Boston: New England Historic Genealogical Society, 1892), 17.
31. Ibid., 15–18.
32. Ibid., 19; Charles W. Akers, *Called unto Liberty: A Life of Jonathan Mayhew, 1720–1766* (Cambridge, Mass.: Harvard University Press, 1964), 205; Knollenberg, "Thomas Hollis and Jonathan Mayhew," 105; Douglas Adair and John A. Schutz, eds., *Peter Oliver's Origin and Progress of the American Revolution: A Tory View* (San Marino, CA: Huntington Library, 1961), 44; Morgan, "Thomas Hutchinson and the Stamp Act," 471; for a full discussion of the relation of Mayhew's sermon to the Hutchinson Riot, and the argument that Mayhew's sermon was not the inspiration for the riot, see J. Patrick Mullins, "The Sermon That Didn't Start the Revolution: Jonathan Mayhew's Role in the Boston Stamp Act Riots," *Community without Consent: New Perspectives on the Stamp Act*, ed. Zachary McLeod Hutchins (Hanover, N.H.: Dartmouth College Press, 2016), 3–35; for an analysis of the Hutchinson Riot in terms of plebeian politics that discounts any place for Mayhew's sermon in its sources, see Peter Messner, "Stamps and Popes: Rethinking the Role of Violence in the Coming of the Revolution," *Between Sovereignty and Anarchy: The Politics of Violence in the American Revolutionary Era*, ed. Patrick Griffin, Robert G. Ingram, Peter Onuf, and Brian Schoen (Charlottesville: University Press of Virginia, 2015), 114–138.
33. Knollenberg, "Thomas Hollis and Jonathan Mayhew," 178.
34. Ibid., 180–181.
35. John Adams, *Papers of John Adams, Volume 1: September 1755–October 1773*, ed. Robert J. Taylor (Cambridge, Mass.: Harvard University Press, 1977), 104, 117–118n, 122n, 125–126.
36. Ibid., 127–128.
37. Thomas Hollis, *The Memoirs of Thomas Hollis*, ed. Francis Blackburne (London: [publisher not identified], 1780), 281, 291; Knollenberg, "Thomas Hollis and Jonathan Mayhew," 181.

38. Knollenberg, "Thomas Hollis and Jonathan Mayhew," 183–184; Greene, *Colonies to Nation, 1763–1789*, 68–69.
39. William C. Lowe, "Archbishop Secker, the Bench of Bishops and the Repeal of the Stamp Act," *Historical Magazine of the Protestant Episcopal Church* (December 1977): 429–442.
40. Hollis, *Memoirs*, 300; Mayhew Papers, Folder No. 94 (italicized words were underlined in the original).
41. Jonathan Mayhew, *The Snare Broken, a Thanksgiving-Discourse, Preached at the Desire of the West Church, in Boston, N.E., Friday May 23, 1766, Occasioned by the Repeal of the Stamp-Act* (Boston: Richard and Samuel Draper, Edes and Gill, 1766), 2–3.
42. Ibid., 4–5.
43. Ibid., 6–9.
44. Ibid., 18–19.
45. Ibid., 13.
46. Ibid., 13–14.
47. Ibid., 19–21, 33, 41.
48. Alan Heimert, *Religion and the American Mind: From the Great Awakening to the Revolution* (Cambridge, Mass.: Harvard University Press, 1966), 259–261, 274–275, 280, 290–293.
49. Mayhew, *The Snare Broken*, 34.
50. Ibid., 35.
51. Ibid., 36.
52. Ibid., 38–39.
53. Ibid., 42.
54. Maier, *From Resistance to Revolution*, 27.
55. Mayhew Papers, Folder No. 131.
56. Ibid.
57. Ibid.
58. Ibid.; John R. Galvin, *Three Men of Boston: Leadership and Conflict at the Start of the American Revolution* (Washington, D.C.: Brassey's, 1976), 131–132.
59. Mercy Otis Warren, *History of the Rise, Progress and Termination of the American Revolution Interspersed with Biographical, Political and Moral Observations*, ed. Lester H. Cohen (Indianapolis: Liberty Fund, 1989), 348.
60. Heimert, *Religion and the American Mind*, 259–261, 274–275, 280, 290–293; Mayhew Papers, Folder No. 131.

CONCLUSION

1. Jonathan Mayhew Papers, Bortmann Collection, Boston University, Folder No. 98; Charles W. Akers, *Called unto Liberty: A Life of Jonathan Mayhew, 1720–1766* (Cambridge, Mass.: Harvard University Press, 1964), 218–220; Bernhard Knollenberg, ed.,

"Thomas Hollis and Jonathan Mayhew: Their Correspondence, 1759–1766," *Proceedings of the Massachusetts Historical Society*, vol. 69 (1947–1950): 188, 192.

2. Charles W. Akers, *The Divine Politician: Samuel Cooper and the American Revolution in Boston* (Boston: Northeastern University Press, 1982), 72; William H. Bond, ed., "Letters from Thomas Hollis of Lincoln's Inn to Andrew Eliot," *Proceedings of the Massachusetts Historical Society*, vol. 99 (1987): 401; Knollenberg, "Thomas Hollis and Jonathan Mayhew," 188, 192–193.

3. Akers, *Called unto Liberty*, 219–221; Anne Rowe Cunningham, ed., *Letters and Diary of John Rowe, Boston Merchant, 1759–1762, 1764–1779* (Boston: W. B. Clarke, 1903), 103.

4. Thomas Hollis, *The Memoirs of Thomas Hollis*, ed. Francis Blackburne (London: [publisher not identified], 1780), 608.

5. Charles Chauncy, *A Discourse Occasioned by the Death of the Reverend Jonathan Mayhew, D.D., Late Pastor of the West-Church in Boston: Who Departed This Life on Wednesday Morning, July 9, 1766, AETATIS 46. Delivered the Lord's-Day after His Decease* (Boston: Richard and Samuel Draper, Edes and Gill, and Thomas and John Fleet, 1766), 27–28, 39; Hollis, *Memoirs*, 319, 371, 608; [Benjamin Church], *Elegy on the Death of the Reverend Jonathan Mayhew, D.D., Who Departed This Life July 9th, Anno Domini, 1766, Aetatis suae 46* (Boston: Edes and Gill, 1766), 10–11; Mayhew Papers, Folder No. 123.

6. John Adams, *Diary and Autobiography of John Adams, Volume 2: Diary 1771–1781*, ed. Lyman H. Butterfield (Cambridge, Mass.: Harvard University Press, 1961), 55, 75, 95.

7. Bernard Mason, ed., *The American Colonial Crisis: The Daniel Leonard–John Adams Letters to the Press, 1774–1775* (New York: Harper and Row, 1972), 119.

8. John Adams, *The Works of John Adams*, vol. 10, ed. Charles Francis Adams (Boston: Little and Brown, 1856), 287–288; Adams, *Diary and Autobiography of John Adams: Diary 1782–1804, Autobiography Part One to October 1776*, ed. Lyman H. Butterfield (Cambridge, Mass.: Harvard University Press, 1961), 286.

BIBLIOGRAPHY

NEWSPAPERS AND JOURNALS
American Magazine
Boston Evening-Post
Boston Gazette, and The Country Journal
Boston Gazette, or, Weekly Journal
The Monthly Review, or, Literary Journal

MANUSCRIPT COLLECTIONS
Benjamin Colman Papers, Massachusetts Historical Society
Fulham Papers, 1700–1800, Lambeth Palace Library
H. H. Edes Papers, Massachusetts Historical Society
Jasper Mauduit Papers, Massachusetts Historical Society
Jonathan Mayhew Papers, Bortmann Collection, Boston University
Mayhew Family Papers, Houghton Library, Harvard University
Mayhew Sermon Transcripts, Huntington Library
Otis Family Papers, Massachusetts Historical Society
Robert Treat Paine Papers, Massachusetts Historical Society
Thomas Hollis Papers, Massachusetts Historical Society
William Cushing Papers, Massachusetts Historical Society

ARTICLES
Bailyn, Bernard. "Religion and Revolution: Three Biographical Studies." *Perspectives in American History*, vol. 4 (1970): 111–139.
Beneke, Chris. "The Critical Turn: Jonathan Mayhew, the British Empire, and the Idea of Resistance in Mid-Eighteenth-Century Boston." *Massachusetts Historical Review*, vol. 10 (2008): 23–56.
Bond, William H., ed. "Letters from Thomas Hollis of Lincoln's Inn to Andrew Eliot." *Proceedings of the Massachusetts Historical Society*, vol. 99 (1987): 76–167.
Bradley, James E. "The Anglican Pulpit, the Social Order and the Resurgence of Toryism during the American Revolution." *Albion*, vol. 21 (1989): 361–388.
Bremer, Francis. "In Defense of Regicide: John Cotton on the Execution of Charles I." *William and Mary Quarterly* (January 1980): 103–124.
Christie, Ian R. "Was There a 'New Toryism' in the Earlier Part of George III's Reign?" *Journal of British Studies*, vol. 5, no. 1 (1965): 60–75.
Clark, Jonathan. "The American Revolution: A War of Religion?" *History Today*, 39 (December 1989): 10–16.
Cushing, John D. "Notes on Disestablishment in Massachusetts, 1780–1833." *William and Mary Quarterly* (April 1969): 169–172.
Ditchfield, G. M. "'The Right of Private Judgement, with the Care of the Public

Safety': The Church of England's Perceptions of Protestant Dissent in the Later Eighteenth Century." *Enlightenment and Dissent*, vol. 28 (2012): 1–23.

Eliot, Andrew. "Letters from Andrew Eliot to Thomas Hollis." *Collections of the Massachusetts Historical Society*, 4th ser., vol. 4, 407. Boston: Massachusetts Historical Society, 1858.

Ferguson, Robert A. "The Dialectic of Liberty: Law and Religion in Anglo-American Politics." *Modern Intellectual History*, vol. 1, no. 1 (2004): 27–54.

Gerardi, Donald F. M. "Samuel Johnson and the Yale 'Apostasy' of 1722." *Historical Magazine of the Protestant Episcopal Church* (June 1978): 153–176.

Gerlach, Don R., and George DeMille. "Samuel Johnson and the Founding of King's College, 1751–1755." *Historical Magazine of the Protestant Episcopal Church* (September 1975): 335–352.

Hogue, William M. "The Religious Conspiracy Theory of the American Revolution: Anglican Motive." *Church History*, vol. 45, no. 3 (September 1976): 277–292.

Hooker, Richard James. "The Mayhew Controversy." *Church History*, vol. 5, no. 3 (September 1936): 239–255.

"Jasper Mauduit: Agent in London for the Province of Massachusetts-Bay, 1762–1765." *Collections of the Massachusetts Historical Society*, vol. 74. Boston: Massachusetts Historical Society, 1918.

Knollenberg, Bernhard, ed. "Thomas Hollis and Jonathan Mayhew: Their Correspondence, 1759–1766." *Proceedings of the Massachusetts Historical Society*, vol. 69 (1947–1950): 102–193.

Lowe, William C. "Archbishop Secker, the Bench of Bishops and the Repeal of the Stamp Act." *Historical Magazine of the Protestant Episcopal Church* (December 1977): 429–442.

Lubert, Howard L. "Jonathan Mayhew: Conservative Revolutionary." *Journal of Political History*, vol. 32 (Winter 2011): 589–616.

Maier, Pauline. "The Pope at Harvard: The Dudleian Lectures, Anti-Catholicism, and the Politics of Protestantism." *Proceedings of the Massachusetts Historical Society*, vol. 97 (1985): 16–41.

Mayhew, Jonathan. "Letter of Rev. Jonathan Mayhew to Richard Clarke, 1765." *New England Historical and Genealogical Register* (1892): 15–20.

"Memoirs of Prince's Subscribers." *New England Historical and Genealogical Register* (July 1859): 248.

Mills, Frederick, V., Sr. "The Internal Anglican Controversy over an American Episcopate, 1763–1775." *Historical Magazine of the Protestant Episcopal Church* (September 1975): 257–276.

Morgan, Edmund S. "Review of Alan Heimert's *Religion and the American Mind*." *William and Mary Quarterly* (July 1967): 454–459.

———. "Thomas Hutchinson and the Stamp Act." *New England Quarterly* (December 1948): 459–492.

Mullins, J. Patrick. "'A Kind of War, Tho' Hitherto an Un-Bloody One': Jonathan Mayhew, Francis Bernard, and the Indian Affair." *Massachusetts Historical Review*, vol. 11 (2009): 27–56.

Rand, Benjamin. "Philosophical Instruction in Harvard University from 1636 to 1900." *The Harvard Graduates' Magazine* (September 1928): 296–301.

"Records of the West Church, Boston." *New England Historical and Genealogical Register* (July 1939): 259–260.

"Researches among Funeral Sermons." *New England Historical and Genealogical Register* (July 1853): 250.

Rossiter, Clinton. "The Life and Mind of Jonathan Mayhew." *William and Mary Quarterly* (October 1950): 531–558.

Spurr, John. "Rational Religion in Restoration England." *Journal of the History of Ideas*, vol. 49, no. 4 (October–December 1988): 563–585.

Taylor, Stephen. "Whigs, Bishops, and America: The Politics of Church Reform in Mid-Eighteenth-Century England." *Historical Journal* (June 1993): 331–356.

Tiedemann, Joseph S. "Presbyterianism and the American Revolution in the Middle Colonies." *Church History*, vol. 74, no. 2 (June 2005): 306–344.

Van Tyne, C. H. "Influence of the Clergy, and of Religious and Sectarian Forces, on the American Revolution." *American Historical Review* (October 1913): 44–64.

Waters, John J., and John A. Schutz. "Patterns of Massachusetts Colonial Politics: The Writs of Assistance and the Rivalry between the Otis and Hutchinson Families." *William and Mary Quarterly* (October 1967): 543–567.

Winship, Michael P. "Godly Republicanism and the Origins of the Massachusetts Polity." *William and Mary Quarterly* (July 2006): 427–462.

Wood, Gordon S. "Conspiracy and the Paranoid Style: Causality and Deceit in the Eighteenth Century." *William and Mary Quarterly* (July 1982): 402–441.

———. "Rhetoric and Reality in the American Revolution." *William and Mary Quarterly* (January 1966): 4–32.

BOOKS AND PAMPHLETS

Adair, Douglas, and John A. Schutz, eds. *Peter Oliver's Origin and Progress of the American Revolution: A Tory View*. San Marino, CA: Huntington Library, 1961.

Adams, John. *Diary and Autobiography*, vols. 1–3. Edited by Lyman H. Butterfield. Cambridge, Mass.: Harvard University Press, 1961.

———. *Papers of John Adams, Volume 1: September 1755–October 1773*. Edited by Robert J. Taylor. Cambridge, Mass.: Harvard University Press, 1977.

———. *The Works of John Adams*. 10 vols. Edited by Charles Francis Adams. Boston: Little and Brown, 1856.

Akers, Charles W. *Called unto Liberty: A Life of Jonathan Mayhew, 1720–1766*. Cambridge, Mass.: Harvard University Press, 1964.

———. *The Divine Politician: Samuel Cooper and the American Revolution in Boston.* Boston: Northeastern University Press, 1982.
Anderson, Fred. *Crucible of War: The Seven Years' War and the Fate of Empire in British North America, 1754–1766.* New York: Random House, 2000.
[Aplin, John.] *Verses on Doctor Mayhew's Book of Observations on the Charter and Conduct of the Society for the Propagation of the Gospel in Foreign Parts: With Notes, Critical and Explanatory.* Providence, R.I.: William Goddard, 1763.
Apthorp, East. *Considerations on the Institution and Conduct of the Society for the Propagation of the Gospel in Foreign Parts.* Boston: Green and Russell, Thomas and John Fleet, 1763.
Ashcraft, Richard. *Revolutionary Politics and Locke's Two Treatises of Government.* Princeton, N.J.: Princeton University Press, 1986.
Bailyn, Bernard. *Faces of Revolution: Personalities and Themes in the Struggle for American Independence.* New York: Random House, 1990.
———. *The Ideological Origins of the American Revolution.* Cambridge, Mass.: Harvard University Press, 1992 [1967].
———. *The Ordeal of Thomas Hutchinson.* Cambridge, Mass.: Harvard University Press, 1974.
———, ed. *Pamphlets of the American Revolution, 1750–1776, Volume I, 1750–1765.* Cambridge, Mass.: Harvard University Press, 1965.
Baldwin, Alice M. *The New England Clergy and the American Revolution.* Durham, N.C.: Duke University Press, 1928.
[Baron, Richard, ed.] *The Pillars of Priestcraft and Orthodoxy Shaken, Volume II.* London: R. Griffiths, 1752.
Barrington, John Shute. *The Rights of Protestant Dissenters.* London: n.p., 1704.
Bartol, Cyrus. *The West Church and Its Ministers: The Fiftieth Anniversary of the Ordination of Charles Lowell, D.D.* Boston: Crosby, Nicholas, 1856.
Beard, Charles A. *An Economic Interpretation of the Constitution of the United States.* New York: Macmillan, 1913.
Becker, Carl L. *The History of Political Parties in the Province of New York, 1760–1776.* Madison: University of Wisconsin Press, 1908.
Beiser, Frederick C. *Sovereignty of Reason: The Defense of Rationality in the Early English Enlightenment.* Princeton, N.J.: Princeton University Press, 1996.
Bell, James B. *Empire, Religion and Revolution in Early Virginia, 1607–1786.* Houndmills, U.K.: Palgrave Macmillan, 2013.
———. *The Imperial Origins of the King's Church in Early America, 1607–1783.* Houndmills, U.K.: Palgrave McMillan, 2004.
———. *A War of Religion: Dissenters, Anglicans, and the American Revolution.* Houndmills, U.K.: Palgrave McMillan, 2008.
Beneke, Chris. *Beyond Toleration: The Religious Origins of American Pluralism.* Oxford: Oxford University Press, 2006.
Benton, William Allen. *Whig-Loyalism: An Aspect of Political Ideology in the Amer-

ican Revolutionary Era. Rutherford, N.J.: Fairleigh Dickinson University Press, 1969.

Bilder, Mary Sarah. *The Transatlantic Constitution: Colonial Legal Culture and the Empire*. Cambridge, Mass.: Harvard University Press, 2004.

Bloch, Ruth H. *Visionary Republic: Millennial Themes in American Thought, 1756–1800*. Cambridge: Cambridge University Press, 1985.

Bonomi, Patricia U. *Under the Cope of Heaven: Religion, Society, and Politics in Colonial America*. New York: Oxford University Press, 1986.

Bradford, Alden. *Memoir of the Life and Writings of Rev. Jonathan Mayhew, D.D.* Boston: Little, 1838.

Bradley, James E. *Religion, Revolution, and English Radicalism: Nonconformity in Eighteenth-Century Politics and Society*. Cambridge: Cambridge University Press, 1990.

Bradley, James E., and Dale K. Van Kley, eds. *Religion and Politics in Enlightenment Europe*. Notre Dame, Ind.: University of Notre Dame Press, 2001.

Breen, T. H. *American Insurgents, American Patriots: The Revolution of the People*. New York: Hill and Wang, 2010.

Bridenbaugh, Carl. *Mitre and Sceptre: Transatlantic Faiths, Ideas, Personalities, and Politics, 1689–1776*. New York: Oxford University Press, 1962.

[Browne, Arthur.] *Remarks on Dr. Mayhew's Incidental Reflections, Relative to the Church of England, As Contained in His Observations on the Charter and Conduct of the Society, &c.* Portsmouth, N.H.: Fowle, 1763.

Bulman, William J., and Robert G. Ingram, eds. *God in the Enlightenment*. Oxford: Oxford University Press, 2016.

Bushman, Richard L. *From Puritan to Yankee: Character and the Social Order in Connecticut, 1690–1765*. Cambridge, Mass.: Harvard University Press, 1967.

———. *King and People in Provincial Massachusetts*. Chapel Hill: University of North Carolina Press, 1985.

Butler, Joseph. *Sermons*. Oxford: Clarendon Press, 1896.

Butterfield, Lyman, ed. *Adams Family Papers*, vol. 1. Cambridge, Mass.: Harvard University Press, 1963.

Byrd, James P. *Sacred Scripture, Sacred War: The Bible and the American Revolution*. Oxford: Oxford University Press, 2013.

[Caner, Henry.] *A Candid Examination of Dr. Mayhew's Observations on the Charter and Conduct of the Society for the Propagation of the Gospel in Foreign Parts, to Which Is Added, a Letter to a Friend, Containing a Short Vindication of the Said Society against the Mistakes and Misrepresentations of the Doctor in His Observations on the Conduct of That Society, by One of Its Members [Samuel Johnson]*. Boston: Thomas and John Fleet, Green and Russell, Edes and Gill, 1763.

Cappon, Lester J., ed. *The Adams-Jefferson Letters: The Complete Correspondence between Thomas Jefferson and Abigail and John Adams*. Vol. 2. Chapel Hill: University of North Carolina Press, 1999.

Champion, J. A. I. *The Pillars of Priestcraft Shaken: The Church of England and Its Enemies, 1660–1730.* Cambridge: Cambridge University Press, 1992.

Channing, Edward, and Archibald Cary Coolidge, eds. *The Barrington-Bernard Correspondence and Illustrative Matter, 1760–1770.* Cambridge, Mass.: Harvard University Press, 1912.

Chauncy, Charles. *A Discourse Occasioned by the Death of the Reverend Jonathan Mayhew, D.D., Late Pastor of the West-Church in Boston: Who Departed This Life on Wednesday Morning, July 9, 1766, AETATIS 46. Delivered the Lord's Day after His Decease.* Boston: Richard and Samuel Draper, Edes and Gill, and Thomas and John Fleet, 1766.

[Church, Benjamin.] *Elegy on the Death of the Reverend Jonathan Mayhew, D.D., Who Departed This Life July 9th, Anno Domini, 1766, Aetatis suae 46.* Boston: Edes and Gill, 1766.

Clark, J. C. D. *English Society, 1660–1832: Ideology, Social Structure, and Political Practice during the Ancien Regime.* Cambridge: Cambridge University Press, 2000 [1985].

———. *The Language of Liberty, 1660–1832: Political Discourse and Social Dynamics in the Anglo-American World.* Cambridge: Cambridge University Press, 1994.

Clarke, Samuel. *The Works of Samuel Clarke.* New York: Garland Publishing, 1978.

Cogley, Richard W. *John Eliot's Mission to the Indians before King Philip's War.* Cambridge, Mass.: Harvard University Press, 1999.

Cogliano, Francis D. *No King, No Popery: Anti-Catholicism in Revolutionary New England.* Westport, Conn.: Greenwood Press, 1995.

Colbourn, Trevor. *The Lamp of Experience: Whig History and the Intellectual Origins of the American Revolution.* Indianapolis: Liberty Fund, 1998 [1965].

Colley, Linda. *Britons: Forging the Nation, 1707–1837.* New Haven, Conn.: Yale University Press, 1992.

Cooper, James F., Jr. *Tenacious of Their Liberties: The Congregationalists in Colonial Massachusetts.* New York: Oxford University Press, 1999.

Corrigan, John. *The Hidden Balance: Religion and the Social Theories of Charles Chauncy and Jonathan Mayhew.* Cambridge: Cambridge University Press, 1987.

———. *The Prism of Piety: Catholick Congregational Clergy at the Beginning of the Enlightenment.* Oxford: Oxford University Press, 1991.

Cross, Arthur Lyon. *The Anglican Episcopate and the American Colonies.* London: Longmans, Green, 1902.

Cunningham, Anne Rowe, ed. *Letters and Diary of John Rowe, Boston Merchant, 1759–1762, 1764–1779.* Boston: W. B. Clarke, 1903.

Davidson, Philip. *Propaganda and the American Revolution, 1763–1783.* Chapel Hill: University of North Carolina Press, 1941.

Dickerson, Oliver M. *The Navigation Acts and the American Revolution.* Philadelphia: University of Pennsylvania Press, 1951.

Dickinson, H. T. *Liberty and Property: Political Ideology in Eighteenth-Century Britain.* London: Methuen, 1979 [1977].

Doll, Peter M. *Revolution, Religion, and National Identity: Imperial Anglicanism in British North America, 1745–1795*. Madison, N.J.: Fairleigh Dickinson University Press, 2000.

Dworetz, Steven M. *The Unvarnished Doctrine: Locke, Liberalism, and the American Revolution*. Durham, N.C.: Duke University Press, 1990.

Eliot, Andrew. *A Sermon Preached before His Excellency Francis Bernard, Esq.; Governor, the Honorable His Majesty's Council, and the Honorable House of Representatives, of the Province of the Massachusetts-Bay in New-England, May 29th, 1765. Being the Anniversary for the Election of His Majesty's Council for the Province*. Boston: Green and Russell, 1765.

Eliot, Samuel A. *Heralds of a Liberal Faith, Volume One: The Prophets*. Boston: American Unitarian Association, 1910.

Elliott, Kenneth R. *Anglican Church Policy, Eighteenth Century Conflict, and the American Episcopate*. New York: Peter Lang, 2011.

Engeman, Thomas S., and Michael P. Zuckert, eds. *Protestantism and the American Founding*. Notre Dame, Ind.: University of Notre Dame Press, 2004.

Ferguson, Robert A. *The American Enlightenment, 1750–1820*. Cambridge, Mass.: Harvard University Press, 1997.

Foote, Henry Wilder, ed. *The Annals of Kings Chapel: From the Puritan Age of New England to the Present Day*. Vol. 2. Boston: Little and Brown, 1896.

Fowler, William W., Jr. *Empires at War: The French and Indian War and the Struggle for North America, 1754–1763*. New York: Walker, 2005.

Frazer, Gregg L. *The Religious Beliefs of America's Founders: Reason, Revelation, and Revolution*. Lawrence: University Press of Kansas, 2012.

Freeman, Joanne B. *Affairs of Honor: National Politics in the New Republic*. New Haven, Conn.: Yale University Press, 2001.

Galvin, John R. *Three Men of Boston: Leadership and Conflict at the Start of the American Revolution*. Washington, D.C.: Brassey's, 1976.

Gascoigne, John. *Cambridge in the Age of the Enlightenment: Science, Religion, and Politics from the Restoration to the French Revolution*. Cambridge: Cambridge University Press, 1989.

Gay, Ebenezer. *The Alienation of the Affections from Ministers Consider'd, and Improv'd: A Sermon Preach'd at the Ordination of the Reverend Mr. Jonathan Mayhew to the Pastoral Care of the West-Church in Boston, June 17, 1747*. Boston: Rogers and Fowle, 1747.

Gay, Peter. *The Enlightenment: The Rise of Modern Paganism*. New York: Alfred A. Knopf, 1966.

Gibson, William. *Enlightenment Prelate: Benjamin Hoadly, 1676–1761*. Cambridge: James Clarke, 2004.

Gish, Dustin, and Daniel Klinghard, eds. *Resistance to Tyrants, Obedience to God: Reason, Religion, and Republicanism at the American Founding*. Lanham, Md.: Lexington Books, 2013.

Greaves, Richard L. *Deliver Us from Evil: The Radical Underground in Britain, 1660–1663*. Oxford: Oxford University Press, 1986.

———. *Secrets of the Kingdom: British Radicals from the Popish Plot to the Revolution of 1688–1689*. Stanford, Calif.: Stanford University Press, 1992.

Greene, Jack P., ed. *Colonies to Nation, 1763–1789: A Documentary History of the American Revolution*. New York: Norton, 1967.

Gregory, Brad S. *The Unintended Reformation: How a Religious Reformation Secularized Society*. Cambridge, Mass.: Harvard University Press, 2012.

Griffin, Patrick, Robert G. Ingram, Peter Onuf, and Brian Schoen. *Between Sovereignty and Anarchy: The Politics of Violence in the American Revolutionary Era*. Charlottesville: University Press of Virginia, 2015.

Guttridge, G. H. *English Whiggism and the American Revolution*. Berkeley: University of California Press, 1963.

Haakonssen, Knud, ed. *Enlightenment and Religion: Rational Dissent in Eighteenth-Century Britain*. Cambridge: Cambridge University Press, 1996.

Haley, K. H. D. *The First Earl of Shaftesbury*. Oxford: Clarendon Press, 1968.

Hartz, Louis B. *The Liberal Tradition in America: An Interpretation of American Political Thought since the Revolution*. San Diego, CA: Harcourt, Brace, 1991 [1952].

Hatch, Nathan O. *The Sacred Cause of Liberty: Republican Thought and the Millennium in Revolutionary New England*. New Haven, Conn.: Yale University Press, 1977.

Haydon, Colin. *Anti-Catholicism in Eighteenth-Century England, c. 1714–80*. Manchester: Manchester University Press, 1983.

Heimert, Alan. *Religion and the American Mind: From the Great Awakening to the Revolution*. Cambridge, Mass.: Harvard University Press, 1966.

Heimert, Alan, and Andrew Delbanco, eds. *The Puritans in America: A Narrative Anthology*. Cambridge, Mass.: Harvard University Press, 1985.

Heimert, Alan, and Perry Miller, eds. *The Great Awakening: Documents Illustrating the Crisis and Its Consequences*. Indianapolis: Bobbs-Merrill, 1967.

Herman, Arthur. *How the Scots Invented the Modern World*. New York: Three Rivers Press, 2001.

Hoadly, Benjamin. *The Works of Benjamin Hoadly*. Edited by John Hoadly. London: W. Bowyer and J. Nichols, 1773.

Holifeld, E. Brooks. *Theology in America: Christian Thought from the Age of the Puritans to the Civil War*. New Haven, Conn.: Yale University Press, 2003.

Hollis, Thomas. *Letters from Thomas Hollis of Lincoln's Inn to Andrew Eliot*. Edited by William H. Bond. Cambridge, Mass.: The Houghton Library, 1988.

———. *The Memoirs of Thomas Hollis*. Edited by Francis Blackburne. London, 1780.

Howe, Daniel Walker. *The Unitarian Conscience: Harvard Moral Philosophy, 1805–1861*. Middletown, Conn.: Wesleyan University Press, 1988.

Hutchins, Zachary McLeod, ed. *Community without Consent: New Perspectives on the Stamp Act*. Hanover, N.H.: Dartmouth College Press, 2016.

Hutchinson, Thomas. *The History of the Colony and Province of Massachusetts-Bay*.

Vol. 3. Edited by Lawrence Shaw Mayo. Cambridge, Mass.: Harvard University Press, 1936.
Ingram, Robert G. *Religion, Reform and Modernity: Thomas Secker and the Church of England*. London: Boydell, 2007.
Isaac, Rhys. *The Transformation of Virginia, 1740–1790*. Chapel Hill: University of North Carolina Press, 1999.
Jacobson, David L., ed. *The English Libertarian Heritage: From the Writings of John Trenchard and Thomas Gordon in The Independent Whig and Cato's Letters*. San Francisco: Fox and Wilkes, 1994 [1965].
Jameson, J. Franklin. *The American Revolution Considered as a Social Movement*. Princeton, N.J.: Princeton University Press, 1926.
Jefferson, Thomas. *Thomas Jefferson: Writings*. Edited by Merrill D. Peterson. New York: Library of America, 1984.
Jones, J. R. *Country and Court: England, 1658–1714*. Cambridge, Mass.: Harvard University Press, 1978.
———. *The First Whigs: The Politics of the Exclusion Crisis, 1678–1683*. London: Oxford University Press, 1961.
Jones, J. W. *The Shattered Synthesis: New England Puritanism before the Great Awakening*. New Haven, Conn.: Yale University Press, 1973.
Kenyon, J. P. *Revolution Principles: The Politics of Party, 1689–1720*. Cambridge: Cambridge University Press, 1977.
Kepel, Gilles. *The Revenge of God: The Resurgence of Islam, Christianity, and Judaism in the Modern World*. Translated by Alan Braley. University Park: Pennsylvania State University Press, 1994.
Kidd, Thomas S. *The Great Awakening: The Roots of Evangelical Christianity in America*. New Haven, Conn.: Yale University Press, 2007.
———. *The Protestant Interest: New England after Puritanism*. New Haven, Conn.: Yale University Press, 2004.
Kishlansky, Mark. *A Monarchy Transformed: Britain, 1603–1714*. London: Penguin Books, 1996.
Knight, Janice. *Orthodoxies in Massachusetts: Rereading American Puritanism*. Cambridge, Mass.: Harvard University Press, 1994.
Kurtz, Steven G., and James H. Hutson, eds. *Essays on the American Revolution*. Chapel Hill: University of North Carolina Press, 1973.
Landsman, Ned C. *From Colonials to Provincials: American Thought and Culture, 1680–1760*. Ithaca, N.Y.: Cornell University Press, 1997.
Langguth, A. J. *Patriots: The Men Who Started the American Revolution*. New York: Simon and Schuster, 1989.
Levy, Leonard W. *The Establishment Clause: Religion and the First Amendment*. New York: Macmillan, 1986.
Lincoln, Anthony. *Some Political and Social Ideas of English Dissent*. Cambridge: Cambridge University Press, 1938.

Lippy, Charles H. *Seasonable Revolutionary: The Mind of Charles Chauncy.* Chicago, 1981.

Livingston, William. *The Independent Reflector: or, Weekly Essays on Sundry Important Subjects More Particularly Adapted to the Province of New-York.* Edited by Milton M. Klein. Cambridge, Mass.: Harvard University Press, 1963.

Locke, John. *An Essay Concerning Human Understanding.* Edited by Peter H. Nidditch. Oxford: Clarendon Press, 1975.

———. *Political Essays.* Edited by Mark Goldie. Cambridge: Cambridge University Press, 1997.

———. *Two Treatises of Government.* Edited by Peter Laslett. Cambridge: Cambridge University Press, 1992 [1960].

———. *The Works of John Locke.* Vols. 1–3. London: W. Taylor, 1722.

Maier, Pauline. *From Resistance to Revolution: Colonial Radicals and the Development of American Opposition to Britain, 1765–1776.* New York: Random House, 1972.

Manning, Bernard Lord. *The Protestant Dissenting Deputies.* Edited by Ormond Greenwood. Cambridge: Cambridge University Press, 1952.

Marsden, George M. *Jonathan Edwards: A Life.* New Haven, Conn.: Yale University Press, 2003.

Mason, Bernard, ed. *The American Colonial Crisis: The Daniel Leonard–John Adams Letters to the Press, 1774–1775.* New York: Harper and Row, 1972.

Mather, Cotton. *The Christian Philosopher.* Edited by Winton U. Solberg. Urbana: University of Illinois Press, 1994.

May, Henry F. *The Enlightenment in America.* Oxford: Oxford University Press, 1976.

Mayhew, Experience. *A Discourse Shewing That God Dealeth with Men as with Reasonable Creatures.* Boston: Green, 1720.

Mayhew, Jonathan. *Christian Sobriety: Being Eight Sermons on Titus II:6, Preached with a Special View to the Benefit of the Young Men Usually Attending the Public Worship at the West Church in Boston.* Boston: Richard and Samuel Draper, Edes and Gill, and Thomas and John Fleet, 1763.

———. *A Defence of the Observations on the Charter and Conduct of the Society for the Propagation of the Gospel in Foreign Parts, against an Anonymous Pamphlet Falsely Intitled, A Candid Examination of Dr. Mayhew's Observations, &c., and Also against the Letter to a Friend Annexed Thereto, Said to Contain a Short Vindication of Said Society, by One of Its Members.* Boston: Richard and Samuel Draper, Edes and Gill, and Thomas and John Fleet, 1763.

———. *A Discourse Concerning Unlimited Submission and Non-Resistance to the Higher Powers.* Boston: Daniel Fowle, 1750.

———. *A Discourse Occasioned by the Death of the Honourable Stephen Sewall, Esq.; Chief-Justice of the Superiour Court of Judicature, Court of Assize, and General-Goal-Delivery; as Also a Member of His Majesty's Council for the Province of the Massachusetts-Bay in New-England: Who Departed This Life on Wednesday-Night, September 10, 1760, Delivered the Lord's-Day after His Decease.* Boston: Richard Draper, Edes and Gill, and Thomas and John Fleet, 1760.

———. *A Discourse Occasioned by the Death of King George II and the Happy Accession of His Majesty King George III to the Imperial Throne of Great Britain, Delivered January 4th, 1761*. Boston: Edes and Gill, 1761.

———. *A Discourse on Rev. XV, 3rd and 4th, Occasioned by the Earthquakes in November 1755*. Boston: Edes and Gill, 1755.

———. *Observations on the Charter and Conduct of the Society for the Propagation of the Gospel in Foreign Parts: Designed to Shew Their Non-Conformity to Each Other*. Boston: Richard and Samuel Draper, Edes and Gill, and Thomas and John Fleet, 1763.

———. *Popish Idolatry: A Discourse Delivered in the Chapel of Harvard College in Cambridge, New-England, May 8, 1765, at the Lecture Founded by the Honorable Paul Dudley, Esquire*. Boston: Richard and Samuel Draper, Edes and Gill, and Thomas and John Fleet, 1765.

———. *Remarks on an Anonymous Tract, Entitled an Answer to Dr. Mayhew's Observations on the Charter and Conduct of the Society for the Propagation of the Gospel in Foreign Parts, Being a Second Defence of the Said Observations*. Boston: Richard and Samuel Draper, Edes and Gill, and Thomas and John Fleet, 1764.

———. *A Sermon Preach'd in the Audience of His Excellency, William Shirley, Esq.; Captain General, Governour and Commander in Chief, the Honourable His Majesty's Council, and the Honourable House of Representatives of the Province of the Massachusetts-Bay, in New-England, May 29, 1754. Being the Anniversary for the Election of His Majesty's Council for the Province*. Boston: Samuel Kneeland, 1754.

———. *A Sermon Preached at Boston in New-England, May 26, 1751, Occasioned by the Much-Lamented Death of His Royal Highness Frederick, Prince of Wales*. Boston: Richard Draper and Daniel Gookin, 1751.

———. *Sermons upon the Following Subjects*. Boston: Richard Draper, 1755.

———. *Seven Sermons upon the Following Subjects*. Boston: Rogers and Fowle, 1749.

———. *The Snare Broken, a Thanksgiving-Discourse, Preached at the Desire of the West Church, in Boston, N.E., Friday May 23, 1766, Occasioned by the Repeal of the Stamp-Act*. Boston: Richard and Samuel Draper, Edes and Gill, 1766.

———. *Two Discourses Delivered November 23rd, 1758, Being the Day Appointed by Authority to Be Observed as a Day of Public Thanksgiving: Relating, More Especially, to the Success of His Majesty's Arms, and Those of the King of Prussia, the Last Year*. Boston: Richard Draper, Edes and Gill, and Green and Russell, 1758.

———. *Two Discourses Delivered October 9th, 1760. Being the Day Appointed to Be Observed as a Day of Public Thanksgiving for the Success of His Majesty's Arms, More Especially in the Intire Reduction of Canada*. Boston: Edes and Gill, 1760.

———. *Two Discourses Delivered October 25th, 1759, Being the Day Appointed by Authority to Be Observed as a Day of Public Thanksgiving, for the Success of His Majesty's Arms, More Particularly in the Reduction of Quebec, the Capital of Canada, with an Appendix*. Boston: Richard Draper, Edes and Gill, and Thomas and John Fleet, 1759.

McConville, Brendan. *The King's Three Faces: The Rise and Fall of Royal America, 1688–1776*. Chapel Hill: University of North Carolina Press, 2008.
Miller, John C. *Sam Adams: Pioneer in Propaganda*. Boston: Little and Brown, 1936.
Miller, Perry. *Errand into the Wilderness*. Cambridge, Mass.: Harvard University Press, 1956.
Milton, John. *Political Writings*. Edited by Martin Dzelzainis. Cambridge: Cambridge University Press, 1991.
Moore, Frank, ed. *The Patriot Preachers of the American Revolution, with Biographical Sketches*. New York: Charles T. Evans, 1862.
Morgan, Edmund S. *The Challenge of the American Revolution*. New York: Norton, 1976.
———. *The Puritan Dilemma: The Story of John Winthrop*. Boston: Little and Brown, 1958.
Nash, Gary B. *The Urban Crucible: Social Change, Political Consciousness, and the Origins of the American Revolution*. Cambridge: Harvard University Press, 1979.
Nicolson, Colin. *The "Infamas Govener": Francis Bernard and the Origins of the American Revolution*. Boston: Northeastern University Press, 2000.
Nieuwentyt, Bernard. *The Religious Philosopher: Or, the Right Use of Contemplating the Works of the Creator*. Translated by John Chamberlayne. London: T. Wood, J. Senex, and W. Taylor, 1719.
Noll, Mark. *America's God: From Jonathan Edwards to Abraham Lincoln*. Oxford: Oxford University Press, 2002.
Oakes, John. "Conservative Revolutionaries: A Study of the Religious and Political Thought of John Wise, Jonathan Mayhew, Andrew Eliot, and Charles Chauncy." Ph.D. dissertation, Simon Fraser University, 2008.
O'Gorman, Frank. *The Long Eighteenth Century: British Political and Social History, 1688–1832*. London: Arnold, 1997.
Osbaldeston, Richard. *A Sermon Preached before the House of Lords, in the Abbey-Church of Westminster, on Saturday, January 30th, 1747: Being the Day Appointed to Be Observed as the Day of the Martyrdom of King Charles I*. London: John Oliver, 1748.
Paine, Robert Treat, Jr. *The Works in Verse and Prose, of the Late Robert Treat Paine, Junior, Esquire, with Notes, to Which Are Prefixed, Sketches of His Life, Character and Writings*. Boston: J. Belcher, 1812.
Pascal, Blaise. *Pensees and Other Writings*. Translated by Honor Levi. Oxford: Oxford University Press, 1995.
Pestana, Carla Gardina. *Protestant Empire: Religion and the Making of the British Atlantic World*. Philadelphia: University of Pennsylvania Press, 2009.
Pickering, Thomas. *A Sermon Preach'd before the Right Honourable, the Lord Mayor, the Aldermen and Citizens of London, in the Cathedral Church of St. Paul, on Tuesday, January the 30th, 1749–50*. London: John Clarke, 1750.
Plumstead, A. W., ed. *The Wall and the Garden: Selected Massachusetts Election Sermons, 1670–1775*. Minneapolis: University of Minnesota Press, 1968.

Pocock, J. G. A. *The Machiavellian Moment: Florentine Political Thought and the Atlantic Republican Tradition.* Princeton, N.J.: Princeton University Press, 1975.

Pope, Alexander. *Essay on Man and Other Poems.* New York: Dover, 1994.

Potter, Janice. *The Liberty We Seek: Loyalist Ideology in Colonial New York and Massachusetts.* Cambridge, Mass.: Harvard University Press, 1983.

Quincy, Josiah, Jr. *Reports of Cases Argued and Adjudged in the Superior Court of Judicature of the Province of Massachusetts Bay, between 1761 and 1772.* Edited by Samuel M. Quincy. Boston: Little, Brown, and Company, 1865.

Ralegh, Walter. *The Historie of the World, in Five Books.* London: Robert White, John Place and George Dawes, 1666.

Ray, John. *Three Physico-Theological Discourses.* London: William Innys, 1732.

———. *The Wisdom of God Manifested in the Works of the Creation.* London: Samuel Smith, 1691.

Rhoden, Nancy L. *Revolutionary Anglicanism: The Colonial Church of England Clergy during the American Revolution.* New York: New York University Press, 1999.

Robbins, Caroline. *The Eighteenth-Century Commonwealthman.* Indianapolis: Liberty Fund, 2004 [1959].

Rossiter, Clinton. *Seedtime of the Republic: Origin of the American Tradition of Political Liberty.* New York: Harcourt, Brace, 1953.

Sandoz, Ellis, ed. *Political Sermons of the American Founding Era, 1730–1805.* Indianapolis: Liberty Fund, 1991.

Savelle, Max. *Seeds of Liberty: The Genesis of the American Mind.* New York: A. A. Knopf, 1948.

Schlesinger, Arthur Meier. *The Colonial Merchants and the American Revolution, 1763–1776.* New York: Columbia University Press, 1917.

Scott, Jonathan. *Algernon Sidney and the Restoration Crisis, 1677–1683.* Cambridge: Cambridge University Press, 1991.

[Secker, Thomas.] *An Answer to Dr. Mayhew's Observations on the Charter and Conduct of the Society for the Propagation of the Gospel in Foreign Parts.* Boston: Reprinted by Richard and Samuel Draper, Edes and Gill, and Thomas and John Fleet, 1764.

Sell, Alan P. F. *John Locke and the Eighteenth-Century Divines.* Cardiff: University of Wales Press, 1997.

Shain, Barry Alan. *The Myth of American Individualism: The Protestant Origins of American Political Thought.* Princeton, N.J.: Princeton University Press, 1994.

Shalev, Eran. *American Zion: The Old Testament as a Political Text from the Revolution to the Civil War.* New Haven, Conn.: Yale University Press, 2013.

Shipton, Clifford K. *Sibley's Harvard Graduates, Volume 5, 1701–1712.* Boston: Massachusetts Historical Society, 1937.

———. *Sibley's Harvard Graduates, Volume 8, 1726–1730.* Boston: Massachusetts Historical Society, 1951.

———. *Sibley's Harvard Graduates, Volume 11, 1741–1745.* Boston: Massachusetts Historical Society, 1960.

Smith, M. H. *The Writs of Assistance Case.* Berkeley: University of California Press, 1978.

Speck, William A. *Reluctant Revolutionaries: Englishmen and the Revolution of 1688.* Oxford: Oxford University Press, 1989.

Spellman, W. M. *The Latitudinarians and the Church of England, 1660–1700.* Athens: University of Georgia Press, 1993.

Starkie, Andrew. *The Church of England and the Bangorian Controversy, 1716–1721.* London: Boydell, 2007.

[Steele, Richard.] *The Ladies' Library.* Vols. 1–3. London: Jacob Tonson, 1732.

Stewart, Matthew. *Nature's God: The Heretical Origins of the American Republic.* New York: W. W. Norton, 2014.

Stout, Harry S. *The New England Soul: Preaching and Religious Culture in Colonial New England.* New York: Oxford University Press, 1986.

Thompson, C. Bradley. *John Adams and the Spirit of Liberty.* Lawrence: University Press of Kansas, 1998.

Thornton, John Wingate. *The Pulpit of the American Revolution, or the Political Sermons of the Period of 1776.* Boston: Gould and Lincoln, 1860.

Trebeck, Andrew. *A Sermon Preach'd before the Honourable House of Commons, at St. Margaret's Westminster, on Friday, January 30, 1746–7.* London: L. Gulliver and W. Owne, [1747].

Voltaire. *Treatise on Tolerance and Other Writings.* Edited by Simon Harvey. Cambridge: Cambridge University Press, 2000.

Walett, Francis G., ed. *The Diary of Ebenezer Parkman, 1703–1782, Part One: 1719–1755.* Worcester, Mass.: American Antiquarian Society, 1974.

Ward, Lee. *The Politics of Liberty in England and Revolutionary America.* Cambridge: Cambridge University Press, 2004.

Warren, Mercy Otis. *History of the Rise, Progress and Termination of the American Revolution Interspersed with Biographical, Political and Moral Observations.* Edited by Lester H. Cohen. Indianapolis: Liberty Fund, 1989.

Watts, Isaac. *Logick: or, the Right Use of Reason in the Enquiry after Truth, with a Variety of Rules to Guard against Error, in the Affairs of Religion and Human Life, as Well as in the Sciences.* London: T. Longman, T. Shewell, and J. Brackstone, 1745.

Weiss, John. *Life and Correspondence of Theodore Parker, Volume 1.* New York: D. Appleton and Company, 1864.

Whitehill, Walter Muir, and Lawrence W. Kennedy. *Boston: A Topographical History.* Cambridge, Mass.: Harvard University Press, 2000.

Wills, Garry. *Inventing America: Jefferson's Declaration of Independence.* Boston: Houghton Mifflin, 1978.

Wilson, Robert J., III. *The Benevolent Deity: Ebenezer Gay and the Rise of Rational Re-*

ligion in New England, 1696–1787. Philadelphia: University of Pennsylvania Press, 1984.

Wood, George Arthur. *William Shirley, Governor of Massachusetts, 1741–1756: A History*. 2 vols. New York: Columbia University Press, 1920.

Wood, Gordon S. *The Creation of the American Republic, 1776–1787*. Chapel Hill: University of North Carolina Press, 1969.

Wright, Conrad. *Beginnings of Unitarianism in America*. Boston: Beacon Press, 1955.

Yirush, Craig. *Settlers, Liberty, and Empire: The Roots of Early American Political Theory, 1675–1775*. Cambridge: Cambridge University Press, 2011.

Yolton, John L., ed. *John Locke: Problems and Perspectives. A Collection of New Essays*. Cambridge: Cambridge University Press, 1969.

Young, Alfred F. *Liberty Tree: Ordinary People and the American Revolution*. New York: New York University Press, 2006.

Zobel, Hiller B. *The Boston Massacre*. New York: W. W. Norton, 1970.

Zuckert, Michael P. *The Natural Rights Republic: Studies in the Foundation of the American Political Tradition*. Notre Dame, Ind.: University of Notre Dame Press, 1996.

INDEX

Aberdeen University, honorary degree, 40, 62, 68–69, 76
Act of Union (1707), 137
Adams, John
    on armed resistance, 3
    on Bishop Controversy, 140, 149, 154
    family, 41
    on intellectual origins of Revolution, 10, 16, 44
    legal career, 42
    on Mayhew, 3, 4, 60, 179–180
    Mayhew's influence, 3, 41–42, 43, 63–64, 65, 166–167, 180, 181
    political principles, 15–16
    on private judgment, 42
    on Stamp Act, 166–168
    on western expansion, 90–91
Adams, Samuel, 3, 15–16, 175, 176
Akers, Charles W., 10
Albany Congress, 85, 175
Albany Plan of Union, 85, 90–91, 175
Allen, William, 3, 154–155
Allison, Francis, 147
American Revolution
    Adams on, 10, 16, 44
    Congregationalist clergy and, 7–9, 10–16, 64–65
    intellectual origins of, 3, 4, 7–15, 17, 44
    postrevisionism, 14–16
    religion and, 15–16
    republican revisionism, 11, 12, 14
    as return to roots of colonies, 45
    Whig interpretation, 7–11, 12
Ames, William, 21
anarchy, distinction from civil liberty, 2, 161
Anglicans. *See* Episcopal Church
Answer to Dr. Mayhew's Observations (Secker), 139–140, 141, 143

Aplin, John, 132–133
Appleton, Nathaniel, 23, 30, 31, 178
Apthorp, Charles, 126
Apthorp, East, 126–127, 129–130, 131, 139, 148
Arians, 28, 29, 40, 68–69
Aristotle, 7, 9
Arminian theology, 20, 25, 38, 41
Atterbury, Francis, 141
Avery, Benjamin, 40, 48, 62, 68–69, 76, 94, 119

Bailyn, Bernard, 1, 11, 56, 65, 156–157
Baldwin, Alice M., 8–9, 14
Baptists, 46–47, 137
Barnard, John, 23–24
Baron, Richard, 63
Barrington, Lord, 48, 98, 101
Bartol, Cyrus, 8
Beard, Charles A., 9
Bell, James B., 15–16
Bellamy, Joseph, 147
Benson, George, 29, 40, 48, 62, 68, 69, 70, 87, 94
Bernard, Francis
    background, 98
    Bishop Controversy and, 97
    criticism of Mayhew, 3
    Eliot's election sermon and, 157
    on Glorious Revolution, 114
    government reform proposals, 101, 175
    as Massachusetts governor, 98–99, 100, 101, 110–111
    Mayhew and, 5–6, 112–117, 118–120, 121
    on Mayhew's Stamp Act sermon, 2, 6
    opposition to, 97, 100–101, 107, 110, 112, 118–120, 121
    on political authority, 115, 121
    servant, 105, 111–112

[229]

Bernard, Francis, *continued*
    Society for Propagating Christian Knowledge among the Indians of North America incorporation, 128
    suspected affinity for Stuarts, 113
    See also Indian Affair
Bill of Rights, English, 48, 156
Bishop Controversy
    fear of political power of bishops, 123, 141–142, 146–149, 150, 154
    First (1763–1764), 124, 139–149, 150
    Mayhew's position, 123, 131–132, 141–142, 147
    as political dispute, 15, 124, 145–147, 150, 153
    political results, 6, 149–150
    proposal, 6, 97, 118, 125, 126, 131, 139
    results, 146–148, 167
    Secker's position, 125–126, 133–134, 138–140
    Second, 148–149
    Stamp Act Crisis and, 120, 153–154, 156, 166–167, 169
    supporters of bishops, 125–127, 128–129, 133, 135
    See also Episcopal bishops; *Observations on the Charter and Conduct of the Society for the Propagation of the Gospel*
Bollan, Jeremiah, 40
Bollan, William, 119
Bonomi, Patricia U., 12
Boston
    Congregationalist churches, 29–30, 31
    earthquakes, 86
    First Great Awakening, 24–25
    Hutchinson Riot, 1–2, 6, 7, 96, 97, 122, 162–165, 170
    King's Chapel, 51, 126, 127
    Port of, 98, 99
    Stamp Act protests, 96, 97, 153, 158, 162
Boston Association of Ministers, 31–32, 77

Boston Evening-Post, 60–61
Boston Gazette, 1, 3, 61, 127, 129, 166–167
Boucher, Jonathan, 149
Bowdoin, James, 3, 85, 104, 119, 128
Braddock, William, 86
Bradford, Alden, 8
Bradley, James E., 13
Braintree church, 41–42, 64, 109
Breen, T. H., 16
Briant, Lemuel, 31, 41–42, 109
Bridenbaugh, Carl, 4, 11, 145, 148
Britain
    Act of Union (1707), 137
    constitution of, 58, 71, 79–80, 93, 114
    loyalty to, 5, 151
    Mayhew's supporters, 3–4, 40
    persecution of Puritans, 46–47, 130, 136, 139
    Revolution Settlement, 45–46, 47–48, 54, 64, 80, 112–114
    Test and Corporation Acts, 36, 46–47, 48, 49, 50, 93, 94, 138
    Toleration Act, 48, 49, 50, 156
    wars with France, 75
    See also English Civil War; Episcopal Church; French and Indian War; Protestant dissenters
British Board of Trade, 85
British Empire
    annexation of French territory, 91
    colonial policy under George III, 155
    constitutional relationship, 15, 135–136, 137–138, 145, 153–154
    expansion as God's will, 90–91, 92
    governors, 110–111
    Mayhew on, 5, 90, 91
    seen as morally corrupt, 68
British monarchy
    constitutional, 5, 58, 75, 79–80, 93, 114
    Protestantism and, 92
    Protestant Succession, 48, 49, 50–51, 59, 156

See also Glorious Revolution; Hanoverian dynasty; Stuart dynasty
British Parliament
  elections, 80–81
  Episcopal bishops, 71
  Sugar Act, 120, 153
  See also Stamp Act
Brockwell, Charles, 51–53, 59, 60–61
Brown, John, 30
Browne, Arthur, 133
Burnet, Gilbert, 113–114
Burr, Aaron, 41
Bute, John Stuart, earl of, 155, 156, 158
Butler, Joseph, 29, 32, 33
Byrd, James P., 14–15

Calvinism
  covenant theology, 21–22
  enforcement of orthodoxy, 36–37
  justification by faith, 38–39, 40
  Mayhew's rejection of, 5, 20, 38–39, 40–41
  moderate, 23–24, 29
  in New England, 21, 36, 69–70
  original sin doctrine, 21, 27, 29, 33–34
  See also Puritans
Cambridge
  Christ Church, 126–127, 131, 148
  potential bishop's palace, 131, 141
  See also Harvard College
Camm, John, 149
Canada
  British annexation of French territory, 91
  Quebec City, 88–90, 91
  Roman Catholic Church, 146
Caner, Henry
  Bishop Controversy and, 149
  Cambridge mission, 126
  A Careful Examination of Dr. Mayhew's Observations, 134–135, 137, 138
  Congregationalists and, 51

  criticism of Mayhew, 3, 119, 128, 134
  on Mayhew's responsibility for Hutchinson Riot, 164
  on Mayhew's Stamp Act sermon, 2
Canterbury, archbishop of. *See* Laud, William; Secker, Thomas
Catholics. *See* Roman Catholic Church
Cato's Letters (Trenchard and Gordon), 49, 52, 73, 92, 108
Chandler, Thomas Bradbury, 148, 149
Channing, Edward, 98
Charles I, King
  anniversary of execution, 46, 49–51, 53, 59–60, 64
  Episcopal clergy and, 59, 124
  execution, 45, 55, 59–60
  as martyr, 59–61
  Mayhew on, 44, 45, 92
  persecution of Puritans, 46
  reign, 52
  Scotland and, 132
  seen as martyr, 51
  tyranny, 57, 58
  See also English Civil War
Charles II, King, portrait, 113
Chauncy, Charles
  as clergyman, 29, 31
  heterodoxy, 19
  Mayhew and, 3, 119
  on Mayhew, 103
  Mayhew's death and, 178, 179
  missionary society and, 128
  political role, 7, 12
  political sermons, 64–65
  Second Bishop Controversy, 148
Christ Church (Cambridge), 126–127, 131, 148
Christian Sobriety (Mayhew), 71–72
Church, Benjamin, 3, 179
Church of England. *See* Episcopal Church
Cicero, 7, 9, 17, 18, 71–72

civil liberty
  English Bill of Rights, 48, 156
  gradual erosion of, 142
  happiness and, 66
  illegal searches, 101
  Mayhew on, 2, 18, 67, 137–138, 159–165, 172–174, 179
  religious liberty and, 39, 147, 150, 154
  resisting encroachments, 53, 170, 173–174
  virtue and, 66, 91
  See also freedom of speech, in Indian Affair
Clark, J. C. D., 13, 15
Clarke, John, 102
Clarke, Richard, 163–164
Clarke, Samuel, 20, 24, 28, 29, 32, 37, 47, 48
Colbourn, Trevor, 11
Committee of Dissenting Deputies, 68
committees of correspondence, 174–176
common law, application to colonies, 135
Congregationalism
  churches, 29–30
  at Harvard, 23–24
  in New England, 5, 49, 145–146
  Rational Dissent, 13
Congregationalist clergy
  Boston Association of Ministers, 31–32, 77
  Mayhew's influence, 6, 156–157
  political activities, 97–98, 146, 147, 150, 156
  political sermons, 8–9, 14, 16, 64–65
  role in Revolution, 7–9, 10–16, 64–65
  Rutland ecclesiastical council, 174, 177
Congregationalists
  Bishop Controversy and, 124
  in England, 46–47
  in New England, 124, 127
  relations with Episcopalians, 46, 51, 61
consent of governed
  British monarchy and, 58, 71
  civil liberty and, 161
  Mayhew on, 39, 74, 77, 78, 92–93, 159–160
  as Real Whig principle, 20, 67, 93, 181
  taxation without representation principle, 2, 153, 161, 168, 170, 171, 183n2
Cooper, Samuel
  as clergyman, 29, 31
  at Harvard, 25, 28–29
  Mayhew's death and, 177–178
  Mayhew's influence, 3
  political role, 7, 12
  political sermons, 65
Cornthwaite, Robert, 70
Corrigan, John, 13
corruption
  in Britain, 80–81, 86–87, 170
  in customs service, 100–101, 110
  power and, 72–73, 74, 116
  See also Indian Affair; morality
Cotton, John, 45
Country Whiggism, 49, 67. *See also* Whigs
covenant theology, 21–22, 25
Cranch, Richard, 3, 41, 42, 43
Cromwell, Oliver, 106, 113, 133

Davidson, Philip, 10
Death of Prince Frederick, The (Mayhew), 72–74, 115–116
Declaration of Independence, 4, 7, 9, 10
Defence of the Observations (Mayhew), 135–138, 140, 143
Discourse Concerning Unlimited Submission (Mayhew)
  on dissenters in England, 60, 71
  on Episcopal clergy, 123–124
  harshness, 62
  historical background, 52
  influence, 3, 8, 11, 44–45, 63–64, 65, 157, 166
  on loyalty, 151

on popular sovereignty, 45, 67, 74
on private judgment, 39
publication, 39, 63
responses, 60–62, 63
as response to Brockwell, 51–52
revolution principles, 45–46, 63, 66–67
on right of resistance, 52–60
on trust in rulers, 72
Discourse Occasioned by the Death of King George II, 92–94, 114
Discourse on Rev. XV, A, 86–87
dissenters. *See* Protestant dissenters
divine right of kings, 46, 48, 49–50, 58, 59, 74–75, 77
Dudleian Lecture, Harvard College, 148, 166, 180
Dworetz, Steven M., 14

Edes, Benjamin, 3
Edwards, Jonathan, 24, 41
Eliot, Andrew
　　election sermon (1765), 156–157
　　on Hutchinson Riot, 163
　　Mayhew and, 119
　　Mayhew's death and, 177–178
　　Mayhew's influence, 3
　　missionary society and, 128
　　political sermons, 16, 64–65
Eliot, Samuel A., 8
English Civil War
　　histories of, 52
　　Massachusetts conflict compared to, 106, 112–113, 121
　　Parliamentarians, 52, 54, 57–58
　　regicide, 45, 55, 59–60
Enlightenment, American, 15, 24
Enlightenment, British, 13, 24, 26, 29, 32, 67, 68. *See also* natural religion
Episcopal bishops
　　Mayhew's opposition to, 5
　　political power, 123, 141–142, 146–149, 150, 154
　　political roles in England, 71, 123, 139, 141, 142–143
　　See also Bishop Controversy; Secker, Thomas
Episcopal Church
　　Charles I and, 59, 124
　　church-state relations, 124, 149
　　clergy, 31, 51, 59, 123–127, 133–134, 137
　　compared to Catholic Church, 143, 147
　　ecclesiastical courts, 98
　　in England, 36, 46–48, 49–51
　　as established church, 71
　　hierarchy, 13, 131, 143
　　latitudinarians, 47, 48
　　Mayhew's criticism of, 123–124, 127, 131–132, 138
　　sermons on anniversary of Charles I's death, 46, 49–51, 53, 59–60, 64
　　theologians, 29
　　tolerance of Catholic Church, 143–147, 148
　　Tory principles and, 114, 123–125
　　See also Protestant dissenters
Episcopal Church, in American colonies
　　Boston churches, 31
　　as established church, 133, 134, 137
　　low-church laymen, 148–149
　　missionaries, 119, 127, 139
　　in New England, 61, 135–136
　　political split between high-church and low-church members, 149–150
　　relations with Congregationalists, 46, 51, 61
　　vestries, 148
　　See also Bishop Controversy; Society for the Propagation of the Gospel in Foreign Parts
equalitarianism, 39, 42

Ferguson, Robert A., 15
Flucker, Thomas, 104
Flynt, Henry, 25

Foster, James, 29, 40, 68
France
    Catholic absolutism, 5, 67–68, 75, 83, 84, 85
    Fort Duquesne, 75
    imperialism, 75, 82
    Jesuit missionaries, 82
    Protestants, 37, 144
    See also French and Indian War
Franklin, Benjamin, 85, 148
Frazer, Gregg L., 15
Frederick, prince of Wales, 72, 73–74, 93–94
Frederick the Great, king of Prussia, 87
freedom. *See* civil liberty; religious liberty
freedom of speech, in Indian Affair, 105–106, 108–109, 112, 117–118, 121
Freeman, Joanne B., 111
French and Indian War
    British victories, 87, 88–92
    Catholic expansionism feared, 5, 146
    French victories, 85–87
    as moral contest, 67–68, 85, 86–87, 89
    Peace of Paris, 129
    political sermons, 67–68, 86–90
    preparations, 82–85
Frink, Thomas, 177

Galatians, epistle to, 159, 161
Gay, Ebenezer, 19, 30, 31, 103, 178
George I, King, 48–49. *See also* Hanoverian dynasty
George II, King
    archbishop of Canterbury appointed, 125
    death, 92
    Mayhew's praise of, 53, 87, 93
    reign, 45
    son, 72, 73–74
George III, King
    coronation, 92
    Mayhew on, 93–94
    power of clergy and Tories under, 142, 155–156
    prime ministers, 155, 165
    Stamp Act and, 168, 170
Gill, John, 3
Glorious Revolution
    liberties gained, 54
    Mayhew on, 57, 58–59, 64
    political gains from, 63, 156
    Protestant reactions, 47–48
    Real Whig interpretation, 5, 48, 49, 92, 113–114
    See also Revolution Settlement; William of Orange
Gordon, Thomas
    Cato's Letters, 49, 52, 73, 92, 108
    The Independent Whig, 49, 61, 63, 123
    on popular sovereignty, 113
Gordon, William, 147
government
    common good as goal, 77–78, 79
    morality and, 78, 79
    religion and, 78–79
    trust in, 39, 56, 67, 72
    See also consent of governed; tyranny
governors, 98, 110–111. *See also* Bernard, Francis
Gray, Harrison
    Indian Affair and, 104, 107, 120
    Mayhew and, 3, 102, 104, 119
    Observations pamphlet and, 132
    as provincial treasurer, 76, 101, 104, 110
    West Church founding, 30
Gray v. Paxton, 101, 104, 107, 110
Great Awakening, First, 12, 24–25, 26, 125
Grenville, George, 155, 158, 165, 168
Gridley, Jeremiah, 100, 106
Gridley and Otis, 106–107

Haakonssen, Knud, 13
Hallowell, Benjamin, 96, 162

Hancock, John, 3, 31, 169
Hanoverian dynasty
　legitimacy, 59
　Mayhew's support, 45–46, 79–80, 88, 92–94, 113, 151
　Protestant allies, 48–49, 50–51
　Protestantism, 48, 75, 93, 94
　religious liberty and, 93
　See also British monarchy; George II, King; George III, King
happiness, 33, 35–36, 66, 77–78
Harrison, Peter, 126–127
Harvard College
　Board of Overseers, 118–119, 127, 162
　Dudleian Lecture, 148, 166, 180
　Episcopalians and, 127
　honorary degree for Experience Mayhew, 23
　Mayhew's education at, 4, 18, 20, 23–25, 26–29, 99
Hatch, Nathan O., 12, 91–92, 146
Heimert, Alan, 12, 62, 172
Henry, Patrick, 4, 44
heterodoxy. *See* Protestant dissenters
Hitchcock, Gad, 64–65
Hoadly, Benjamin
　influence in America, 9
　Mayhew and, 40, 62, 69
　on popular sovereignty, 113
　on resistance, 152
　on revolution principles, 48
　writings, 29, 52, 54, 61
Hollis, Thomas
　admiration of Mayhew, 3
　Bishop Controversy and, 128–129, 132, 138–139, 140
　on British politics, 155–156
　correspondence with Mayhew, 97, 118, 119, 155–156, 157–158, 162, 165–166, 167, 168, 177
　death, 179
　Mayhew's death and, 179

political influence, 167
Stamp Act opposition, 167–168
Holyoke, Edward, 23–24
Hooper, William, 30–31
Huguenots, 37
Hutchinson, Eliakim, 127
Hutchinson, Thomas
　at Albany Congress, 85
　as chief justice, 100, 101
　house destroyed by mob, 1–2, 96, 97, 162–165
　Indian Affair and, 97, 105, 107, 109, 111, 120
　Mayhew and, 3, 6, 162–163, 164–165
　proposed college and, 119
　Shirley and, 99
　Stamp Act protests and, 158
Hutchinson Riot, 1–2, 6, 7, 96, 97, 122, 162–165, 170

Independent Whig, The (Trenchard and Gordon), 49, 52, 53, 61, 63, 123
Indian Affair
　conclusion, 111–112, 120
　effects on Mayhew, 97–98, 117–118, 121
　Hutchinson on, 97
　as ideological conflict, 98, 115, 116, 120–121
　Mayhew's letter to Bernard on, 108–109, 112–113
　Mayhew's memorandum on, 102, 103–106, 109–110, 111–112, 113, 115, 116, 117–118, 120
　Tallman's story, 97, 102–103, 104, 108, 111–112, 116, 117
Indians
　missionaries to, 20–21, 23, 82, 90, 119, 127
　Wampanoag, 20–21, 23
　See also French and Indian War
Ingram, Robert G., 148
Iroquois Confederation, 75

Jacobite Rebellion, 49–50, 54, 63, 80
James II, King
　Catholic Church and, 47
　France and, 75
　grandson, 49
　Mayhew on, 92
　overthrow of, 55, 58, 59, 64
　portrait, 113
　Whig resistance to, 54
　See also Glorious Revolution
Jefferson, Thomas, 7, 63–64
Jesuit missionaries, 82
Johnson, Samuel, 3, 124–126, 129
judgment, private. *See* private judgment

King's Chapel (Boston), 51, 126, 127
King's College, 125

Lardner, Nathaniel, 29, 40, 68
Laud, William, 46, 52, 57
Leonard, Daniel, 180
liberty. *See* civil liberty; religious liberty
Livingston, William, 3
Locke, John
　Essay Concerning Human Understanding, 24, 35, 71
　influence in America, 7, 9, 10
　influence on Mayhew, 32, 39, 52, 56
　Mayhew's study of, 29
　natural rights philosophy, 14, 16
　on resistance, 152
　Second Treatise of Government, 52, 78
　Thoughts on Education, 71
London Chronicle, 167–168
Louis XIV, king of France, 37, 75
Louis XV, king of France, 88
Loyalists, 7, 149–150. *See also* Tories
loyalty
　to British Crown, 5, 79–80, 151
　conditional, 72, 80, 93, 94, 181
　consistency with freedom, 151–152
Luther, Martin, 38, 39

Macaulay, Catherine, 3
Maccarty, Thaddeus, 30
MacSparran, James, 61, 137
Maier, Pauline, 146, 152, 153, 174
Martha's Vineyard, 20–21, 23, 99, 107, 111
Marvell, Andrew, 142
Massachusetts
　Albany Congress delegation, 85
　colonial government, 76–77
　frontier defenses, 83–84
　governorship, 75, 98, 110–111
Massachusetts Charter, 75, 110, 137–138
Massachusetts Council
　college proposal, 118–119
　General Court sessions, 75–76, 77
　Indian Affair and, 107, 120
　members, 75, 99, 100, 103–104, 175
Massachusetts Gazette, 146, 178, 179
Massachusetts General Court
　church rate cases, 137
　composition, 75
　election sermon (Eliot, 1765), 156–157
　election sermon (Mayhew, 1754), 75–85
　power and, 110
　SPCK incorporation, 119, 128
Massachusetts House of Representatives, 75, 101, 110, 118–119, 174, 175
Massachusetts State House, 113
Massachusetts Superior Court, 99–100
Mather, Cotton, 21
Mauduit, Israel, 119, 128, 133–134, 140
Mauduit, Jasper, 87, 119, 128, 132
Mayhew, Elizabeth Clarke, 102
Mayhew, Experience, 20–23, 25–26, 30, 31, 99, 127
Mayhew, Jonathan
　Anglophilia, 68, 70–71
　biographies, 8, 10
　conservatism and radicalism, 151, 172, 181, 182
　death and funeral, 3, 177–179
　decision to become clergyman, 25–26

early life, 20–21, 23
education, 4, 17–18, 20, 23–25, 26–29, 99, 180–181
family, 20–23, 25–26, 30, 41
frankness, 103
heterodox views, 19, 20, 27–29, 32, 33–34, 70–71
indentured servant, 102–103
influence, 3–4, 6, 7–16, 41–43, 44–45, 63–65, 156–157, 170, 181
influences on, 17–18, 180–181
intellectual development, 26–29
isolation from Boston clergy, 31–32
loyalty to British Crown, 5, 151
marriage and children, 102
ordination, 30, 31
political principles, 3, 5, 9, 10, 67, 170, 181
religious beliefs, 4–5, 10, 25
reputation, 65, 109, 148
training as preacher, 29–30
See also Bishop Controversy; Indian Affair; sermons; Stamp Act; West Church (Boston)
Mayhew, Nathan, 23, 99
Mayhew, Remember, 20, 23
Mayhew, Zachariah, 23, 25, 26, 107, 111
Miller, Ebenezer, 129
Miller, John C., 9–10
Milton, John, 52
missionaries
 Catholic, 20, 82
 Episcopalian, 119, 124–125, 127, 139
 French, 82
 to Indians, 20–21, 23, 82, 90, 119, 127
 Protestant, 82, 90
 See also Society for the Propagation of the Gospel
monarchies
 divine right of kings, 46, 48, 49–50, 58, 59, 74–75, 77
 French, 5, 67–68, 75, 83, 84, 85
 hereditary, 73

popular sovereignty and, 160
See also British monarchy
Montcalm, Marquis de, 88–90
Moore, Frank, 8
morality
 Christian, 71–72, 79
 decline of British, 68, 86–87
 in French and Indian War, 67–68, 85, 86–87, 89
 good works, 38–39
 government and, 78, 79
 of humble men, 73
 Mayhew on, 71–74, 81–82
 natural order, 22
 rationality and, 4, 27–28, 32–33, 71–72
 of rulers, 72–74
 See also corruption; virtue
moral sense, 33, 66
Morgan, Edmund S., 154

natural liberty, 159
natural religion
 Congregationalist clergy and, 14
 at Harvard, 24
 of Mayhew, 5, 20, 26, 39
 rationality, 5, 21, 22
 readings on, 26, 27–28
 virtue, 66
 See also rationality
natural rights, 9, 14, 16, 20, 135, 169–170, 181
natural theology, 24, 26, 32
Netherlands, United Provinces of the, 84–85
New England
 conservative clergy, 69–70, 71
 political institutions, 81
 popular sovereignty, 65
 religious liberty, 60, 135, 137–138
 right of resistance, 65
 Whig revolution principles, 9, 14–15, 156–157, 169–170
 See also Massachusetts

New Light revivalism, 5, 12
Newport Mercury, 132–133
Nicolson, Colin, 114
Noll, Mark, 14
Nonconformists. *See* Protestant dissenters

obedience, 53, 54, 55–56. *See also* Tory obedience principles
Observations on the Charter and Conduct of the Society for the Propagation of the Gospel (Mayhew), 130–134
  Caner's reply, 134–135, 137, 138
  Defence of the Observations, 135–138, 140, 143
  influence, 166
  London publication, 138–139
  Secker's *Answer*, 139–140, 141, 143
obsta principiis (resist first beginnings), 53–54, 118, 142, 154–155, 181
Oldfield, Joshua, 27
Oliver, Andrew
  house, 158
  Indian Affair and, 97, 103, 104, 105, 109, 111
  Otis and, 100
  Stamp Act protests and, 96, 158, 163
Oliver, Peter, 7, 16, 165
Ossoit, Judah, 103, 111, 112
Otis, James, 100
Otis, James, Jr.
  Bernard and, 175
  grave, 179
  at Harvard, 25, 29
  Indian Affair and, 106–107
  intellectual leadership, 4, 7
  Mayhew and, 3, 6, 118–120, 121–122, 174–176
  opposition to Bernard, 97, 100–101, 104, 110, 118–119
  Rights of the British Colonies Asserted and Proved, 120

Otis, Jonathan Mayhew, 107
Otis, Samuel Allyne, 3, 106–107

Paine, Robert Treat, 3, 19, 41, 42–43, 179, 181
Paine, Thomas, *The Nature and Progress of Liberty*, 19
Parker, Theodore, 8
Parliament. *See* British Parliament
Paul, apostle, 54, 55–56, 159, 161
Paxton, Charles, 99, 100, 101, 104, 110
Pemberton, Ebenezer, 41, 178
Pennsylvania
  Fort Duquesne, 75
  Presbyterian party, 6, 154–155
Pickering, Thomas, 50, 51, 59
Pillars of Priestcraft and Orthodoxy Shaken, The, 63
Pitt, William, 155, 168, 170, 177
Pokanauket Indians, 99. *See also* Indians; Tallman, James
popular sovereignty
  conflict with parliamentary sovereignty, 114–115
  delegation of power to king-in-Parliament, 114
  Mayhew on, 67, 74, 77, 92–93, 114–116, 160
  in New England, 65
  rational deliberation, 67
  as Real Whig principle, 20, 67, 71, 77, 113
  Revolution Settlement and, 114
Pownall, Thomas, 99, 100
Presbyterians
  Arians, 28, 29, 40, 68–69
  clergy, 8–9, 12, 147, 150
  in England, 46–47, 69, 87
  in mid-Atlantic colonies, 6, 16, 154–155
  in New England, 6, 49, 61, 124, 145–146
  in Scotland, 132, 137
Price, Richard, 3–4

Priestley, Joseph, 3
private judgment
   Adams on, 42
   churches restricting, 36–37
   exercising, 34, 37–38
   happiness as goal, 35–36
   Mayhew's confidence in, 5, 19–20, 28–29, 31, 35, 74, 180–181
   Mayhew's sermons on, 32–39
   morality and, 39
   as obligation, 34–36, 42
   in politics, 39–40
   rational basis, 34
   in religious matters, 5, 47, 48
   right of, 20, 34, 36, 39–40, 42, 152, 166
   See also rationality
Protestant dissenters
   anti-Trinitarianism, 5, 13, 20, 87, 134
   Arians, 28, 29, 40, 68–69
   Committee of Dissenting Deputies, 68
   in England, 13, 45–47, 50–51, 53, 64, 94–95, 138
   Hoadly's support, 40, 69
   laws limiting rights, 36, 40, 46–47, 48, 49, 64, 71, 138
   Mayhew and, 4, 53, 63, 68–70, 71, 148
   Mayhew's correspondence with English, 68–70, 87, 94–95, 119
   in New England, 94–95, 135
   religious liberty, 93
   right of resistance, 53–54, 55
   Toleration Act, 48, 49, 50, 156
Protestantism
   British defense of, 75
   denominational differences, 16, 46
   established denominations, 136–137
   in France, 37, 144
   political principles associated with, 74
   rationality and, 4–5, 13, 15
   revivalism, 5, 12, 24–25, 26, 125
   right of private judgment, 38
   See also individual denominations

Protestant Succession, 48, 49, 50–51, 59, 156
Puritans
   covenant theology, 21–22, 25
   English Parliamentarians, 50, 52
   missionaries, 20–21, 23
   New England settlers, 81, 130, 136
   persecution in Britain, 46–47, 130, 136, 139
   See also Calvinism

Quakers, 46–47, 137
Quebec Act of 1774, 146
Quebec City, 88–90, 91
Quincy, Edmund, 3, 41, 43, 179, 181
Quincy, Josiah, Jr., 1, 3, 41, 162, 179, 181
Quincy, Samuel, 3, 41

radical Whigs. *See* Real Whigs
Rational Dissent, 13
rationality
   as basis of Mayhew's thought, 5, 14, 180–181
   covenant theology, 21–22, 25
   God-given capacity, 5, 20, 21–22, 26–28, 33–34, 39–40, 152
   logic, 28
   Mayhew's graduate thesis, 29
   Mayhew's reading on, 17–18, 26–28
   morality and, 4, 27–28, 32–33, 66, 71–72
   in natural religion, 5, 21, 22
   popular sovereignty and, 67
   Protestantism and, 4–5, 13, 15
   See also private judgment
Real Whig principles
   American Revolution and, 3, 14
   in Glorious Revolution, 64
   of Mayhew, 3, 20, 39–40, 52, 63, 66–67, 170, 181
   obsta principiis, 53–54, 118, 142, 154–155, 181
   of Otis, 101

Real Whig principles, *continued*
  restraint, 152, 153, 174
  See also consent of governed; popular sovereignty; resistance, right of; Whig revolution principles
Real Whigs
  Mayhew as, 94
  view of Glorious Revolution, 48, 49, 92, 113–114
  See also Whigs
reason. *See* rationality
Reduction of Quebec, The (Mayhew), 89–90, 91
regicide, 64. *See also* Charles I, King
religious liberty
  civil liberty and, 39, 147, 150, 154
  in colonies, 49, 83
  in England, 48, 60, 93, 138
  importance of, 66
  Mayhew on, 38, 60, 78, 121, 132, 136, 143–144, 179
  in New England, 60, 135, 137–138
  of Puritans, 130, 136
  See also private judgment
Remarks on an Anonymous Tract (Mayhew), 140–145, 148, 153, 156
representative government, 159–160
resistance, right of
  Adams on, 166
  of dissenters, 53–54, 55
  grounded in Britain, 45–46, 48, 166
  loyalty and, 151–152
  Mayhew on, 5, 10, 15, 52–60, 152, 161–162, 170
  in New England, 65
  obsta principiis, 53–54, 118, 142, 154–155, 181
  Paul on, 54, 55–56
  Whig principle, 20, 64–65, 152, 153, 174
Revelations, Book of, 86–87, 89–90, 146
Revere, Paul, 3, 41, 43, 179, 181

revivalism
  First Great Awakening, 12, 24–25, 26, 125
  New Light, 5, 12
Revolution Settlement, 45–46, 47–48, 54, 64, 80, 112–114
Rhoden, Nancy L., 149
rights. *See* civil liberty; freedom of speech, in Indian Affair; natural rights; private judgment; religious liberty; resistance, right of
Rights of the British Colonies Asserted and Proved (Otis), 120
Rockingham, Marquis of, 165, 167, 168
Roman Catholic Church
  anti-Catholicism in New England, 146–147
  bishops, 143
  in Canada, 146
  conflict with Protestants in England, 46–47, 143–144, 146
  in England, 140, 143–147, 148, 150
  English laws on public worship, 143–144
  Inquisition, 36, 52
  Mayhew on, 87–89, 143–147, 148
  missionaries, 21, 82
  papal authority, 75, 85, 88, 143–144
  political principles associated with, 74–75
Romans, epistle to, 54, 55–56
Rossiter, Clinton, 10, 145
Rowe, John, 178
rulers. *See* monarchies; obedience; tyranny

Sacheverell, Henry, 48, 141
Sandercock, Edward, 69, 70
science, 24, 28, 37
Scotland
  Act of Union (1707), 137
  Presbyterian Church, 132, 137

searches. *See* writs of assistance
Secker, Thomas
   Answer to Dr. Mayhew's Observations, 139–140, 141, 143
   as archbishop, 125–126, 128, 129
   criticism of Mayhew, 3
   missionaries and, 133–134
   on Stamp Act repeal, 168
   See also Bishop Controversy
self-government, 161
Sermon . . . Occasioned by the Much-Lamented Death of His Royal Highness Frederick, Prince of Wales, A. See Death of Prince Frederick, The
sermons
   Death of King George II, 92–94, 114
   early, 29–30
   on earthquakes (1755), 86–87
   election (1754), 75–85
   funeral of Sewall, 99–100
   on Hutchinson Riot, 164
   political, 67–68, 72–74, 86–90, 115–116, 152–153
   on Stamp Act (August 25, 1766), 2, 6, 96, 159–165
   on Stamp Act repeal, 169–174, 177
   of thanksgiving (1760), 91–92
   on war (1758), 87–88
   on war (1759), 88–90
   See also individual titles
Sermons upon the Following Subjects (Mayhew, 1755), 40–41, 87
Seven Sermons (Mayhew), 20, 28, 32–39, 40, 56, 62, 66, 69, 74, 78
Sewall, Samuel, 21, 99
Sewall, Stephen, 76, 99–100
Shalev, Eran, 14
Sherwood, Samuel, 146
Shirley, William, 68, 76, 83, 85, 86, 99, 100
Shirley, William, Jr., 86
Sidney, Algernon, 7, 9, 10, 52

slavery, Stamp Act compared to, 2, 160–161, 165–167, 171
smugglers, 99, 100, 101, 162
Snare Broken, The (Mayhew), 8, 17, 18, 53, 169–174, 177
sobriety. See *Christian Sobriety*
Society for Propagating Christian Knowledge among the Indians of North America (SPCK), 119, 128, 132
Society for the Propagation of the Gospel in Foreign Parts (SPG)
   Apthorp's pamphlet on, 129–130
   competitor, 119
   Mayhew's criticism of, 82, 127–128, 129, 130–134
   missionaries, 61, 63, 124–125, 133–134
   Secker's defense of, 139
   Tories, 51
SPCK. *See* Society for Propagating Christian Knowledge among the Indians of North America
SPG. *See* Society for the Propagation of the Gospel in Foreign Parts
Sprat, Thomas, 60
Stamp Act
   boycott in response to, 154–155, 166, 168, 170
   clergy opposing, 156–157
   Mayhew's sermon on, 2, 6, 96, 159–165
   Otis pamphlet on, 120
   passage, 120, 150, 153, 156
   protests, 1–2, 6, 96, 97, 153, 158, 162–165, 170, 171–172
   public reaction in colonies, 157–158, 165–166, 168
   repeal, 6, 167–170
   revenues, 170–171
   tax collectors, 158, 165
Stamp Act Congress, 165, 174
Steele, Richard, 26–27, 28, 33
Stiles, Ezra, 130, 147
Story, William, 96, 97, 104, 109, 111, 162

Stout, Harry S., 12–13
Stuart dynasty
    Catholic Church and, 144
    corruption, 73
    Jacobite Rebellion, 49–50, 54, 63, 80
    Pretender, 49, 80, 87, 88, 113, 170
    Restoration, 46
    supporters, 59, 87, 113
    See also Charles I, King; James II, King
Sugar Act, 120, 153

Tallman, James, 97, 103, 104, 108, 111–112, 116. See also Indian Affair
taxation without representation principle, 2, 153, 161, 168, 170, 171, 183n2
taxes, church rates, 137. See also Stamp Act
Tennent, Gilbert, 25
Test and Corporation Acts, 36, 46–47, 48, 49, 50, 93, 94, 138
Tiedemann, Joseph, 16
Tillotson, John, 20, 24, 27, 38, 47, 48
Tories
    in England, 48, 114, 142, 150, 155–156
    Episcopal Church and, 16, 123–125
    Glorious Revolution interpretation, 114
    in New England, 61, 63, 124–125
    on political authority, 115, 124, 150
    Stuart dynasty and, 47
    See also Bernard, Francis
Tory obedience principles
    in America, 51
    Bishop Controversy and, 133, 134
    conflict with Whig positions, 150
    Episcopal clergy supporting, 46, 48, 49, 51, 114, 123
    George III and, 156
    Mayhew's opposition to, 54, 55, 59, 63, 123
    popular opposition, 158

Towgood, Michaijah, 168–169
trade
    boycott of English goods, 154–155, 166, 168, 170
    customs service, 100–101, 110
    Port of Boston, 98, 99
    smugglers, 99, 100, 101, 162
Trebeck, Andrew, 50
Trenchard, John
    Cato's Letters, 49, 52, 73, 92, 108
    The Independent Whig, 49, 52, 53, 61, 63, 123
    on popular sovereignty, 113
Trinitarianism, 5, 20, 40–41, 48, 138
Trinity Church (Boston), 31
truth, 32, 34. See also private judgment
Two Discourses Delivered November 23rd, 1758, 87–88, 151–152
Two Discourses Delivered October 9th, 1760, 91–92
Two Discourses Delivered October 25th, 1759, 88–90, 91
tyranny
    of Charles I, 57, 58
    ecclesiastical, 53–54, 123–124, 148–149
    resisting, 5, 151–152
    resisting from beginning, 53, 142, 154–155
    submission to, 156–157
Tyrrell, James, 113–114

unity, political, 84–85, 174

violence, Mayhew's opposition to, 2, 164, 171–172. See also Hutchinson Riot
virtue
    civil liberty and, 66, 91
    classical, 4, 27, 35, 39, 66, 79, 88
    happiness and, 35–36, 78
    military victories and, 88
    of New Englanders, 81

searches. *See* writs of assistance
Secker, Thomas
   Answer to Dr. Mayhew's Observations, 139–140, 141, 143
   as archbishop, 125–126, 128, 129
   criticism of Mayhew, 3
   missionaries and, 133–134
   on Stamp Act repeal, 168
   See also Bishop Controversy
self-government, 161
Sermon . . . Occasioned by the Much-Lamented Death of His Royal Highness Frederick, Prince of Wales, A. See *Death of Prince Frederick, The*
sermons
   Death of King George II, 92–94, 114
   early, 29–30
   on earthquakes (1755), 86–87
   election (1754), 75–85
   funeral of Sewall, 99–100
   on Hutchinson Riot, 164
   political, 67–68, 72–74, 86–90, 115–116, 152–153
   on Stamp Act (August 25, 1766), 2, 6, 96, 159–165
   on Stamp Act repeal, 169–174, 177
   of thanksgiving (1760), 91–92
   on war (1758), 87–88
   on war (1759), 88–90
   See also individual titles
Sermons upon the Following Subjects (Mayhew, 1755), 40–41, 87
Seven Sermons (Mayhew), 20, 28, 32–39, 40, 56, 62, 66, 69, 74, 78
Sewall, Samuel, 21, 99
Sewall, Stephen, 76, 99–100
Shalev, Eran, 14
Sherwood, Samuel, 146
Shirley, William, 68, 76, 83, 85, 86, 99, 100
Shirley, William, Jr., 86
Sidney, Algernon, 7, 9, 10, 52

slavery, Stamp Act compared to, 2, 160–161, 165–167, 171
smugglers, 99, 100, 101, 162
Snare Broken, The (Mayhew), 8, 17, 18, 53, 169–174, 177
sobriety. See *Christian Sobriety*
Society for Propagating Christian Knowledge among the Indians of North America (SPCK), 119, 128, 132
Society for the Propagation of the Gospel in Foreign Parts (SPG)
   Apthorp's pamphlet on, 129–130
   competitor, 119
   Mayhew's criticism of, 82, 127–128, 129, 130–134
   missionaries, 61, 63, 124–125, 133–134
   Secker's defense of, 139
   Tories, 51
SPCK. *See* Society for Propagating Christian Knowledge among the Indians of North America
SPG. *See* Society for the Propagation of the Gospel in Foreign Parts
Sprat, Thomas, 60
Stamp Act
   boycott in response to, 154–155, 166, 168, 170
   clergy opposing, 156–157
   Mayhew's sermon on, 2, 6, 96, 159–165
   Otis pamphlet on, 120
   passage, 120, 150, 153, 156
   protests, 1–2, 6, 96, 97, 153, 158, 162–165, 170, 171–172
   public reaction in colonies, 157–158, 165–166, 168
   repeal, 6, 167–170
   revenues, 170–171
   tax collectors, 158, 165
Stamp Act Congress, 165, 174
Steele, Richard, 26–27, 28, 33
Stiles, Ezra, 130, 147
Story, William, 96, 97, 104, 109, 111, 162

Stout, Harry S., 12–13
Stuart dynasty
    Catholic Church and, 144
    corruption, 73
    Jacobite Rebellion, 49–50, 54, 63, 80
    Pretender, 49, 80, 87, 88, 113, 170
    Restoration, 46
    supporters, 59, 87, 113
    See also Charles I, King; James II, King
Sugar Act, 120, 153

Tallman, James, 97, 103, 104, 108, 111–112, 116. *See also* Indian Affair
taxation without representation principle, 2, 153, 161, 168, 170, 171, 183n2
taxes, church rates, 137. *See also* Stamp Act
Tennent, Gilbert, 25
Test and Corporation Acts, 36, 46–47, 48, 49, 50, 93, 94, 138
Tiedemann, Joseph, 16
Tillotson, John, 20, 24, 27, 38, 47, 48
Tories
    in England, 48, 114, 142, 150, 155–156
    Episcopal Church and, 16, 123–125
    Glorious Revolution interpretation, 114
    in New England, 61, 63, 124–125
    on political authority, 115, 124, 150
    Stuart dynasty and, 47
    See also Bernard, Francis
Tory obedience principles
    in America, 51
    Bishop Controversy and, 133, 134
    conflict with Whig positions, 150
    Episcopal clergy supporting, 46, 48, 49, 51, 114, 123
    George III and, 156
    Mayhew's opposition to, 54, 55, 59, 63, 123
    popular opposition, 158

Towgood, Michaijah, 168–169
trade
    boycott of English goods, 154–155, 166, 168, 170
    customs service, 100–101, 110
    Port of Boston, 98, 99
    smugglers, 99, 100, 101, 162
Trebeck, Andrew, 50
Trenchard, John
    Cato's Letters, 49, 52, 73, 92, 108
    The Independent Whig, 49, 52, 53, 61, 63, 123
    on popular sovereignty, 113
Trinitarianism, 5, 20, 40–41, 48, 138
Trinity Church (Boston), 31
truth, 32, 34. *See also* private judgment
Two Discourses Delivered November 23rd, 1758, 87–88, 151–152
Two Discourses Delivered October 9th, 1760, 91–92
Two Discourses Delivered October 25th, 1759, 88–90, 91
tyranny
    of Charles I, 57, 58
    ecclesiastical, 53–54, 123–124, 148–149
    resisting, 5, 151–152
    resisting from beginning, 53, 142, 154–155
    submission to, 156–157
Tyrrell, James, 113–114

unity, political, 84–85, 174

violence, Mayhew's opposition to, 2, 164, 171–172. *See also* Hutchinson Riot
virtue
    civil liberty and, 66, 91
    classical, 4, 27, 35, 39, 66, 79, 88
    happiness and, 35–36, 78
    military victories and, 88
    of New Englanders, 81

private judgment and, 39
sobriety and, 71–72
See also morality
Voltaire
The Age of Louis XIV, 79
Treatise on Tolerance, 144

Walpole, Robert, 48, 49
Wampanoag Indians, 20–21, 23. *See also* Indians
Warren, Mercy Otis, 3, 176
Washington, George, 75, 82–83
Watts, Isaac, 27, 28, 33, 34
West, Samuel, 64–65
West, Thomas G., 14
West Church (Boston)
deacons, 104
founding, 30
Mayhew as pastor, 30, 31–32, 102, 109–110
members, 41, 76, 99, 101, 102, 106–107, 163–164
relations with other Boston churches, 30–31
Whig dilemma, 152, 153
Whig revolution principles
Bishop Controversy and, 150
government by consent, 181
Hanoverian support, 152, 155
Mayhew's commitment, 5, 6, 63, 181
natural rights, 9, 14, 16, 181
in New England, 9, 14–15, 156–157, 169–170
opponents, 50–51
rational basis, 152
sermons on, 64–65
Stamp Act protests and, 156–157, 158
See also popular sovereignty; Real Whig principles; resistance, right of
Whigs
American, 7, 16, 17, 49
in England, 47, 48–49, 114, 150, 155
moderate, 114, 165
Protestant clergy, 49
See also Real Whig principles
Whitefield, George, 24–25, 147
Whitelock, Bulstrode, 52, 57
Whiting, John, 24
William of Orange (King William), 47–48, 54, 58, 75, 88, 92, 114. *See also* Glorious Revolution
Williams, Abraham, 29
Williams, Isaac, 118
Wingate, John Thornton, 8
Winthrop, John, 24, 178, 179
Wolfe, James, 88, 89, 91, 94
Wolsey, Charles, 26
Worcester, Congregational church, 30
writs of assistance, 99, 100, 101

Zobel, Hiller B., 98
Zuckert, Michael P., 14